FOURTH INDUSTRIAL REVOLUTION TECHNOLOGIES

Maritime and Naval Operations

FOURTH INDUSTRIAL REVOLUTION TECHNOLOGIES

Maritime and Naval Operations

Vijay Sakhuja

Vivekananda International Foundation
New Delhi

PENTAGON PRESS LLP

Fourth Industrial Revolution Technologies: Maritime and Naval Operations
By Vijay Sakhuja

ISBN 978-93-90095-19-3

First Published in 2021

Published by
PENTAGON PRESS LLP
206, Peacock Lane, Shahpur Jat
New Delhi-110049
Phones: 011-64706243, 26491568
Telefax: 011-26490600
email: rajan@pentagonpress.in
website: www.pentagonpress.in

Printed at Aegean Offset Printers, Greater Noida, U.P.

For

Kabir and Myra

CONTENTS

FOREWORD

The 4th Industrial Revolution, 4IR, driven by artificial intelligence, machine learning, big data, 3D printing, blockchain, quantum computing, 5G high-speed communication, Internet of Things, and a host of other technologies is revolutionising the world. The day is not far off when machines may overtake humans in intelligence and become autonomous in decision-making. Driverless cars, autonomous drones and robots are already a reality. Being dual-use technology, 4IR technologies have applications in the civilian as well as military domains.

The race for 4IR technologies is hotting up. The technology landscape changes every few months as new products are brought to the market. The USA, China, France, Japan, the UK, South Korea and Israel have taken the lead in the development of these technologies. Others are catching up. The world's largest tech companies are spending large sums of money in R&D and product development.

4IR technologies have tremendous application in civilian and military maritime domains. Smart ports, autonomous ships, drone swarms, unmanned underwater surveillance and weapon systems are being developed and deployed. 4IR technologies promise to change naval warfare in a significant way.

The onset of autonomous weapon systems like the "killer robot" which take decisions based on algorithms, independent of human intervention, has raised many troubling questions. The fear that autonomous systems will make humans redundant has led to debates on ethical and moral and legal issues. The UN has been engaged in discussing the way to regulate autonomous weapon systems.

India cannot remain oblivious to these revolutionary developments. Poised to become the third largest economy in the world in a few years, India should focus on 4IR technologies more seriously. It needs to develop a modern, competitive shipping industry using 4IR technologies as also smart ports which are more efficient and productive.

India's security environment is changing rapidly. The Indian Ocean has been rapidly transformed into a global trade and energy artery. The oceans are also being militarised. China has embarked upon a major programme of military modernisation which includes the modernisation of its navy. It has taken a lead in the development and application of 4IR technologies to make autonomous ships, data-driven weapon systems and underwater drones, among others.

India has also recognised the importance of 4IR. Prime Minister Modi has spoken about making India a hub of artificial intelligence technologies. Several government departments have come up with recommendations for incorporating 4IR in their respective fields of work. The Ministry of Defence has set up an Artificial Intelligence Council to ensure that IR technologies are incorporated in the Indian defence forces.

The Vivekananda International Foundation had requested Dr. Vijay Sakhuja, a Navy veteran and a noted academic, to look into the global 4IR landscape and its impact on the maritime domain. We are happy to publish Dr. Sakhuja's work, *Fourth Industrial Revolution Technologies: Maritime and Naval Operations*. After a thorough scan of open source material, he has identified the key technologies and tracked the state of their development. He has also looked at how different countries are employing these technologies.

While the Indian Government has taken note of the importance of artificial intelligence, a lot needs to be done to build the requisite ecosystem from research and development to commercialisation of technologies. The Indian record of mastering the entire technology cycle has not been inspiring. Despite the lead we had in information and communication technologies, we cannot develop globally competitive products or companies like Google and Facebook. One hopes that India will not miss the 4IR revolution. The enormous Indian talent has drained away due to the lack of opportunities in the country.

Time is the essence. Urgent policy, technological, financial, legal and regulatory interventions will be needed to be established to build a robust ecosystem for the development, production and deployment of 4IR technologies. We must pay special attention to the application of 4IR technologies in the military domain. Dr. Sakhuja's book alerts the government that it is necessary to act now. He warns that "the unmanned arms-race has already begun and the Indian Navy would have to reassess its future requirements of conventional assets. The remedy lies in both rethinking priorities as also the design of future ship classes focused on 4IR".

We hope that this book, which deals with a new, relatively unexplored field, will be found useful by the general reader, academics as well as policymakers.

Arvind Gupta
Director
Vivekananda International Foundation
New Delhi, October 2020.

ACKNOWLEDGEMENTS

Scientific and technological advancements have been an important feature of maritime-naval transformation, and the associated industrial complexes have drawn immensely from the prevalent Industrial Revolutions. There are now clear trends of widespread digitalization and Fourth Industrial Revolution (4IR) technologies are disrupting every aspect of maritime and naval activity. I decided to study, understand and write about maritime and naval related 4IR issues in an incremental way and various think tanks and journals published my research.

I place on record the support provided by the Vivekananda International Foundation, New Delhi for accepting my research proposal to pursue the subject and publish a volume.

A number of practitioners, experts and scholars have supported me in the above pursuit and I am grateful to them: Vice Admiral M P Muralidharan, former Director General, Indian Coast Guard, by giving a practitioners' perspectives on the role of 4IR technologies in maritime and naval operations; and Dr W. Lawrence, S, Prabhakar, Advisor, Centre for Public Policy Research, Kochi by sharing an academic critique on the volume.

Several other practitioners and experts painstakingly read the manuscript and offered their valuable comments and these have added immense value to the volume. Captain Anand Dixit, President, Indian Maritime Foundation, Pune; Rear Admiral Dr. S Kulshrestha (retd.); Commodore KM Ramakrishnan; and Captain Himadri Das.

My wife Sangeeta has always stood by me in my academic pursuits and being patient with my work schedules.

Vijay Sakhuja

INTRODUCTION

Commercial and military operations at sea and ashore across the globe are in the throes of technological and organisational transformation. During the last few decades, the commercial maritime domain successfully assimilated information and communication technologies (ICT) that resulted in 'digitization'[1] of all its sectors including supply chains. Significantly, digitization and the ever-expanding use of data transformed the way merchant ships began to operate at sea using digital systems for navigation, machinery management, cargo handling and for safety and security resulting in 'digitalization'.[2]

Besides, there were simultaneous advancements in automation[3] onboard ships which not only enhanced operational efficiency but also helped seafarers overcome fatigue from monotonous and physically and mentally challenging tasks undertaken onboard ships. There is now a desire to go beyond automation-digitization and building a fleet of autonomous[4] ships albeit with varying degrees of autonomy, that not only perform various tasks and operations automatically but are also capable of conducting operations through self-learning.

Similarly, shore based supporting infrastructure has been operating through data networks that feature a high degree of system integration of ship and port operations along with the associated supply chains. These were 'security hardened' against cyber threats that can cause major disruption across the supply chain eco-system. The maritime industry also adapted to both internal and external changes and responded with new human resource strategy and skill development.

The maritime industry is now preparing for 'digital transformation'[5] to integrate Fourth Industrial Revolution (4IR) technologies. These are smart, intelligent and use predictive-cognitive tools and algorithms and drive autonomous, unmanned and remote controlled platforms, robots and machines. Some of the frontline technologies of 4IR are Artificial Intelligence, Machine Learning, Big Data, Cloud Computing, Augmented Reality, Quantum Computing, Cognitive Computing (CC) and Internet of Things (IoT) and they are gathering momentum and finding use to support maritime operations. Technology developers have also successfully developed wearable technologies including person-embedded sensors and human mounted computers.

There are now clear trends of widespread digitization, digitalization and digital transformation across the maritime commercial domain and these are impacting every aspect of the industry from commercial operations, onboard technology management, maintenance processes, use in fintech to support banking and financial services, new business models through analytics, and human resource management that will bring about radical changes in the maritime industry. Simultaneously, there will be challenges for human resources both at sea and ashore that would require 'up-skilling, re-skilling and retooling'[6] to embrace 4IR technologies. The industry leaders too have recognized the importance of educating themselves and using new technologies as also adopting innovative models for their operations.

Likewise, warfare at sea has been in the continuous process of technological transformation and the 'envelop of warfare at sea' has expanded. In the 16th century, cannons came to be carried onboard ships, duels with guns took place within visual range; but over the years these became obsolescent and substituted with missiles that are launched at targets on land from as far as 3,000 kilometres in the sea. The current techno-naval transformation is on 4IR technology and several navies are developing new strengths in war fighting. They have shifted their operations from platform-centric to network-centric warfare and now towards autonomous warfare that pivots on complex integration of unmanned-autonomous platforms at sea, in the air, underwater, ashore and even in outer space. There is strong evidence of 'desire and quest' among some navies to achieve technological proficiency and translate 4IR technology into operational competence, so that the enemy could be engaged further out in the sea and on shore, with limited or even 'no-contact' with the platform resulting in a new type of warfare.

The desire to modernize armed forces to obtain a competitive edge and the increase in military spending by States on 4IR-enabled platforms is expected to give stimulus to a new form of war fighting. Such trends are already visible in the militaries of the USA, the UK, Russia, China, Israel, Japan and South Korea, and these countries are investing on 4IR research and development to compete and maintain a favourable balance of power at the regional and global levels.

Advanced navies have already begun to ride on the new revolution that is marked by autonomous platforms, intelligent systems, smart devices, artificial intelligence and machine learning, and cognitive technologies. They also see Big Data as a solution to a number of combat and non-combat operations. Naval planners are keen to harness the benefits of 4IR-enabled weapon systems, 'mobile and wearable devices', integrated robotics and Artificial Intelligence, as part of their war fighting menu for the overall management of the battle space.

The navies are also embracing commonly used and commercially available communication devices such as smart phones, tablets and hybrid devices. These are faster, cheaper and flexible devices that supplement the existing high-speed wireless equipment and other sophisticated communications technologies. Perhaps, wearable devices such as smart watches, smart glasses, health monitors, and activity trackers are changing the way militaries access, use and exchange information to enhance the effectiveness of existing technologies. For instance, modern-day soldiers carry micro-UAVs as portable gear which falls in the category of wearable technologies.

While that is true in the case of advanced navies, small and medium naval powers too have realised the significance of 4IR technologies in naval warfare and are beginning to see them as game changers. There is now visible proliferation of UAVs, drones and smaller unmanned platforms which are being acquired from commercial markets and are being modified or tailor-made to meet the specific needs of their naval environment.

At another level, large numbers of devices, equipment and machineries will be connected to the Internet, facilitating access from multiple locations across different mediums. Maritime digital connectivity will advance and upgrade beyond 5G technology to 6G, 7G, or another 'G',[7] and will dramatically transform the way the marine and maritime world manages information.

The new maritime digital ecosystem in both physical and virtual form is expanding and supporting multi-domain operations in the oceanic domain. This composite physical-digital is also called the Cyber-Physical System (CPS) and is enabled by a complex structure of sensors-actuators that bring together diverse constituents which work together, i.e., the "physical world with the virtual world of information processing through software systems, communications technology, and sensors/actuators including embedded technologies".[8] For instance, inputs from machinery sensors and control systems can be accessed by multiple agencies such as port operators, stevedore services, shore-based ancillary and support companies, Customs authorities, port health organizations, shipping agents and supply chain managers, etc., resulting in a marine-maritime ecosystem that would enhance efficiency and productivity.

The history of modernization of the shipping industry and navies leads to a conviction that innovation is the key for tactical advantage and an operational edge. Furthermore, business processes and policy formulation, the other two critical determinants for the transformation of any navy, require continuous evolution towards building a powerful force. It is fair to contend that it also requires a resolute and determined leadership to ensure transformation of the force and guarantee that various initiatives reach the logical and desired end state.

The trends indicate that in the future, navies will harness the potential of 4IR technologies and transform by building and operating 4IR-enabled naval platforms. There are also fears that these technologies will have a profound impact on the way war is waged and would require international regulatory mechanisms. In essence, 4IR technologies have created a new digital-cyber-physical-humanitarian-legal ecosystem taking warfare to new frontiers.

The overarching objective of this volume is to contribute to a better understanding of 4IR technologies in the maritime-commercial and military-naval domains including operations at sea and ashore. It is divided into eleven sections including introduction, conclusion and an appendix that expounds on the impact of 4IR-related developments in maritime commercial and naval domains.

The first chapter identifies several 4IR technologies that are in use or have potential use in the maritime-naval domain. It makes the argument that 4IR technologies will transform commercial maritime business operations at sea and ashore, and navies across the globe are preparing to understand, acquire and assimilate 4IR-enabled warfare.

Chapter 2 offers insights into the unique opportunities that accrue from 4IR and these can potentially revolutionize the entire maritime supply chain ecosystem built around multiple stakeholders such as shippers, freight forwarders, port operators, carriers (ships, trucks, and rail) and other connected service providers such as Customs, security agencies and emergency services that are connected to each other in real-time.

Chapter 3 is an exposition of the ongoing 4IR technological transformation in the naval domain and provides an overview of how 4IR technologies present newer challenges for war fighting doctrines, concept of operations and command and control. It explains the ongoing trends among navies to harness the benefits of the upcoming 4IR transformations as part of their war fighting blackboard, for the management of the battle space, and operational support functions.

Chapter 4 notes that the Western navies have taken the lead in 4IR technology development and it is featuring in their naval strategies and concept of operations which could be the beginning of '4IR rivalry' resulting in geopolitical and geostrategic contestations among themselves as also with other major navies across the globe.

Chapter 5 is focused on 4IR-related naval developments in Asia and highlights the current trends in strategic thinking and naval orders of battle of acquisition of 4IR-enabled platforms, and ongoing changes in the navies of China, India, Japan, Korea and Singapore.

Chapter 6 is a detailed account of 4IR technological related developments in the Indian Navy. This chapter highlights issues of integration of 4IR in strategic thought and operations at sea as also using them to enhance organisational efficiency.

Chapter 7 illustrates the manifold capabilities of 4IR technologies to gain a deeper knowledge of the oceans for development of a Blue Economy. It notes that these technologies help to identify and harness the goods and services provided by the seas and oceans in a sustainable manner as also contribute to a better knowledge of the physical state, chemical composition and biological conditions of the oceans and seas.

Chapter 8 is an elucidation of various legal and ethical matters associated with 4IR technologies. In particular, it delves into the ethics and morality in any 4IR-led war and legal issues concerning 4IR-enabled maritime platforms.

Chapter 9 serves as the 'conclusion of the volume' and in its policy-prescriptive nature, this chapter offers recommendations for a number of stakeholders from the commercial maritime domain and naval specialist and policy makers. The study also lists market trends of many of the 4IR technologies and has been put together as an appendix. This will enable Indian industry to understand the future growth in the 4IR technology domain and define their participation in the Indian defence market.

4IR is a wide domain with large numbers and varied issues, and these cannot be articulated in one breath and written in one go. During the last three years I published op-eds, commentaries and articles on the subject that helped me to develop a fairly good understanding of the subject. Armed with these modest publications and a reasonably good understanding of 4IR related maritime and naval issues, I approached the Vivekananda International Foundation, New Delhi, to pursue the subject in further detail and attempt a book.

It is my hope that this volume will attract the attention of strategic thinkers, maritime and naval practitioners, industry stakeholders, academics, analysts and policy makers who are interested in future operational and organisational dynamics of the commercial and naval aspects in the seas and oceans.

Vijay Sakhuja

NOTES

1. "Digitization is the conversion of analog to digital, whereas digitalization is the use of digital technologies and digitized data to impact how work gets done, transforms how customers and companies engage and interact, and creates new (digital) revenue streams. Colleen Chapco-Wade "Digitization, Digitalization, and Digital Transformation: What's the Difference?", https://medium.com/@colleenchapco/digitization-digitalization-and-digital-transformation-whats-the-difference-eff1d002fbdf (accessed 15 September 2019).
2. "Digitization refers to the internal optimization of processes (e.g., work automation, paper minimization) and results in cost reductions. Conversely, digitalization is a strategy or process that goes beyond the implementation of technology to imply a deeper, core change to the entire business model and the evolution of work", Colleen Chapco-Wade "Digitization, Digitalization, and Digital Transformation: What's the Difference?", https://medium.com/@colleenchapco/digitization-digitalization-and-digital-transformation-whats-the-difference-eff1d002fbdf (accessed 15 September 2019).
3. Automation onboard ships can be understood as the "management, monitoring and maintenance of a vessel's cargo operations, propulsion systems and power generation and distribution remotely from one or more consoles". See "Automation at Sea", https://www.ship-technology.com/features/feature77533/ (accessed 15 September 2019).
4. "An autonomous ship is a water craft piloted by artificial intelligence (AI) and can potentially be unmanned and function autonomously as a type of seafaring drone". See "Autonomous Ship", https://whatis.techtarget.com/definition/autonomous-ship (accessed 15 September 2019).
5. "Digital transformation is more about people than it is about digital technology. It requires organizational changes that are customer-centric, backed by leadership, driven by radical

challenges to corporate culture, and the leveraging of technologies that empower and enable employees". Colleen Chapco-Wade "Digitization, Digitalization, and Digital Transformation: What's the Difference?", https://medium.com/@colleenchapco/digitization-digitalization-and-digital-transformation-whats-the-difference-eff1d002fbdf (accessed 15 September 2019).

6. "Seafarers and Digital Disruption", https://www.ics-shipping.org/docs/default-source/resources/ics-study-on-seafarers-and-digital-disruption.pdf?sfvrsn=3 (accessed 30 June 2020).
7. Tim Fisher, "6G: What it is & When to Expect it", https://www.lifewire.com/6g-wireless-4685524 (accessed 21 April 2020).
8. Christopher Greer, Martin Burns, David Wollman, and Edward Griffor "Cyber-Physical Systems and Internet of Things", https://nvlpubs.nist.gov/nistpubs/SpecialPublications/NIST.SP.1900-202.pdf (accessed 21 April 2020).

CHAPTER 1

Fourth Industrial Revolution Technologies

Technology is central to human development, and mankind has benefitted from it in all facets of its existence. Furthermore, the modern timeline is replete with examples of scientific and technological innovations that facilitated industrialization, economic development and human growth.[1] The First Industrial Revolution was centred on water, and coal-steam as the primary source of energy and the prime driver of industrialization, manufacturing and transportation; the Second Industrial Revolution harnessed electric power to facilitate mass and rapid production; and the Third Industrial Revolution or the Digital Revolution, i.e., from analog to digital systems and processes, is more recent and focuses on information and communication technology (ICT) to augment production through computerized processes. The world is now witnessing transition towards the Fourth Revolution, also referred to as Industry 4.0,[2] which is a fusion of technologies that permeate the 'physical, digital, and biological' domains but are tethered to the Third Industrial Revolution technologies, i.e., ICT.

It is important to note that the period between each of the revolutions lessened, and the time of invention and its implementation has been shrinking.[3] For instance, "the time between invention and widespread use was cut from about 80 years for the steam engine to 40 years for electricity, and then to about 20 years for IT"; and "the implementation lag for AI-related technologies will be about 10 years".[4]

There is ample historical evidence now of the 'zestful desire and visible quest' among militaries to achieve proficiency in war fighting through technological competence. In the naval domain, the First Industrial Revolution was marked by changes in propulsion from wind-sail power to coal-fired steam engines to drive ships. The Second Industrial Revolution witnessed ships built first with iron and then with the widespread use of steel. There were simultaneous technological developments marked by the internal combustion engine and the use of radio for communications. For war fighting, cannons were carried onboard albeit with limitations of weight, challenges of gun-recoil and difficulties of safe storage of gunpowder. The Third Industrial Revolution witnessed rapid growth in ICT featuring transition from platform-centric to network-centric warfare. Merchant vessels too benefitted from ICT technologies and improved navigation, communications and machinery management.

The Fourth Industrial Revolution (4IR) is potentially disruptive and is led by Artificial Intelligence, Big Data, Quantum Communications, Additive Manufacturing, etc. Perhaps it is instructive to note that it is exponential in nature and marked by 'velocity of change, scope, and systems-wide impact with massive disruptions'.[5]

Artificial Intelligence and Machine Learning

One of the leading and promising 4IR technologies of current times is Artificial Intelligence (AI). It is central to any commercial and military discussion, policy formulation and strategy development of future military platforms, tactics, techniques, and procedures. There are several definitions, interpretations and understanding of AI and these have evolved since the 1950s based on "more-specialized sub-categories of the field, but each is useful for providing guidelines and goals for researchers".[6] A more precise yet general understanding of the AI would be that it is a self-learning system and employs tools and algorithms that make any software smart; it uses 'data mining, pattern recognition and natural language processing that helps it to build a human-like response'.[7]

The "Discussion Paper: National Strategy for Artificial Intelligence" published by the NITI (National Institution for Transforming India) Aayog, a policy think tank of the Government of India, states that "AI refers to the ability of machines to perform cognitive tasks like thinking, perceiving, learning, problem solving and decision making. Initially conceived as a technology that could mimic human intelligence, AI has evolved in ways that far exceed its original conception".[8]

The 2018 US Department of Defence Artificial Intelligence Strategy defines Artificial Intelligence as "the ability of machines to perform tasks that normally require human intelligence —for example, recognizing patterns, learning from experience, drawing conclusions, making predictions, or taking action—whether digitally or as the smart software behind autonomous physical systems".[9]

Another definition of AI concerning the oceanic domain with particular reference to commercial operations at sea is "Artificial Intelligence is a system that undertakes navigational tasks, provides exemplar ship maintenance, executes safe cargo handling, transportation and shore operations and establishes successful security of ships, while preventing from rendering itself dangerous to environment and other objects".[10]

AI is being used in naval warfare in all mediums, i.e., surface, sub-surface, air and space and "helps the command team make informed decisions faster; rapidly detect and evaluate potential threats removing anomalies. It is inherently designed to integrate itself into existing warship equipment suits to optimize their exploitation".[11] Closely associated with AI is Machine Learning (ML) wherein machines possess an ability to learn and improve automatically without human intervention or a new programme.[12] For instance, "a machine learning algorithm can be trained to find a warship in an image or video"[13] a task undertaken by humans who would sift through a library of thousands of images of warships and aircraft.

Suffice to say, AI and ML have crossed over from the laboratory to the battle field, taken on new identities and promising roles, and permeated into maritime operations and naval warfare. The market size of Artificial Intelligence in the military domain could touch US$ 18.82 billion by 2025, at a CAGR of 14.75 per cent from 2017 to 2025.[14]

However, it is important to note and fair to argue that AI and ML have limitations too given that they function on the accuracy and format of data. For instance, any inaccuracy in data will appear in the results; further, an algorithm is designed and programmed to serve a single purpose and may not be useful for other purposes, i.e., an algorithm for logistic management may not be useful for the human resource organisation. Therefore, it is highly specialized and narrow in its use and may not achieve the human capability to perform multiple tasks at any given time. However, this may change in the future as machines become more intelligent.

Big Data

Another important 4IR technology is Big Data. It involves systematically analysing large and complex datasets and extracting information given that traditional data-processing methodologies and application software are not primed to undertake such tasks. Significantly, the challenge is of five 'V's, i.e., volume, variety, velocity, veracity and value.[15] The science of 'Big Data analytics' is critical due to the exponential availability of data from multiple sources and numerous organizations which must be processed to "predict and anticipate political crises, disease outbreaks, economic instability, resource shortages, and natural disasters".[16]

Likewise, the algorithm, also referred to as the 'invisible hand', links the data, establishes an order behind the scenes. It is critical in any military operational process and both "algorithms and Big Data make battlefield data and information orderly and effective" and "good algorithm can activate the data to make it valuable in combat".[17]

The maritime ecosystem is a repository of large volumes of data which is exchanged among stakeholders and stored for posterity. Most of the data is stored in silos and it is difficult to collate and obtain knowledgeable economic trends and market assessments. Integration of Big Data therefore becomes critical as commercial maritime operations undergo transformation and enable companies, shippers and other multiple stakeholders along the supply chain. A variety of data is obtained from ships such as about the performance of the machinery, nature of cargo, and voyage data to improve efficiency and enhance its overall performance. In essence, maritime Big Data is a "combination of cutting-edge data analytics and shipping expertise".[18]

Big Data is a high priority issue for the military to remain relevant in the 21st century. For instance, C4ISR data collected in the past, non-military data such as that from oceanography and space, to name a few of the sources, is enormous and requires systems and processes to generate up-to-date and actionable information. It is not surprising then that there are clear trends of a rise in military focus on information processing and analytics. The militaries are using AI-integrated systems to process data and get timely predictions. In essence, "the convergence of AI and Big Data has transformed the existing methods of Intelligence exploitation and data analytics".[19]

Experts argue that colossal amounts of data generated onboard a warship from diverse and disparate sources would necessitate "data handling capacity as well as the analysis of this data in real-time to provide actionable inputs for decision making. The knowledge-based approach to warfare has already made inroads into the development of situational awareness systems and decision-making tools coupled with high bandwidth requirements and associated communication networks".[20] Furthermore, "modern warfare on the big data battlefield relies on insights extracted from ever-growing volumes of unstructured, time-critical data".[21] Big Data and Artificial Intelligence applications are able to fulfil unique computing requirements and ensure tactical reliability. It must also embed "security in the hardware as opposed to simply bolting it on".[22]

The integration of AI and Big Data in warfare will be a game changer in any future combat settings as "platforms become smarter and more capable, greater on-board AI and big processing in general is required to handle the torrents of sensor and situational awareness data for autonomous decision-making and effective control.... As the number of smart platforms grows, so does the need for a greatly expanded, distributed fog layer with big processing capability that safely and efficiently manages the increased traffic".[23]

Blockchain

Blockchain technology made its debut in the financial sector and was designed to ensure secure, efficient, encrypted and tamper-proof transactions between two entities. It was invented in 2009 by a Japanese group of scientists with the pseudo name of 'Satoshi Takemoto' and was a "way to digitally and anonymously send payments between two parties without needing a third party to verify the transaction".[24] At the heart of this technology is the idea that it enables financial transactions with great speed and without intervention of a third party, across borders and in this case, the State or the bank. Simply put, Blockchain is a "digital ledger on a Blockchain-as-a-Service (BaaS) platform", is made of "data blocks" that are linked together with "cryptographic validation" that are not stored in a master location, serve the purpose of security, and are "not managed by any single entity".[25]

Blockchain is a "disruptive technology"[26] and "a new Internet that puts the users first".[27] A large number of sectors such as education, healthcare, aviation and power grid management are using Blockchain to provide administrative support[28] and, interestingly, its use in diplomacy is also being explored. The foremost features of Blockchain are privacy and security while transacting data on "land titles, loans, trades, intellectual property, identities, votes, etc".[29]

Blockchain technology is slowly being explored by maritime stake holders in a number of sectors like marine insurance, supply chains, management of container shipping that are introducing this technology in operations making it more transparent, efficient, and secure.

Militaries too see several uses and it will become an important technology for a number of naval activities and operations. Blockchain also impacts on naval planning involving combat operations, Intelligence, surveillance and reconnaissance, logistics and supply chains, engineering and maintenance, and human management. It is useful for supply chains and logistic networks, and advanced Western militaries of the USA and NATO members see several uses particularly when they engage in global operations. Blockchain can also help secure communications through "military-related Apps built on Blockchain".[30]

Blockchain can also be an important tool for nuclear weapon launch decision-making process. Given that the decision to launch is made after serious consideration by a number of responsible people in the national decision-making apparatus, the decision-making process can be based on Blockchain technology and digital signatures. According to DARPA's program manager behind the Blockchain effort, "whenever weapons are employed...it tends to be a place where data integrity in general is incredibly important" such as "nuclear command and control, satellite command and control, command and control in general, [information integrity] is very important".[31] The current trends in the use of Blockchain technology are indeed promising and the Blockchain market is estimated to grow to over US$ 23.3 billion in size by 2023.[32]

Virtual Reality and Augmented Reality

The launch of Pokemon Go, a free-to-play, location-based game, in 2016 was a seminal moment for Augmented Reality (AR).[33] It involved a Pokémon appearing on Google Maps[34] and then allowing the gamers to use their browsers to search for it in real-world positions and physically reaching up. The gamer would then hit an icon on the screen, and be rewarded with items and experience points. Ghost-type Pokémon appeared in different locations including military establishments forcing the US military's Joint Base Lewis-McChord near Tacoma, Washington, to issue a warning not to "chase Pokémon into controlled or restricted areas, office buildings, or homes on base"[35] forcing the Pentagon to announce rules for playing Pokemon Go in and around its premises

The technology showcased that it is possible to overlay virtual objects on real world places thus augmenting it into a new reality.[36] However, it is useful to mention that AR systems are not new and these have seen many applications for specific systems and were naturally exclusive and therefore very expensive.

It is important to define various types of 'Reality'. Virtual Reality (VR) "is an artificial, computer-generated simulation or re-creation of a real life environment or situation. It immerses the user by making them feel like they are experiencing the simulated reality first hand, primarily by stimulating their vision and hearing".[37] It produces environment in which the user "interacts with virtual content and the participant-observer is totally immersed in, and able to interact with, a completely synthetic world".[38]

Unlike VR, Augmented Reality (AR) "layers computer-generated enhancements atop an existing reality in order to make it more meaningful through the ability to interact with it. AR is developed into apps and used on mobile devices to blend digital components into the real world in such a way that they enhance one another".[39] It achieves this by combining the virtual with the real and is used on small hand-held devices with cameras. However, it is useful to mention that VR and AR are two sides of the same coin; the former brings the interaction into the 3D virtual world and the latter provides virtual objects in the real world. In recent times, the boundaries of VR and AR have seen some blurring to emerge as 'Mediated or Mixed' Reality or 'Hybrid Reality'.[40]

The defence sector has closely watched the usage and growth of VR/AR devices and the military is keenly exploring vistas for its usage in battle space management; training on military equipment; logistics supply chains; and maintenance of machinery.[41] The role of AR for Situational Awareness is a significant development and it is now possible for a combatant to be informed about its surroundings. Its usage in covert operations and amphibious landings is noteworthy.

AR has an enormous potential for a variety of naval functions that span tactical operations, training, maintenance and supply chain management. It can also help achieve information superiority over opponents. However, 'right skills in the right place' are critical and integrating them with existing systems and processes would require innovative ways.

Additive Manufacturing or 3D Printing Technology

Additive Manufacturing, or 3D printing, is a method of using traditional materials such as metals, plastics, polymers, porcelain and other by-products to make three-dimensional solid objects using a digital file of the design. The process is similar to brick-laying in which an object is created by placing layers of material on the previous layer until the object is created. It is possible to "produce intricate and complex objects of complex geometry, shape, contour and mould with cavities hitherto involving traditional manufacturing methods by using the cast and forging process. These had several limitations in terms of type of materials, temperature, difficulties of handling hazardous and dangerous materials and, above all, material waste and time losses".[42] 3D printing is generally for lower volumes of products and is most suitable for innovations, prototyping, and production of parts at low-cost and can potentially disrupt large manufacturing operations.

Among the many uses of 3D printing, the most common is manufacturing machinery parts and equipment to support various industries such as automotive and aerospace. The maritime industry is exploring the use of 3D printing technology to build, repair and maintain ships and platforms. It is becoming a common practice now to produce 3D printed parts which also eliminate human error from interpretation of drawings and descriptions. The 3D printers have already been proved in the production of auxiliary components, particularly spare parts for pumps, valves, heat exchangers, engines, propellers and catalysers. Many companies and businesses have now chosen to install 3D printers' onboard ships and platforms to prevent interruption and disruption. It not only cuts down costs and delivery time, it improves efficiency.

In the marine construction sector, in the section of ships and offshore platforms, it has been argued that distinct applications of 3D have impacted both "warship-building and merchant shipbuilding industries, specifically refits and repairs in these segments. The use of 3D technologies for prototypes has speeded up the research and development process in shipbuilding, enabling a larger number of iteration cycles. Early in the design stage, promotional models are possible for better appreciation. This technology complements lean and "just in time" processes and one-piece flow in warship constructions. Three-dimensional printing is being increasingly used to manufacture one-of-a-kind interim products, micro-panel profiles, non-standard brackets and outfitting equipment like double bottoms, side shells, single and double skins, decks and longitudinal bulkheads. A major advantage is that it provides a capability to manufacture one-of-a-kind steel parts or smaller and complex parts without having to machine or order them, reducing the cost substantially".[43] It is now possible to build full boats using 3D printers.[44] For instance, the University of

Maine's Advanced Structures and Composites Centre produced the largest 3D-printed boat in 72 hours.[45] The vessel is named 3Dirigo and measures 25 feet in length and is made from 5,000-pounds of material.

3D printed technologies are being harnessed to produce onboard defence systems like unmanned vessels armed with weapons, and micro-drones for reconnaissance and data-gathering or vehicle escort missions. These technologies require 3D printing technology to create shapes that may not be previously possible.

Although 3D technology is moving at a rapid pace, there are misgivings about products manufactured by using this technology. "We're still paving the road because the Navy, rightfully so, has to pay a lot of attention to the reliability of the parts, safety of their sailors and operability of their ships.... So, the technical work that we've done over the last, really, four years is all aligned toward making the Navy comfortable with the parts that are going on their ships".[46]

5G or Fifth Generation Wireless Communications Technologies

The Internet global system of interconnected computer networks, World Wide Web (www), the global collection of documents and hyperlinks and Uniform Resource Locators (URLs) are the lexicon of modern-day communications. The number of users of the above systems and processes is expanding rapidly and this is expected to create a "massive web of interconnected devices spanning everything from smart phones to kitchen appliances".[47] The number of IoT-connected devices across the globe will grow from 7.6 billion in 2019 to 24.1 billion in 2030.[48] Experts are of the view that future networks could be transmitting zettabytes (ZB) of data[49] and by 2025 the "storage industry will ship 42 ZB of capacity over the next seven years (beginning 2018); 90 ZB of data will be created on IoT devices by 2025; 49 per cent of data will be stored in public Cloud environments; and nearly 30 per cent of the data generated will be consumed in real-time by 2025".[50] This exponential growth in devices and data will increase the demand for bandwidth for expansion of various services and speed.

The Fifth Generation wireless communications technology is four times faster than 4G LTE (Long Term Evolution). Some of the key technical features of 5G are: (a) support one million connected devices per square kilometre; (b) 1-millisecond latency; (c) peak data download rate of up to 20 gigabits per second; and (d) greater efficiency in terms of power and use of radio spectrum.[51] Among the many commercial uses of 5G, it will enable quick access to data along the supply chain, i.e., ship-port-transport-production zone and vice versa. It is noted that "automated port control centre and operators can perform operations such as video security monitoring, real-time data collection and disposal by using mobile terminals. These operations require a reliable low-latency network with real-time access to Cloud data, and a system with high-level information security protection, where the 5G Edge-Cloud Solution can play an important part".[52]

Similarly, high bandwidth and low latency have enormous advantages for the military particularly in the battlefield where operations are conducted with high speed and platforms that are auto-driven such as armoured vehicles and unmanned aerial vehicles such as drones. Another interesting use of 5G would be in counter-terrorism that would involve sending acoustics of gunfire data rapidly to rear formations for analysis and guidance. Closely associated with this would be to send a drone through an opening such as a window to accurately send back the location of the snipers.

5G would potentially bring enormous economic and social benefits, but its spill-over into military operations is unfolding. Undeniably, it would help in the development of cutting-edge AI systems that can crunch through vast amounts of data which the military receives through a multitude of sensors and sources for its operations. It will also help in real-time analytics, cut latency, and cull most suitable data to enable an effective kinetic response. A vast network of sensors, robots and autonomous vehicles would be connected through sophisticated artificial intelligence, which could be the future of faster, deadlier, and may be partial autonomous, warfare.

5G may be a technological marvel but it is also an issue that has attracted geopolitical undercurrents. The advancement in 5G is supported by the Chinese government, and Huawei and ZTE are leaders who make necessary equipment for the technology. However, both companies are under scrutiny in the USA; in August 2018, the USA enacted the Foreign Investment Risk Review Modernization Act which applies to a country of "special concern that has a demonstrated or declared strategic goal of acquiring a type of critical technology or critical infrastructure that would affect United States leadership in areas related to national security".[53] Meanwhile, in July 2020, the UK announced cancellation of 5G contracts to Huawei and Oliver Dowden, minister in charge of telecommunications, informed the British House of Commons, "This has not been an easy decision, but it is the right one for the U.K.'s telecoms networks, for our national security and our economy, both now and indeed in the long run..."[54]

Underwater Fibre Optic Cables

Information technology has facilitated seamless connectivity over long distances resulting in instant communications through computers and rapid dissemination of information and data through Internet. These are supported by satellites, digital networks and complex integrating systems to transport large volumes of information across the globe in a short time. It is estimated that nearly 90 per cent of data transmission involves submarine cables.

Submarine cables are not new and have been used to carry data in telegraphic mode since the 1850s. The first such cable was laid between England and France and was capable of carrying only 10 words per minute. The underwater telegraph cable systems witnessed expansion rapidly and by 1900 these cables were crisscrossing the oceans and facilitating connectivity between all the continents other than Antarctica.

Since then, there has been a rapid expansion of the underwater cable network, and today nearly 95 per cent of data transmission worldwide takes place through 406 globally active submarine cables measuring 1.2 million kilometres with about 1,000 landing stations.[55] The longest submarine cable networks Southeast Asia–Middle East–Western Europe (SEA-ME-WE 3) is spread across the oceans and covers over 39,000 kilometres from Norden, Germany, to Keoje, South Korea, and connects 33 countries.[56]

The global demand for cable networks is growing and according to a market report the submarine cable system market will touch US$ 22.0 billion by 2025 from US$ 10.3 billion in 2019; it is expected to grow at a CAGR of 11.1 per cent from 2020 to 2025 due to "surge in global bandwidth demand, increasing Internet connection worldwide, increasing new offshore wind capacity additions, and growing demand for inter-country & island connections are the key factors driving the growth of the submarine cable system market";[57] the report, however, does note that "space-based Internet communication could potentially challenge the growth in submarine communication market".

Major content providers such as Google, Facebook, Amazon and Microsoft have an enormous demand for bandwidth for streaming photos, videos, and other data.[58] These companies have invested in submarine cable systems by directly setting up new networks. Netflix, YouTube and Web-based media streaming are the three major users (as of September 2019) of global traffic taking up nearly 34.1 per cent of the traffic.[59]

Data Storage

As noted earlier, future networks could be transmitting zettabytes (ZB) of data and this huge and monstrous generated-shared-transmitted data would be stored in special storages called Data Centres. These should not only be large but also possess very high-performance capability and capacity. Furthermore, they must be safe, secure and reliable and these stringent requirements necessitate a robust infrastructure. The facility should be 'resistant to seismic activity, flooding, and other types of natural disasters' and the design of the Data Centre should be such that it can be expanded.[60] Further, it should be efficient both in terms of cost of operations as also it should be close to a location that offers a cheap power source to make it more affordable. For instance, Apple built a data centre near hydropower resources in central Oregon, and Facebook has a mega-data centre next to a hydroelectric plant in Luleå, Sweden.[61] Another important consideration for a Data Centre location is fibre networks which should be near the end-user to reduce latency.[62]

The Data Centre generates an enormous amount of heat and requires high quality cooling systems. For instance, in Norway, the Lefdal Mine Data Centre is installed inside an old mine; in the USA, the Bluebird Underground Data Centre in Springfield, Missouri, is 85 feet below the ground and surrounded by solid limestone, leveraging natural resources for cooling and protection;[63] Facebook set up a data centre in the Swedish city of Lulea, in the Arctic Circle;[64] and Microsoft is currently developing a pilot project for an underwater data centre (prefabricated and size of a shipping container) off the coast of Scotland.[65]

In Singapore, Keppel Data Centres and Toll Group plan to install a floating data centre at the Loyang Offshore Supply Base. It is expected to be 'environmentally-friendly and resource-efficient' and would use seawater for cooling and is particularly significant for the island state as it will 'free up valuable land for other urban uses, making it a particularly attractive proposition for land-scarce cities'.[66]

Wearable Technologies

There is an ongoing 'wrist revolution', 'head revolution', and 'clothing revolution'. Numerous varieties of smart and intelligent products such as mobile phones, watches, wrist band, patches, eyewear, hearable, attachable, footwear, or clothing are in use and newer varieties such as ingestible and attachable with sophisticated features are being developed. Besides, these are physically manageable, handy and flexible enough to be worn under and over clothing, and can even be implantable in humans.[67] Also, these can be synchronized with other devices to transfer data both through physical connectors or Wi-Fi. Perhaps what is more interesting is that the developers of these devices have proactively used aesthetics and art to make them appealing to consumers and fashionable to wear.

The sophistication in such types of devices and products are far reaching and it is now possible to ingest micro size devices in the form of pills that run through the body and transmit data through applications embedded in a wearable device. Some of these are even capable of real-time video capture both to the wearer or controller. A number of manufacturing power houses are closely following the growth of these devices, particularly consumer wearables, healthcare-related products, textile and cloth manufacturers, integrated device manufacturers, and wearable electronics technology platform developers.[68]

According to the International Data Corp. (IDC) "Wearable are not just for technophiles", instead, "there is still plenty of room for growth", for the wider population.[69] According to market data, the wearable (smart watches, smart clothing, eyewear, headwear, and footwear) market is expected to grow by US$ 35.48 billion during 2020-2024, progressing at a CAGR of 13 per cent during the forecast period.[70]

Navies are embracing commonly available and commercially used communication devices such as smart phones, tablets, hybrid devices, etc. These are cheaper and flexible devices and supplement the existing high-speed wireless equipment and other sophisticated communications technologies. Perhaps, wearable devices such as smart watches, smart glasses, health monitors, and activity trackers are changing the way people access, use and exchange information to enhance the effectiveness of existing technologies. For instance, modern-day soldiers carry micro-UAVs as portable gear, and these fall in the category of wearable technologies.

However, the navies are not likely to fully rely on touch screen devices. The confidence in these devices came under scrutiny after a US warship was involved in a collision off the coast of Singapore. The US National Transportation Safety Board accident (collision between USS John S. McCain and Alnic MC, a Liberian oil tanker) notes that among many other lapses by the crew, the design of the ship's controls was a factor in the accident. It "points to the touch screens on the bridge" and notes that mechanical throttles are generally preferred because "they provide both immediate and tactile feedback to the operator".[71]

Kirigami, Origami and Warigami

The revolution in hand-held or wearable smart devices and rovers are all inspired by Origami, the traditional Japanese art of folding paper. It is possible to make three-dimensional figures of birds, animals, insects, fish, dinosaurs and even mythical characters. Origami requires ordinary paper but designing a creature or an object takes a lot of time. The physiognomy (structure) of each object is studied in fine detail and precise folds and creases make them look like real objects.

Similarly, the geometric diversity of living creatures is a major source of inspiration for scientists and engineers who study not only their organic composition, but also observe and record the movements in diminutive details. Technology developers build mock-ups and replicas based on these observations; and the up-scaled models result in machineries that operate in similar ways as living organisms.

There is a symbiotic linkage between origami and physiognomy in the development of objects. Technology developers can make objects that not only look similar to living creatures; these are equally precise, compact and foldable. It is the latter that has resulted in "swallowable origami robot made of meat and origami exoskeletons that allow tiny bots to be more versatile".[72] According to Kyu Jin Cho, the director of the Soft Robotics Research Centre at Seoul National University, "folding, packaging of everyday things are everywhere,...Why not for robots?"[73] Also, experts of Origami are upbeat about its use, and a former NASA physicist has stated that by using mathematical tools it is possible to "design artistic Origami to create new folding structures that specifically solve technological problems.... We can draw on ideas, structures and mechanisms that already exist in the world of Origami".[74]

Similarly, Kirigami, the Japanese art of paper cutting can make artificial snakeskin that can be wrapped over a soft robot to crawl forward. According to an expert, "these all-terrain soft robots could one day travel across difficult environments for exploration, inspection, monitoring and search-and-rescue missions or perform complex, laparoscopic medical procedures".[75]

Kirigami and Origami are the future of devices which will find reference in the military. Origami enthusiasts are already putting their 'folding' expertise to make models of fighter jets, battle tanks, missiles and other ground vehicles. This art form is now being labelled as 'Warigami' and there is strong evidence in the drone industry which is inspired by Origami and Kirigami.[76] It has also found reference in products and large structures that are carried or stored by squeezing them into tiny spaces thus saving on space.

Shape-shifting is another facet of the evolving technologies. It has its genesis in popular mystical and mythical stories and folklore. For instance, in ancient Indian mythology Nâga (snakes) could assume human form and shape-shifting Rakshasa (demons) assuming animal forms to deceive humans.[77] It is possible to change the physical form or shape of an object. A "combination of origami and digital weaving can help sculpt complex forms which will be compact to transport and easy to deploy through inflatable, pop-up or robotic mechanisms".[78] Apparently, these shape-shifting materials can be useful for solar panels and follow the sun throughout the day which in the future will be a source of power for many military devices, platforms and other associated infrastructure.

Biomimetics

Humankind has mimicked nature, both life-forms and non-living, and learnt to jump, crawl, roll, swim and more recently, fly. Furthermore, living-life is being minutely observed and objects and machines are produced through replication which can take several years to polish to be made into exact copies with similar functions. Apparently, Leonardo da Vinci designed something like an aircraft to enable humans to fly by flapping large artificial wings. He was obviously inspired by the movement of bats, birds, and insects; but it was finally the Wright brothers who built and flew a motor-operated airplane.

The science of mimicking life-forms and building innovative objects/ machines is labelled Biomimicry or Biomimetics; it can be broken up to read as 'bio for life' and 'mimesis for imitation'. According to the Biomimicry Institute, Biomimicry can be defined as "an approach to innovation that seeks sustainable solutions to human challenges by emulating nature's time-tested patterns and strategies. The goal is to create products, processes, and policies—new ways of living—that are well-adapted to life on Earth over the long haul.[79] It involves looking at Nature in fine detail, making an engineering design of the object and creating solutions to solve human problems. It is inherently interdisciplinary and is based on "principles from engineering, chemistry and biology" that are creatively put to use for the "synthesis of materials, synthetic systems or machines that have functions that mimic biological processes".[80] As far as materials used for Biomimicry are concerned, they can be natural or synthetic, but should be able to naturally interact with any portion or section of a biological system. There has been a surge in the number of patents for biomimetic technologies and from fewer than 500 in 1997 it has grown to almost 7,000 by 2017.[81]

Militaries are inspired by Nature and have put to use pets, animals, birds, fishes and mammals to perform a number of activities such as delivery of messages (pigeons), mine detection (dolphins), bats (to carry incendiary bombs) and dogs (detecting explosives), etc. Besides they have also explored the possibility of imitating life-forms to build tools of warfare. It is natural that sea-based life-forms would be the best choice for navies. For instance, a submarine derives its hull-form from the sunfish.[82] It is the heaviest bony fish with the 'exact same body density' as seawater which gives it 'neutral buoyancy' at any depth. Furthermore, it has no 'gas-filled swim bladder' that helps it to 'withstand volume changes from pressure in deep water'. Similarly, sound waves are used for communication purposes underwater as also for detecting underwater objects/obstructions/enemy submarines. This is inspired by dolphins that use sound waves to communicate with other members of the family. Likewise, bats make sounds, listen to echoes, and then see outlines of objects which is the principle used in depth measuring devices which use sound energy underwater.

UAVs and Drones

The skies have traditionally been ruled by aircraft (invented by the Wright brothers in 1903 and helicopters (invented in 1939 by Igor Sikorsky) and in recent times, unmanned aircraft have made their debut adding to the inventory of flying machines. The latter are fast finding place in inventories of a large number of militaries primarily due to their "low weight, small size, and ability to carry a variety of payloads and ordnance".[83] These have been broadly designated as unmanned aerial vehicles (UAVs) and drones and have proved their efficacy and successes in a number of roles such as delivering ordnance, Intelligence, surveillance and reconnaissance (ISR) duties and their performance in missions in a number of conflicts in Afghanistan, West Asia and the Middle East are noteworthy. The UAVs are generally larger in size and are comparatively expensive. According to assessments, the global military UAV market is set to grow from US$ 10.9 billion in 2019 to US$ 14.8 billion in 2029 at a compound annual growth rate (CAGR) of 3.14 per cent.[84] Similarly, the drone market is set to grow in value from US$ 7.93 billion in 2018 to US$ 21.76 billion by 2026 at a CAGR of 12.4 per cent during the forecast period.[85]

Drones are smaller and cheaper than UAVs and are commercially available and therefore are an attractive option. Drones, if operated in swarms like bees or locusts, fly long distances without colliding. For instance, the US Office of Naval Research has developed Low-Cost UAV Swarming Technology (LOCUST) wherein 'swarm of drones' is mimicked based on locust swarms.[86] It is based on the understanding that "fish, birds, insects and even humans naturally form groups...like all groups, when the density gets to a certain point, a collective consciousness occurs, rather than individual thought. This can be witnessed when a flock of birds changes direction, for example, or when a school of fish forms a giant ball when under attack".[87] "Swarm drones are programmed to follow very simple commands that do not require advanced computers and sensors, and therefore their collective numbers could be of the order of hundreds and potentially thousands, which can conjure a lethal force on the battlefield".[88] Furthermore, they can 'self-organise" and be a game-changer in military and naval operations, achieved through coordinated and distributed attacks to saturate defences and breaching an adversary's A2/AD strategy.

Although drones have recorded several successes in various crisis situations, at least three counter-droning techniques are being developed: (a) hard-kill shooting by anti-aircraft guns, missiles, air-burst ammunition and lasers; (b) non-kinetic ways involving cyber-attacks or electronic jamming; and (c) physical barriers that act as traps against drones.[89]

While drones are well known for their operations in the air, these small platforms are now being explored for underwater use. In 2016, during the House Armed Services Committee hearing, Rear Admiral Michael Jabaley, the US Navy's program executive officer for submarines, made an interesting statement that he would like "some organic means of designing the submarine from the ground up that would seamlessly integrate UUVs".[90] He was inspired by 'remoras', a small fish also called 'sharksucker or suckerfish', that attaches itself to a big fish and free rides along and "when it's time for them to go do something, they do and then come back".[91] It was also his belief this would help to launch and recover UAVs as convenient and would be useful for carrying out operations over a larger area in the oceans.

Counter-drone technologies are being developed amid the fear of drone swarms that are becoming popular tools of warfare. The anti-drone market is expected to grow from US$ 342.6 million in 2016 to US$ 1,571.3 million by

2023, at a compound annual growth rate (CAGR) of 25.9 per cent between 2017 and 2023.[92]

Another innovative option offered by Rear Admiral Michael Jabaley was to design a new propulsion system which would eliminate drive shaft and blades of the propeller which would result in "revolutionary leap in acoustic performance"[93] as also reduce underwater noise which is the major source of being detected by enemy submarines. Jabaley believed that advances in Biomimetics would result in a new design for platforms that would take underwater warfare into a new realm. There is also a view that future submarines could shelve mechanical drives because it has reached "limits in terms of acoustic performance".[94]

Digital Twinning

Digital Twining is a process in which a solid object is digitally mapped, mirrored and monitored using data from sensors fitted in the equipment. The sensors then send data through a Cloud-based system before being "analyzed, using machine learning algorithms in cases where there are more complicated variables and a harder-to-discover linear relation. The changes identified are then replicated in the twin. The twin can vary widely in complexity".[95] A 'digital twin' of an offshore platform or a ship can help obtain real-time performance or parameters of various onboard machinery or systems. It "helps predict breakdowns before the equipment fails, and enables remedial measures through replacements and repair, thereby enhancing operational efficiency".[96]

Cloud Computing

Cloud computing is a general term "inspired by the Cloud symbol that's often used to represent the internet in flowcharts and diagrams" and involves the use of Internet to deliver hosted services.[97] It is built around: (a) infrastructure as a service (IaaS); (b) platform as a service (PaaS); and (c) software as a service (SaaS).[98] The German Cloud-based software service provider Hanseaticsoft notes that Cloud computing technology "solves a major problem facing the maritime industry because it facilitates increased ship capacity without requiring expensive infrastructure investments, or personnel training".[99]

Cloud-based management helps in monitoring shipping operations and shipbuilding. Although the shipping industry, including supply chain managers, were initially hesitant, they have slowly started using Cloud computing services to securely store data, which allows industry executives to understand and address market and operational risks effectively.[100] For instance, the United Arab Shipping Co. which operates a fleet of 70 vessels, saved bunker fuel costs by 3 to 5 per cent by using a Cloud. As far as shipbuilding is concerned, Cloud computing is making promising inroads. Samsung Heavy Industries has turned to Amazon Web Services (AWS) as a digitalisation platform and uses its services of Cloud computing and data storage to expand its smart shipping capabilities.[101]

At the operational level, Cloud computing is being put to use in autonomous ships that use enormous amounts of data from numerous sources including on-board systems to detect, identify and track objects. For instance, Rolls-Royce is partnering with Google for its Cloud Machine Learning Engine to train Rolls-Royce's AI-based object classification system.[102]

Chatbots

Messaging applications such as WhatsApp, Messenger, Facebook, etc., are very popular and help interaction among people, shoppers, companies, customers, etc. However, it is now time to say 'goodbye, apps', instead use 'hello, bots'.[103] Chatbot is a conversation tool for automating conversation and comes in countless forms and frameworks. There are two main categories, i.e., Rule-based Chabot and Machine learning-based Chatbot. The former "use keywords to complete scripted actions. It has gained popularity in e-commerce not only because it is easier to build but also because it can get simple tasks done" and the latter "are more complex and tend to converse more naturally due to their use of neural networks".[104] Chatbots can soon become "pervasive in day-to-day company-to-customer and online communications"[105] and explode in popularity.

Chatbots work as virtual assistants and are capable of accessing data and answering questions relating to maritime operations. For instance, the VTS-Bot project employs ChatBot which "assists future Officers of the Watch (OOW) in acquiring maritime communication skills as per the SMCP (Standard Marine Communication Phrases) as mandated under communication competencies under the IMO STCW code (Standards of Training, Certification and Watchkeeping, Chapter II, Table A-II/1).[106]

Singularity

The idea of Singularity has been around since the 1950s. During a talk entitled "Intelligent Machinery: A heretical theory," in 1951, Alan Turing observed that "Once the machine thinking method has started, it would not take long to outstrip our feeble powers.... At some stage therefore we should have to expect the machines to take control".[107] In the early 1999s, Vernor Vinge from the Department of Mathematical Sciences, San Diego State University, in a paper argued that it will be technologically possible to create 'superhuman intelligence' and this will mark the beginning of the 'end of the human' era.[108]

In recent times, Raymond Kurzweil , in his book, 'The Singularity in Near' argues that Singularity can be created by a super-human artificial intelligence with the potential to conjure ideas which "no human being has thought about in the past, and will invent technological tools that will be more sophisticated and advanced than anything we have today".[109]

Super-intelligent artificial intelligence can be expected to improve upon itself continuously and create another improved version. This will result in an 'intelligence explosion' and the 'simple, biological machines' that humans are will be left far behind. These fears have also been expressed by Steven Hawking and Elon Musk and they cautioned that super-intelligent artificial intelligence, if allowed to run away, could create many other challenges.[110] For instance, super-human artificial intelligence, when applied to weapons, could even take human life on the battlefield or in policing, border control, or any circumstances without human oversight. It is useful to mention that there is an ongoing agitation against autonomous technologies and an international ban on 'killer robots' as also "a treaty for emerging weapons' is being advocated. This issue is discussed in detail in Chapter 8.

Be that as it may, artificial intelligence specialists are confident about the arrival of Singularity, but differ on the time it will become a reality. Raymond Kurzweil has predicted that machines will match human intelligence by 2029 and will surpass it by 2045.[111] Another prediction by Masayoshi Son, SoftBank CEO, notes that Singularity will arrive by 2047 and artificial enabled machines will constantly improve upon themselves and start controlling and managing connected devices.[112] It is at this point that "a single computer chip will have an IQ of 10,000—far surpassing the most intelligent people in the world".[113] Further, "If this super intelligence goes into moving robots, the world, our lifestyle dramatically changes".

These robots, two, four or 100-legged or winged or with propellers, would be crawling on land, flying in the air, sailing or swimming in water and would be everywhere. Over the next three decades their population will surpass that of humans living on the Earth. Depending on the number of robots that are connected to the Internet, it is plausible that their combined intelligence could be far higher and superior than that of the human population. For instance, it is estimated that by 2020, "50 billion objects will be connected to the Internet. This will result in a smart integrated system of sensors, data and Internet-enabled devices that manage our lives. Over the next 25 years, through technological convergence, the 'Internet of Everything' will enable us to manage all aspects of our lives in real time".[114]

Artificial Intelligence will fundamentally transform warfare from 'informatized' to 'intelligentized'[115] and its usage is beginning to find reference in many facets of naval activity. Swarm drone operations will grow exponentially and underwater drones will operate autonomously and intelligently navigate to avoid obstacles to carry out reconnaissance missions. Future missiles will possess a high degree of artificial intelligence for a number of functions such as mission control, flight management, and target designation. It will be possible to overcome the limitations of 'fire and forget' and control these in real-time as also redirect them to other tasks while in flight. There will be data fusion, synthesis of multi-source data and images, automated target recognition based on machine learning and intelligent sensing in complex electromagnetic environment. Big data analytics would be pivotal enablers who would be able to retrieve massive information, and by using advanced computational capacity make intelligent decisions. While it will be possible to achieve information and data superiority, human physical and psychological shortcomings would need to be compensated by an external and intelligent brain thereby augmenting battle space awareness for quick decision making and hasten the command-cycle by presenting recommendations to the commander. Whenever that happens, Singularity in naval warfare would have arrived and become a reality and would severely challenge human power to micromanage and exercise authority.

Issues of Cyber Warfare

The 4IR enabled battle space at sea will be dotted with an assortment of autonomous and unmanned platforms and diverse devices that would be deployed for varied tasks. While there is a bright future for 4IR technologies, it is equally important to understand that hackers will be on the prowl and data thefts and Ransomware attacks will continue to torment and challenge storage infrastructure and devices. Some of these will run on some version of the World

Wide Web which will pose numerous challenges for tactical commanders. This will entail hardened protection and an unchallengeable recovery plan to regain control over data. Robust cyber warfare capabilities in which the actors (State and non-State) aim to disrupt command and control structures, networks, and systems and gain battle-space superiority and winning the war through asymmetry would need to be addressed.

Artificial Intelligence is also useful for detecting cyber-attacks. By some estimates, the detection rate of cyber-attacks varies between 85 per cent and 99 per cent.[116] However, hackers too can use Artificial Intelligence to systematize cyber-attacks on a massive scale. Furthermore Artificial Intelligence can also be the catalyst for new types of cyber-attacks that would add to the complexity and necessitate new ways to manage the AI-ML-Deep Learning enabled battle space.[117]

Concluding Thoughts

This chapter has expounded on 4IR technologies and their application in commercial maritime operations and naval warfare. The chapter documented several 4IR technologies, their developments, and usage in the maritime and naval domains. It makes the argument that 4IR technologies will transform commercial maritime operations, and navies across the globe are preparing to use 4IR technologies in warfare at sea. The next chapter explores how 4IR technologies are transforming commercial maritime operations and disrupting ship-port-production hubs/zones as also supply chains and their operations/ managers and users.

NOTES

1. Klaus Schwab, *The Fourth Industrial Revolution* (UK: Portfolio Penguin, 2017), pp.6-9.
2. Ibid. The term '4IR' has its genesis in the high-tech strategy of the German government presented at the 2012 Hanover Fair by Siegfried Dais (Robert Bosch GmbH) and Henning Kagermann (Acatech).
3. Indermit Gill, "Whoever Leads in Artificial Intelligence in 2030 will rule the World until 2100", https://www.brookings.edu/blog/future-development/2020/01/17/whoever-leads-in-artificial-intelligence-in-2030-will-rule-the-world-until-2100/ (accessed 19 January 2020).
4. Ibid.
5. Klaus Schwab, *The Fourth Industrial Revolution*, (UK: Portfolio Penguin, 2017), pp.6-9.
6. Heller, Christian H. (2019), "The Future Navy—Near-Term Applications of Artificial Intelligence", *Naval War College Review*: Vol. 72: No. 4, Article 7, https://digital-commons.usnwc.edu/nwc-review/vol72/iss4/7 (accessed 24 February 2020).

7. Amanda Jenner, "The Evolution of Artificial Intelligence", https://tecadmin.net/evolution-of-artificial-intelligence/ (accessed 24 February 2020).
8. "National Strategy for Artificial Intelligence: # AI for All" https://niti.gov.in/writereaddata/files/document_publication/NationalStrategy-for-AI-Discussion-Paper.pdf (accessed 24 February 2020).
9. "Summary of the 2018 Department Of Defence Artificial Intelligence Strategy: Harnessing AI to Advance Our Security and Prosperity", p. 5., https://media.defense.gov/2019/Feb/12/2002088963/-1/-1/1/SUMMARY-OF-DOD-AI-STRATEGY.PDF (accessed 24 February 2020).
10. E. Kulbiej & P. Wo³ejsza, "Naval Artificial Intelligence", https://www.researchgate.net/publication/318655874_Naval_Artificial_Intelligence (accessed 24 January 2020).
11. "Artificial Intelligence to help Indian Navy to deal with Different Threats", https://www.financialexpress.com/defence/artificial-intelligence-to-help-indian-navy-to-deal-with-different-threats/1549959/ (accessed 24 February 2020).
12. "What do you think Artificial Intelligence is?" https://cisse.info/pdf/2019/rr_01_artificial_intelligence.pdf (accessed 23 February 2020).
13. Connor S. Mclemore & Hans Lauzen, "The Dawn of Artificial Intelligence in Naval Warfare", https://warontherocks.com/2018/06/the-dawn-of-artificial-intelligence-in-naval-warfare/ accessed 24 February 2020).
14. "8 Key Military Applications for Artificial Intelligence in 2018", https://blog.marketresearch.com/8-key-military-applications-for-artificial-intelligence-in-2018 (accessed 24 February 2020).
15. "The Big Data battlefield", http://mil-embedded.com/articles/the-big-data-battlefield/ (accessed 24 January 2020).
16. "How AI, Drones and Big Data are Reshaping the Future of Warfare", https://www.forbes.com/sites/bernardmarr/2016/10/06/how-ai-drones-and-big-data-are-reshaping-the-future-of-warfare/#2d9247923fa9 (accessed 23 November 2019).
17. "How Does Big Data Show Up in War?", https://www.rebellionresearch.com/blog/how-does-big-data-show-up-in-war (accessed 24 February 2020).
18. "Maritime Big Data Market 2020 Impressively Grow in Future by Top Companies Analysis By IHS Markit Ltd, Eniram Ltd, ABB, LAROS Technologies, Inmarsat Plc, Ericsson |Global Forecast to 2025", https://www.openpr.com/news/2032538/maritime-big-data-market-2020-impressively-grow-in-future-by-top (accessed 6 May 2020).
19. "Artificial Intelligence in Military Market", https://www.marketsandmarkets.com/Market-Reports/artificial-intelligence-military-market-41793495.html (accessed 24 February 2020).
20. "Latest Engineering Trends in Surface Combatants' Design and Construction", https://www.indrastra.com/2020/05/Latest-Engineering-Trends-in-Surface-Combatants-Design-006-05-2020-0002.html (accessed 6 May 2020).
21. "The Big Data battlefield", http://mil-embedded.com/articles/the-big-data-battlefield/ (accessed 24 January 2020).
22. Ibid.
23. "Artificial Intelligence and Embedded Computing for Unmanned Vehicles", https://www.militaryaerospace.com/unmanned/article/14175187/artificial-intelligence-and-embedded-computing-for-unmanned-vehicles (accessed 24 April 2020).
24. Andrew Meola, "Understanding Blockchain technology, Bitcoins and the rise of Cryptocurrency", https://www.businessinsider.com/blockchain-technology-cryptocurrency-

explained-2017-8?IR=T (accessed 2 May 2020).

25. "What Different Types of Blockchains are There?", https://dragonchain.com/blog/differences-between-public-private-blockchains/ (accessed 23 November 2019).
26. "Why is Blockchain a disruptive technology?:, https://www.projectco3.eu/2019/04/08/why-is-blockchain-a-disruptive-technology/#:~:text=Blockchain%20has%20been%20considered% 20a,the%20Web%20had%20on%20communication. (accessed 23 June 2020).
27. "Blockchain Technology has the Power to let us build an Entirely New Internet", https://futurism.com/blockchain-technology-has-the-power-to-let-us-build-an-entirely-new-internet (accessed 23 November 2019).
28. "MasterCard Announces That Payments can now be made on Blockchain", https://futurism.com/mastercard-announces-that-payments-can-now-be-made-on-blockchainannounces-that-payments-can-now-be-made-on-blockchain (accessed 23 November 2019).
29. Neil Ainger, "SAP unveils Blockchain service in the Cloud", https://www.cnbc.com/2017/05/17/sap-unveils-blockchain-service-in-the-cloud.html (accessed 23 November 2019).
30. "DARPA, NATO Looking at Military Applications of Blockchain Technology", https://bitcoinmagazine.com/articles/darpa-nato-looking-at-military-applications-of-blockchain-technology-1464018766 (accessed 23 November 2019).
31. "Blockchain technology has been slow to gain adoption in non-financial contexts, but it could turn out to have invaluable military applications", https://www.nextgov.com/cio-briefing/2016/10/even-us-military-looking-blockchain-technology-secure-nuclear-weapons/132258/(accessed 23 November 2019).
32. "Size of the Blockchain Technology Market Worldwide from 2018 to 2023", https://www.statista.com/statistics/647231/worldwide-blockchain-technology-market-size/ (accessed 23 November 2019).
33. "The Pokémon GO Experience: A Location-Based Augmented Reality Mobile Game Goes Mainstream", http://library.usc.edu.ph/ACM/CHI%202017/1proc/p2493.pdf (accessed 23 November 2019).
34. "This map can show the exact location of every Pokémon around you", https://www.theverge.com/tldr/2016/7/19/12226958/pokemon-go-google-map-display (accessed 23 November 2019).
35. "Military Base issues 'Pokémon GO' Warning", https://www.foxnews.com/tech/military-base-issues-pokemon-go-warning (accessed 23 November 2019).
36. "The Difference between Virtual Reality, Augmented Reality And Mixed Reality", https://www.forbes.com/sites/quora/2018/02/02/the-difference-between-virtual-reality-augmented-reality-and-mixed-reality/#6e12cc7a2d07 ((accessed 23 November 2019).
37. Alexandra Levit, *Humanity Works: Merging Technologies and People for the Workforce of the Future* (London: Kogan Page, 2019), p. 97.
38. "Mixed Reality", https://en.wikipedia.org/wiki/Mixed_reality#:~:text=%22The%20conventionally%20held%20view%20of,with%2C%20a%20completely%20synthetic%20world (accessed 23 November 2020).
39. Steven Keslowitz, *The Digital Dystopias of Black Mirror and Electric Dreams* (North Carolina: MacFarland & Co, 2020). p.151.
40. "Theory and applications of marker-based augmented reality", https://www.vttresearch.com/sites/default/files/pdf/science/2012/S3.pdf (accessed 23 November 2019).

41. "Augmented Reality in Military: AR Can Enhance Warfare and Training", https://jasoren.com/augmented-reality-military/ (accessed 23 November 2019).
42. Vijay Sakhuja, "Naval Transformation: From Casting and Forging to 3D Printing", http://www.defstrat.com/magazine_articles/naval-transformation-from-casting-and-forging-to-3d-printing/ (accessed 23 November 2019).
43. "Emerging technologies: impact on shipbuilding", http://dx.doi.org/10.1080/09733159.2016.1239359, *Maritime Affairs: Journal of the National Maritime Foundation of India*, 2016.
44. "3D Printed Boat Sets Guinness World Record", https://www.maritime-executive.com/article/3d-printed-boat-sets-guinness-world-record (accessed 16 October 2019).
45. "University of Maine Creates the World's Largest 3D Printed Boat", https://www.3dnatives.com/en/3d-printed-boat-university-of-maine-161020195/ (accessed 16 October 2019).
46. "3-D Printing Might Be a New Future in Navy Ship Construction", https://www.realcleardefense.com/articles/2018/12/31/3-d_printing_might_be_a_new_ future_in_navy_ship_construction__114069.html (accessed 16 October 2019).
47. "IoT connected devices worldwide 2030", https://www.statista.com/statistics/802690/worldwide-connected-devices-by-access-technology/ (accessed 21 April 2020).
48. "The IoT in 2030: 24 billion Connected Things Generating $1.5 trillion" https://iotbusinessnews.com/2020/05/20/03177-the-iot-in-2030-24-billion-connected-things-generating-1-5-trillion/#:~:text=The%20IoT%20in%202030%3A%2024%20 billion %20 connected%20things%20generating%20%241.5%20trillion,-Posted%20by%20IoT& text= By%20Matt%20Hatton%2C%20Founding%20Partner,USD465%20billion%20to%20over%20USD1. (accessed 06 June 2020).
49. A zettabyte is one sextillion bytes and a sextillion is numeral one followed by 21 zeroes. Some of the key technical features of 5G are: (a) support one million connected devices per square kilometer; (b) 1-millisecond latency; (c) peak data download rate of up to 20 gigabits per second; and (d) greater efficiency in terms of power and use of radio spectrum.
50. "IDC: Expect 175 zettabytes of Data Worldwide by 2025", https://www.networkworld.com/article/3325397/idc-expect-175-zettabytes-of-data-worldwide-by-2025.html (accessed 21 April 2020).
51. Dumitrel Loghin, (et al), "The Disruptions of 5G on Data-driven Technologies and Applications", https://arxiv.org/pdf/1909.08096.pdf (accessed 21 April 2020).
52. "China Unicom and Huawei Jointly Launch Industry-First 5G Edge-Cloud Smart Port Solution, Trial Already Started", https://www.huawei.com/en/press-events/news/2018/4/Industry-First-5G-Edge-Cloud-Smart-Port-Solution (accessed 21 April 2020).
53. "CFIUS Reform: Key Takeaways for Investors", https://www.reedsmith.com/en/perspectives/2018/08/cfius-reform-key-takeaways-for-investors (accessed 21 April 2020).
54. "U.K. Bars Huawei for 5G as Tech Battle between China and the West Escalates", https://www.nytimes.com/2020/07/14/business/huawei-uk-5g.html (accessed 1 August 2020).
55. "Submarine Cable 101", https://www2.telegeography.com/submarine-cable-faqs-frequently-asked-questions (accessed 25 March 2020).
56. "Africa Network Connections - SMW3 - SEA-ME-WE3", https://www.cmcnetworks.net/smw3-sea-me-we3.html (accessed 25 March 2020).
57. "The Submarine Cable System Market by Application (Communication (Component, Offering (Installation & Commissioning, Upgrades)), Power (Type, Voltage, End User

(Offshore Wind Power Generation, Offshore Oil & Gas), and Region - Global Forecast to 2025", https://www.businesswire.com/news/home/20200317005632/en/Global-Submarine-Cable-System-Market-2020-2025.

58. "How Google Is Cramming More Data into Its New Atlantic Cable", https://www.wired.com/story/google-cramming-more-data-new-atlantic-cable/ (accessed 25 March 2020).
59. "How the Internet Spans the Globe". https://cacm.acm.org/magazines/2020/1/241709-how-the-internet-spans-the-globe/fulltext (accessed 25 March 2020).
60. 'The Future of Data Centers', https://www.cbinsights.com/research/future-of-data-centers/ (accessed 21 April 2020).
61. Ibid.
62. "How Important Is Location When Choosing a Data Center?", https://www.datacenterknowledge.com/industry-perspectives/how-important-location-when-choosing-data-center (accessed 21 April 2020).
63. "Data Center Services", https://bluebirdnetwork.com/data-center-services/ (accessed 21 April 2020).
64. "That's Really Cool: Facebook Puts Your Photos into the Deep Freeze as it Unveils Massive new Five Acre Data center Near Arctic Circle", https://www.dailymail.co.uk/sciencetech/article-2054168/Facebook-unveils-massive-data-center-Lulea-Sweden.html (accessed 21 April 2020).
65. "Mines, Underwater, Outer Space - the Weirdest Data Centers on Earth and Beyond", https://datacenternews.us/story/mines-underwater-outer-space-the-weirdest-data-centers-on-earth-and-beyond (accessed 21 April 2020).
66. "Floating Data Centers to be Designed for Singapore", https://www.maritime-executive.com/article/floating-data-centers-to-be-designed-for-singapore (accessed 21 April 2020).
67. "Wearable and Implantable Sensors for Biomedical Applications", https://innovate.ee.ucla.edu/wp-content/uploads/2010/03/Ozcan-Group-Annurev-Anchem-Wearable-Implant-2018.pdf (accessed 21 April 2020).
68. "Global Wearable Technology Market Study 2020-2025: Evaluates the Current State of the Wearable Technology Ecosystem Including Devices, Applications and Industry Segments", https://www.businesswire.com/news/home/20200304005515/en/Global-Wearable-Technology-Market-Study-2020-2025-Evaluates (accessed 23 June 2020).
69. "The Worldwide Wearable Market Leaps 126.9% in the Fourth Quarter and 171.6% in 2015 according to IDC", https://www.businesswire.com/news/home/20160223005496/en/Worldwide-Wearables-Market-Leaps-126.9-Fourth-Quarter (accessed 21 April 2020).
70. "Wearable Technology Market 2020-2024", https://www.businesswire.com/news/home/20200207005233/en/Wearable-Technology-Market-2020-2024-Popularity-Wearable-Devices (accessed 21 April 2020).
71. "The US Navy will Replace its Touch Screen Controls with Mechanical ones on its Destroyers", https://www.theverge.com/2019/8/11/20800111/us-navy-uss-john-s-mccain-crash-ntsb-report-touchscreen-mechanical-controls (accessed 6 June 2020).
72. Vijay Sakhuja, "Origami and Kirigami Support Military and Space Innovation", Vol. 13, Mar/Apr, 2019, p.13.
73. "Origami Robots to Help the Scientists", https://medium.com/deepaerodrones/origami-robots-to-help-the-scientists-49c9fdda1043 (accessed 21 April 2020).
74. "6 ways the centuries-old art of origami is bringing us the future", https://www.nbcnews.com/mach/science/6-ways-ancient-art-origami-bringing-us-future-ncna898731 (accessed 21 April 2020).

75. "Soft robots could one day slither and crawl to complete rescue missions", https://www.createdigital.org.au/soft-robots-rescue-missions/(accessed 21 April 2020).
76. Vijay Sakhuja, "Origami and Kirigami Support Military and Space Innovation", Vol. 13, Mar/Apr, 2019, p.13.
77. "The Concept of Transformation Myth in A·chik Culture", https://shodhganga.inflibnet.ac.in/bitstream/10603/253546/9/09_chapter%204.pdf (accessed 21 April 2020).
78. "Origami-inspired Habitats for the Moon and Mars", https://earthsky.org/space/using-origami-to-design-habitats-for-moon-mars (accessed 21 April 2020).
79. "Biomimicry Definition: What Is It, Examples and Areas of Application", https://youmatter.world/en/definition/definitions-what-is-biomimicry-definition-examples/ (accessed 15 February2020).
80. "Bioinspired and Bioderived Materials", https://www.nap.edu/read/10631/chapter/9 (accessed 30 July 2020).
81. "Can Biomimicry Save the Planet? This Exhibition Shows the Green Side of Tech—and Exposes the Greenwashing", https://www.forbes.com/sites/jonathonkeats/2020/07/28/biomimicry-moda/#4921ec525887 (accessed 30 July 2020).
82. "Biomimicry", https://janssenjbiology-history-humanityofwarfar.weebly.com/biomimicry.html (accessed 15 February 2020).
83. "Swarm Drones: Could they Shape the Future of Naval Warfare?", http://www.ipcs.org/comm_select.php?articleNo=5426 (accessed 24 March 2020).
84. "World's top Military UAV Manufacturers and Global Market Insights", https://www.marketresearchreports.com/blog/2019/10/31/worlds-top-military-uav-manufacturers-and-global-market-insight (accessed 24 March 2020).
85. "Military Drone Market Size to Reach USD 21.76 Billion by 2026; Introduction to Advanced Technology will Boost Growth, says Fortune Business Insights", https://www.globenewswire.com/news-release/2020/02/17/1985673/0/en/Military-Drone-Market-Size-to-Reach-USD-21-76-Billion-by-2026-Introduction-to-Advanced-Technology-Will-Boost-Growth-says-Fortune-Business-Insights.html (accessed 24 March 2020).
86. "Navy office awards $30 million contract for drone swarms", https://www.c4isrnet.com/unmanned/2018/06/27/office-of-naval-research-awards-raytheon-30-million-to-develop-locust-swarm/ (accessed 24 March 2020).
87. Rebecca Northfield, "Military by Nature: Biomimetic Inspiration for Future Armies", https://eandt.theiet.org/content/articles/2018/11/military-by-nature-biomimetic-inspiration-for-future-armies/ (accessed 21 February 2020).
88. Vijay Sakhuja, "Swarm Drones: Could they Shape the Future of Naval Warfare?" http://www.ipcs.org/comm_select.php?articleNo=5426 (accessed 24 March 2020).
89. Ibid
90. Dave Majumdar, "US Navy's Next Submarine: Super Stealthy and now Underwater Aircraft Carrier?", https://nationalinterest.org/blog/the-buzz/us-navys-next-submarine-super-stealthy-now-underwater-16978 (accessed 15 February 2020).
91. Ibid.
92. "Anti-drone Market", https://www.marketsandmarkets.com/PressReleases/anti-drone.asp (accesed 24 February 2020).
93. Dave Majumdar, "US Navy's Next Submarine: Super Stealthy and Now Underwater Aircraft

Carrier?", https://nationalinterest.org/blog/the-buzz/us-navys-next-submarine-super-stealthy-now-underwater-16978 (accessed 15 February 2020).

94. Dave Majumdar, "Beyond the Ohio-Class: Inside America's Next-Generation Missile Submarine", https://nationalinterest.org/feature/beyond-the-ohio-class-inside-americas-next-generation-16270 (accessed 15 February 2020).

95. "Beginner's Guide To Digital Twin Technology", https://channels.theinnovationenterprise.com/articles/a-beginner-s-guide-to-digital-twin-technology (accessed 15 March 2020).

96. "Maritime Digital Trends in 2018", http://www.ipcs.org/columns_select.php?column_name=Maritime%20Matters (accessed 15 March 2020).

97. "Cloud Computing", https://searchcloudcomputing.techtarget.com/definition/cloud-computing (accessed 23 March 2020).

98. "SaaS vs PaaS vs IaaS: What's the Difference and How to Choose", https://www.bmc.com/blogs/saas-vs-paas-vs-iaas-whats-the-difference-and-how-to-choose/ (accessed 23 March 2020).

99. "Will Cloud Technology Revolutionise Ship Management?", https://www.ship-technology.com/features/cloud-technology-shipping/(accessed 23 March 2020).

100. Vijay Sakhuja, "Maritime Digital Trends in 2018", http://www.ipcs.org/comm_select.php?articleNo=5417 (accessed 23 March 2020).

101. "Amazon cloud will help shipbuilder develop autonomous shipping", https://www.rivieramm.com/news-content-hub/news-content-hub/amazon-cloud-will-help-shipbuilder-develop-autonomous-shipping-23696 (accessed 23 March 2020).

102. "Rolls-Royce to 'man' Autonomous Ship with Google AI Software", https://www.thehindubusinessline.com/economy/logistics/rollsroyce-to-man-autonomous-ship-with-google-ai-software/article9901368.ece (accessed 23 March 2020).

103. "Hello Bots, Goodbye Apps: How Brands Should Embrace Chat Bots", http://www.adweek.com/digital/michaelaaron-flicker-xenopsi-tuest-post-hello-bots-goodbye-apps/ (accessed 23 March 2020).

104. "Machine Learning Chatbots: What You Should Know about Neural Conversation Agents", https://www.cognillo.com/blog/machine-learning-chatbots-neural-conversation-agents/ (accessed 23 March 2020).

105. "The Rise of Chat Bots and Their Implications for Social Media", https://www.adweek.com/digital/smadar-landau-feelter-guest-post-chat-bots/ (accessed 23 March 2020).

106. "VTS-Bot: Using ChatBots in SMCP-based Maritime Communication", https://www.researchgate.net/publication/303365446_VTS-Bot_Using_ChatBots_in_SMCP-based_Maritime_Communication (accessed 23 March 2020).

107. "What Is the Future of Computers? https://www.livescience.com/23074-future-computers.html (accessed 23 March 2020).

108. "What is The Singularity?", https://mindstalk.net/vinge/vinge-sing.html (accessed 23 March 2020).

109. "Singularity: Explain It to Me Like I'm 5-Years-Old", https://futurism.com/singularity-explain-it-to-me-like-im-5-years-old (accessed 23 March 2020).

110. "Stephen Hawking Warns Artificial Intelligence could end Mankind", https://www.bbc.com/news/technology-30290540https://www.bbc.com/news/technology-30290540 (accessed 23 March 2020).

111. "Can Futurists Predict the Year of the Singularity?", https://singularityhub.com/2017/03/31/can-futurists-predict-the-year-of-the-singularity/#sm.00001pi9kifp7fd26pkedlr2s3ic6 (accessed 21 April 2020).

112. "Softbank CEO: The Singularity Will Happen by 2047", https://futurism.com/softbank-ceo-the-singularity-will-happen-by-2047 (accessed 21 April 2020).
113. "There's a New Prediction for the Singularity: 2047", https://www.inverse.com/article/28386-singularity-2047 (accessed 21 April 2020).
114. "2038: Six Trends for the Next 25 Years", https://www.zenithmedia.com/wp-content/uploads/2014/01/ZO2038TrendsReport.pdf (accessed 21 April 2020).
115. "Battlefield Singularity: Artificial Intelligence, Military Revolution, and China's Future Military Power", https://s3.amazonaws.com/files.cnas.org/documents/Battlefield-Singularity-November-2017.pdf?mtime=20171129235804 (accessed 21 April 2020).
116. Ibid.
117. "How Artificial Intelligence Is Changing Cyber Security Landscape and Preventing Cyber Attacks", https://www.entrepreneur.com/article/339509 (accessed 8 August 2020).

CHAPTER 2

Maritime Commercial Operations

The maritime world is not new to technological revolution. It has evolved from sailing ships that carried 'low volume; high value' cargo (silk, spices, porcelain, etc.) to modern ships that transport 'high volume; low value' (oil and gas tankers and coal and ore carriers) cargo and now container shipping (palletized cargo) which has transformed the way cargo is packaged and carried onboard ships.[1] This has significantly reduced intermodal transportation costs across the supply chain from production zones to ships to the end user. The stage is now set for transition in the nature of cargo from coal for which a high point has already passed, to fossil fuels that would experience peak demand by 2035 and gas could become the world's primary energy source towards 2050.[2]

Likewise, there is an ongoing technological transformation impacting on the way ships are operated, cargo handled at ports and supply chains that go far deep into the heartland. There is widespread automation in nearly all facets of operations and processes enumerated above. Electronic data exchange with real-time feeds among multiple stakeholders (ship, port, shipping company, freight forwarder and end user) along the supply chain has contributed immensely to make the maritime trading ecosystem highly efficient.[3]

Similarly, there are numerous notable advancements in ship navigation such as Global Positioning System (GPS), Electronic Chart Display Systems (ECDIS), Automatic Identification System (AIS), and onboard Voyage Data Recorder (VDR) to record and store data of each voyage in electronic format and Global Maritime Distress and Safety System (GMDSS) for communication, distress signal accurate weather forecasting, a compulsory requirement of the International Convention for the Safety of Life at Sea Convention 1974 (SOLAS), etc.

The 2017 UNCTAD Review of Maritime Transport (RMT), an annual publication of the United Nations Conference on Trade and Development (UNCTAD), acknowledges that "new technologies are transforming the maritime transport industry and providing opportunities to improve economic efficiency, optimize logistics management systems and operations, and expand connectivity, including digital connectivity".[4] Furthermore, remotely operated vessels and unmanned ocean going vessels are the future of shipping and industry experts believe that these could be operational by 2025 and 2030, respectively. In the above contexts, this chapter expounds on the transformative changes in maritime infrastructure led by Industry 4.0 technologies.

Seaports and Port Operations

The maritime trading system is the vanguard of economic development[5] and ports and harbours are central to maritime trade. Since ancient times there have been striking improvements in the way cargo is handled. The earlier practice of manual loading and unloading at anchorages or offshore terminals was a laborious activity; it involved the transfer of cargo from a bigger vessel to boats and vice versa. The ever increasing size of ships and the changing nature of cargo necessitated docks for loading and unloading of goods.

There were simultaneous developments to improve efficiency of ports, and dockside cranes replaced manual loading operations. In contemporary times, cargo has been containerized, ports are highly digitalized and have boosted efficiency of maritime operations. Significantly, modern ports are networked with various industrial centres, Special Economic Zones and manufacturing hubs on land thus creating a digital ecosystem of goods and services.

The table below[6] provides a broad idea of transformation in ports and their operations.

Phase	1st IR	2nd IR	3rd IR	4th IR
Period	18th-19th century	First half of 20th century	Second half of 20th century	Early 21st century
Energy	Coal	Oil &gas	Oil & gas and Nuclear	Renewable Energy
Storage Location for	Coal & iron ore	Oil & gas	Consumer goods	Biomass, Recyclables, Renewables

Phase	1st IR	2nd IR	3rd IR	4th IR
Production System	Mechanical Production	Mass Production Make-to-stock	Mass Customization Make to Order	Distributed Manufacturing
Dominant Transportation Innovation	Rail Steamship	Automobile Truck	Jet aircraft Very Large Vessel	Autonomous Vehicles/ vessels Ultra Large Vessels
Port evolves as location for	Steel Industry	(Petro)chemical industry	Container handling	Bio-based chemicals and Circular industry
Communication	Telegraph	Telephone	Telematics (Internet)	Internet of Things

Source: Ports in the 4th Industrial Revolution – Learning to think in circles", https://safety4sea.com/ports-in-the-4th-industrial-revolution-learning-to-think-in-circles/(accessed 21 September 2019).

In the above context, it has been noted that "introducing IoT techniques into container terminal operations enables port terminal operators and other port related entities to collect, process and store a bulky digitalized data from daily terminal operations on 24 hours and 365 days per year basis without any terminal staff intervention".[7] Furthermore, Artificial Intelligence will "learn port operation skills and practices by analyzing the big data" and automatized container terminal yards "will assist the terminal staff in all their daily operations and management works". Some of the important functions would be assisting terminal planners about stowage and yard plans, crane time optimization, control and processing of container cargo traffic, etc.[8] Many seaports across the globe have begun using 4IR technologies and these have been labelled as 'Smart Ports'; however, the major smart port players are in Europe and the USA, barring one in Asia.[9]

Numerous definitions have been propounded to define the term 'Smart Port' but a simpler version is a port that uses "automation and innovative technologies including Artificial Intelligence (AI), big data, Internet of Things (IoT) and Blockchain to improve its performance"[10] to conduct its operations. At the heart of this definition are two important issues; first, 4IR technologies enable 'efficient data-driven decision making';[11] and the second is about enhancing the efficiency of the supply chain. This is not to suggest that it is only the ports that require 4IR technologies; instead, these technologies are now a prerequisite and must be embedded in every facet and operation in which a port is one of the many stakeholders in the supply chain.

The traditional understanding of a port as a venue for exchange of cargo between a ship and the port, and serve as a transhipment hub for movement of cargo to other destinations is also under transformation. It is seen as a nucleus of information exchange as also to facilitate diverse services to existing clienteles and new customers joining and availing unique digital services of the whole ecosystem.[12] For instance, among the many activities and operations that take place in a port, 'Harbour Pilots' are responsible for moving the ship in/out of the port. In future, this activity "could involve a port-based drone that would fly to a landing pad located above a ship's control bridge" and remotely guide it from a shore station.[13]

The drive to digitalize ports and the shipping industry is gaining momentum. The International Association of Ports and Harbours (IAPH), a leading organization in the shipping industry, has observed that "while some port communities seized the opportunities of the fourth industrial revolution and developed into full-fledged 'smart' ports, many others have barely grasped the essentials of digitalization and continue to struggle with a larger reliance on personal interaction and paper-based transactions as the norms for shipboard, ship-port interface and port-hinterland based exchanges".[14]

However, industry experts believe that "smart ports are the only ports that will survive".[15] It is thus not surprising that the future global market for the smart port segment is very encouraging and is projected to touch US$ 5.3 billion by 2024 from an estimated US$ 1.7 billion in 2019, at a CAGR of 25 per cent; and the Blockchain segment (control over the information, privacy of the user and prevention of manipulation of data) in the smart port ecosystem is expected to be the fastest-growing market from 2019 to 2024.[16]

The commercial maritime world has already embraced Blockchain technology in a few sectors, but its use in other marine related activities and synchronization between the many nodes of the maritime ecosystem across the value chain is becoming critical. All stakeholders including Customs and port authorities would be able to access and share data which would potentially transform the industry, making it more transparent, efficient, and secure.

Fifth Generation (5G) of Wireless Communications Technologies

A container port is a busy hub and facilitates loading and unloading of containers which are moved from ship to shore to a lorry and vice-versa. Further, these boxes are part of the seamless supply chain ecosystem that runs across the shore-ship-shore continuum. This ecosystem also includes data exchange among various stakeholders including those who receive/export raw materials and semi-finished/finished products. This exchange requires a reliable low-latency network with real-time access to Cloud data, and a system with high-level information security protection. 5G enables quick access to data along the supply chain and it is noted that "automated port control centre and operators can perform operations such as video security monitoring, real-time data collection and disposal by using mobile terminals".[17]

In 2017, Port of Qingdao in China was chosen to be upgraded into a fully-automated harbour. Under the 'Smart Port' Demonstration Project, Ericsson and China Unicom, a mobile service provider, were tasked to develop a 5G network for the port in the hope that it would help reduce labour costs by up to 70 per cent. A top functionary of the Market Area North East Asia at Ericsson, stated: "In the Qingdao 5G smart harbour project, we successfully showcased various 5G network capabilities, such as milli-second level end-to-end latency at Gbps level speed. This 5G smart harbour solution is not only applicable to the Port of Qingdao but can also be replicated with many other harbours and industries".[18]

One of the major highlights of the upgrade was that the "automated ship-to-shore (STS) crane successfully lifted a container over a 5G connection operated from the control centre".[19] China is expected to advance 5G to port projects under the Belt Road Initiative. Gwadar in Pakistan would be the most suitable destination given that the Pakistan-China fibre optic cable project stretching over 820 kilometres from Rawalpindi to Khunjerab was made operational earlier this year.[20]

Smart Ships: Autonomous and Unmanned

The most notable development in the shipbuilding industry is the construction of 'smart vessels'. Although technological advancements have been the feature of the shipbuilding industry since the time humans began to use the seas as a medium of transport, the move towards smart vessels has been driven by at least four factors; first is reduction of personnel onboard ships for cost cutting and using their living spaces for cargo; second, reduce accidents given that nearly 70 to 80 per cent of ship accidents at sea are a result of human error; third, harness 4IR technologies for enhancing efficiency, reduce down time through predictive maintenance and harmonize ship operations with the supply chain; and four, is sea piracy involving ransom and crew being held hostage that would be considerably reduced or even eliminated. However, experts are divided over the introduction of smart vessels and firmly believe that the human factor cannot be totally left out of ship operations.

Smart vessels can be divided into at least two categories, i.e., unmanned ships and autonomous ships.[21] Unmanned vessels, as the name suggests, are operated and controlled by an operator who could be sitting in a control centre onshore. On the other hand, an autonomous ship uses an onboard computer and operates it based on relevant decisions concerning the route to be followed, decides on speed based on fuel consumption, predicts maintenance schedules and also berths alongside a jetty in a harbour or a port based on sensors.[22]

The International Maritime Organisation (IMO), the specialist arm of the United Nations, took note of the advent of smart ships. Under the Strategic Plan for the Organization for the six-year period 2018 to 2023, it acknowledged the need for 'new and advancing technologies in the regulatory framework'.[23] It also issued associated safety and security guidelines including classification, and potential impacts on seafarers and the environment.

During its 100th session held on December 3-7, 2018, the IMO's Maritime Safety Committee (MSC) approved the "framework and methodology for the regulatory scoping exercise on Maritime Autonomous Surface Ships (MASS)"[24] and established four degrees[25] of autonomy in ships. Apparently, the MSC discussed automated ships as early as 1964 in the context of trends in increasing automation in shipping.

Furthermore, the MSC defined MASS as a 'ship which, to a varying degree, can operate independently of human interaction'. It has been noted that "autonomy of the shipping industry is expected to reduce the maritime emissions, enable massive fuel savings and save about 20 per cent of the cost incurred for the shipping operators.... This technology is anticipated to apprehend such accidents due to human error on the bridge of the vessel thereby reducing accidents on-board.[26]

The market trends for autonomous ships are indeed very encouraging and according to an estimate this segment is "estimated to be USD 6.1 billion in 2018 and is projected to reach USD 13.8 billion by 2030, at a CAGR of 7.00 per cent from 2018 to 2030"[27] This is driven by a number of factors such as promising outlook for global seaborne shipping, high rate of compliance with maritime safety norms, and growth in maritime tourism. In terms of numbers, by 2020 there could be nearly 100 autonomously operated vessels[28] and by 2025 the number could be of the order of nearly 1,000 autonomous vessels and as many as 2,000 semi-autonomous vessels.

A number of autonomous ship projects are currently underway; for instance, under a Norwegian initiative, *Kongsberg Maritime,* a Norwegian technology enterprise is building the *Yara Birkeland,* an "autonomous electric-powered vessel", capable of carrying 100 to 150 shipping containers which will be completed by 2020.[29] Another Norwegian company called Massterly, a joint venture between the shipping group Wilhelmsen and technology firm Kongsberg, has announced plans to launch a "complete value chain for autonomous ships, from design and development, to control systems, logistics services and vessel operations".[30] This project will involve setting up infrastructure and services to manage and operate these vessels in autonomous mode.

The international technology conglomerate, Rolls-Royce, is among the top pioneers in autonomous ship technology, and in 2016 published a White Paper listing their vision of how remote and autonomous shipping will become a reality.[31] By 2017, the company's 28-metre long *Svitzer Hermod* tugs had completed a number of remotely controlled manoeuvres in Copenhagen harbour while the captain of the vessel was elsewhere at Svitzer headquarters.[32] The company is optimistic about the future of the autonomous vessels and believes that "fully autonomous oceangoing cargo ships [could] be routinely plying the world's seas in 10 or 15 years' time".[33] Rolls-Royce's current €6.6 million project—Advanced Autonomous Waterborne Applications Initiative (AAWA)—is supported by the Finnish Funding Agency for Technology and Innovation to examine the future of autonomous ships.[34]

The European Commission has funded the collaborative project, MUNIN (Maritime Unmanned Navigation through Intelligence in Networks), "to develop and verify a concept for an autonomous ship, which is defined as a vessel primarily guided by automated on-board decision systems but controlled by a remote operator in a shore side control station".[35]

The IBM is supporting the development of a 'five-ton, wing sail/solar/diesel powered' autonomous vessel called 'Mayflower Autonomous Ship (MAS)' capable of moving at 20 knots speed. The MAS is expected to be ready for its maiden voyage in September 2020 and would sail across the Atlantic Ocean. During the voyage, MAS will 'take water samples for research on ocean micro-plastics, and its sensors will return data on water temperature and nutrient levels. For navigation and collision avoidance, it will be equipped with an inertial guidance system, GPS, radar and LIDAR. With a SATCOM link to shore and processors on board, it will use IBM's Power AI Vision technology to evaluate its surroundings and an IBM Deep Learning-powered collision avoidance system to maintain autonomous safety of navigation'.[36]

In Asia, Japan is a leading autonomous ship technology development and a consortium of shipping and engineering companies, research institutes and laboratories that were shortlisted by Japan's Ministry of Land, Infrastructure, Transportation and Tourism to develop a technological concept for autonomous ocean transport system.[37] The project will be based on 4IR technologies and is estimated to cost "tens of billions of yen, or hundreds of millions of dollars, at a minimum".[38]

In 2020, China announced steel cutting for its first autonomous containership named Zhi Fei to be constructed at Qingdao shipyard. This 5,000-ton vessel can carry up to 300 TEUs and is being fitted with intelligent navigation systems. It would have electric propulsion which would reduce noise and advanced systems to reduce NO_x, SO_x and CO_2 gases.[39]

The MASS technology is in its infancy and can be expected to improve in the coming times. However, the major challenge is human resource which would need to be educated and trained for adoption and assimilation of new technologies for which they must develop specialist skills for MASS operations both at sea and ashore. This would entail significant investment in training infrastructure, bridging the digital education divide, and research for this new technological age.

There will also be social challenges on account of existing workers' skills that would require upgrading on a continuing basis, as also for those workers being displaced or having their jobs eliminated.[40] Perhaps the biggest risk is of not being ready for the coming wave of technology which means being left behind in the future shipping environment. Asian shipbuilding giants such as Japan, Korea, China and Singapore are the leading countries on emerging technologies and the gap is widening.

3D Printing and Shipbuilding

The use of 3D printers in ship construction has made a promising debut and a few shipyards have taken the lead. For instance, Innovation Quarters, Havenbedrijf Rotterdam, RDM Makerspace and AEGIR-Marine, a consortium of 27 marine-related companies are doing 3D Printing of Maritime Spare Parts;[41] The China Shipbuilding Industry Corporation (CSIC) had drawn plans to set up a 3D printed manufacturing base in Kunming and a prototype technology centre in Yunnan province;[42] South Korea's Ministry of Trade, Industry and Energy has decided to invest US$ 20 million over five years (2017-2022) for research in 3D printing and 3D manufacturing of ships and offshore equipment;[43] 3D Scanning AS, a subsidiary of The Maritime Group of Norway, has a partnership with 3Discovered of Chicago, a leading industrial 3D printing services platform, to supply 3D printed parts to its cruise/maritime ship repair and retrofit service business;[44] and 3D Matters in Singapore is a long-time established additive manufacturers entity and is helping clients enter and increase their 3D printing needs.[45]

Wearable Technologies for Maritime Operations

The aggressive and sweeping digital transformation in the maritime industry has led to newer Human Machine Interface (HMI) challenges.[46] At its core lies the belief that machines can be made as intelligent as humans through deep learning, and then it is possible to integrate and digitally co-habit crew and machine to work seamlessly across static, mobile and wearable devices.[47] The maritime industry which works fiercely on profits can potentially be a major user of the HMI-driven systems through cutting costs on crew, maintenance, operations and supply chains.[48] Industry experts argue that "compatibility with wearable technology is extremely important for the shipping sector because whether it is today or in three years' time, wearable technology will become widely adopted for any task that requires hands-free operation and communication or remote expert support, such as complex mechanical failures or any mission critical or hazardous jobs where audio visual expertise can be delivered right to the front line where and when it is needed".[49]

"Mobile apps have changed the way we approach everyday tasks, and it's no different when it comes to safety checks," notes the CEO and managing director of BASS, a Norwegian maritime software company that helps "vessel and shore-based personnel go digital when conducting audits and inspections on site".[50] This would help inspectors to obtain data in situ or on site and work with visuals and audio.

From Preventive to Predictive Maintenance

Ship operations are highly maintenance-intensive and 4IR technologies have potential roles in the management of ship-borne equipment. As noted in Chapter 1, Digital twinning[51] offers a new way to design a digital copy of a physical asset. It can also help maintenance during the full life cycle of a product by determining the health or performance of equipment or a machinery part through embed sensors. These continuously transmit to the 'digital twin' located offshore to study and analyse the real-time health of machinery or equipment, and predict breakdowns before they occur. It also enables remedial measures through replacements and repair, thereby enhancing operational efficiency.[52]

For instance, at the global quality assurance company, DNV GL, 'digital twins' are connected to control system software on ships and offshore units, and help in monitoring machinery, equipment and systems on these platforms. The CEO of DNV GL - Oil & Gas has observed that "a single, unscheduled downtime event can cost from $2 to $5 million per day and so better and up-to-date risk information may significantly reduce unplanned or unnecessary downtime".[53]

IoT helps "shore-side experts to conduct root cause assessments and send a software patch remotely. Similarly, ship managers are in the service of vessel availability, and downtime is a huge expense. IoT enables ship managers to better plan in advance for the right parts and service plan to minimize time in port. Shipyards can also benefit from IoT by using it to service the equipment on board, remotely, ensuring all systems are performing as expected and extending their business model into service over the lifetime of the vessel operations".[54]

The market trends for Digital Twinning are very promising and according to a report, "Up to 89% of all IoT Platforms will contain some form of Digital Twinning capability by 2025; Digital twinning will become standard feature/ functionality for IoT Application Enablement by 2027; over 92% of vendors recognize the need for IoT APIs and platform integration with digital twinning functionality for industrial verticals; and nearly 36% of executives across a broad spectrum of industry verticals understand the benefits of digital twinning and 53% of them plan to incorporate within their operations by 2028".[55]

At another level, spare part supply chains which are inherently large and diverse present unique challenges to keep a ship fully operational. The current trends in inventory management are to use a Cloud-based database which contains details of parts and equipment and helps technical managers to manage inventory, predict future requirements for stocking as also support procurement contracts. It also helps managers to service large number of vessels in a fleet and ensures that procurements are based on economies of scale. The software is based on the popular and widely used Internet banking model and clients can have access to data which is centrally stored and controlled. For instance, the MESPAS platform is a good example of a repository and its global master database contains details of "part and component" needed for shipboard equipment including engines, pumps, navigation equipment, etc.[56] Further, over 21,000 maritime suppliers are clients of this Cloud-based platform that has an annual turnover of over US$ 600 million.

Human Resource

The 4IR-led maritime shipping industry (ships and shore operations) is making traditional skills redundant. From the human resource perspective, this should be viewed from at least three perspectives; first, 4IR technologies offer new solutions to complex problems and eliminate the need of performing recurring tasks, thus making work more enjoyable. Second, it would necessitate additional knowledge and competences to perform in the new 4IR-enabled operational environment involving complex systems and devices, new data management skills and understanding and implementing new regulations. Besides, 'sociological challenges too involve 'complex relationships between man and man, and man and machine'.[57] Third is about jobs. It has been argued that "the growing importance of intangible products like smart phone applications, investment management and other higher order services, which require rarer skill sets or talents mean that those made redundant from automated manufacturing might face long-term unemployment, due to the inability to re-skill or be absorbed by new industries".[58]

There are calls urging seafarers to re-skill and preserve their jobs amid fears that 4IR technologies 'may possibly reduce demand for seafarers by 30,000 to 50,000' and shore operations would require "highly skilled remote-operators, pilots of a new kind and riding gangs will be needed to keep ships operational".[59]

Similarly, remote docking without physical attendance of the superintendent for a precise procedure is being explored.[60] Closely associated is the issue of inspection of tank spaces, a task both dangerous and difficult. A promising technology demonstration has shown that it is possible to detect cracks in the structure using drones and interpreting in real-time the pictures taken by using an algorithm.[61] This technology is being developed jointly by Scout Drone Inspection and DNV GL and is expected to save time as well as costs including reducing risks due to human exposure.

4IR-led technological advancements have necessitated new skills; however, the current human resource availability to support the techno-optimism is quite low. The China-based Tencent Research Institute has estimated that there are roughly 300,000 AI researchers and practitioners worldwide, with market demand for millions of roles.[62] The international 4IR technology community is looking towards India and China who are the largest non-US supplier of technology professionals and international students in AI-related fields.

The International Labour Organisation (ILO) has acknowledged that the "movement into integrated technology and automated functions require consideration of how ships are to be manned and operated. The demand for specialized and highly skilled crews will increase as the sector moves towards more digital operating systems on vessels. Technological changes are changing ship management processes and altering the traditional patterns of operating".[63]

Ship Registration

Ship registration is the process by which a ship is assigned a permanent number and given the nationality of the country to which it belongs. International law and practice require every ship that sails on the oceans and seas to have a registration number. This is provided by the IMO and it remains unchanged through the life of the ship and shall never be reassigned to another ship. Blockchain technology is being developed for ship registration and preparations are on for its international adoption. Labelled 'International E-Registry of Ships', the system would 'streamline, standardize and drastically improve the currently laborious ship registration and renewal process' resulting in 'significant reductions in operating costs, timing required, human error and fraud'.[64] The Maritime and Port Authority of Singapore (MPA) is developing Application Programming Interface (API) in the registration process and 'will include automated document checking and API integration from trusted data sources'.[65]

Hyperloop Enabled Maritime Supply Chain

As noted earlier, maritime supply chains are not just limited to the port-ship-port continuum; instead they go deep into the heartland and connect to Inland Container Depots (ICD), railway stowage yards, Special Economic Zones (SEZ), industrial hubs, factories and retail outlets. Perhaps the biggest challenge is the first/last mile (as the lorry moves in/out of the port and cuts through the city/industrial hubs) which can impact on the efficiency of the supply chain for which supply chain mangers seek solutions for the best routes to save time and ensure delivery of cargo at the port/industrial hub.

A number of significant developments are underway for this sector of the supply chain. The real-time information of container location, forecasts of delivery/arrival and integrated flow management are some of the ways by which the supply chain management specialists and practitioners have successfully reduced turnaround times for ships and controlled inefficiencies.[66] They also believe that the transport sector will be disrupted and an "autonomous transport chain will extend from initial loading, stowage, and sailing all the way to unloading directly into autonomous trains and trucks and drone-enabled last mile deliveries".[67] Future ships will be capable of transporting 50,000 twenty-foot equivalent units (TEU) and a 'fully autonomous transport chain will extend from loading, stowage, and sailing to unloading directly onto autonomous trains and trucks, with last-mile deliveries by drones'.[68]

It is not beyond the stretch of imagination that "a terminal with no stacks in the yard; instead, Customs would pre-clear boxes digitally, and autonomous trucks would take them straight from ships and out to customers".[69] Perhaps, by then, these will be supplemented by 'hyperloop' that will enable land-based cargo/container moving at very high speeds comparable with that of commercial aircraft and reduce travel time across destinations and supply chains. By some estimates, the capsules can move at speeds of 600 to 800 miles per hour (900 to 1,287 kilometres per hour) and the distance between Los Angeles and San Francisco would shorten to 30 minutes which is half the time it takes in a plane. Similarly, the transport time between Mumbai and Chennai, two major ports in India, could be 60 minutes, and between Chennai to Bengaluru, an IT and industrial hub of India, just 20 minutes.[70]

The idea of a 'hyperloop' was first introduced in 2013 by Elon Musk and he argued that a capsule (train cars or bogies), when placed in a tube with little or no aerodynamic drag, could be moved at very high speeds. At the heart of this technology is magnetic technology in which capsules levitate passively, move with little friction and the journey is silent and emission-free. Such an innovation has huge benefits across the world[71] given that e-commerce is expected to grow to US$ 4 trillion globally by 2020 and the 'market for express and parcel freight is set to grow to $516 billion by 2025' which will pose challenges to the limited airline/airport capacities.[72]

Hyperloop technology is currently under active consideration by only a few port operators. They see it as critical for the future of maritime supply chains which will shrink the time of transportation as also help integrate ports, shipping, logistics companies and other service providers across the globe. For instance, the 150-kilometre UAE Hyperloop between Dubai and Abu Dhabi would cut travel time to 12 minutes.[73] It is the first commercial venture and would be partly (first 10 kilometres) operational by 2020. It costs between $20 and $40 million per kilometre but this can be recovered in 15 years. In Germany, the Hyperloop Transportation Technologies (HyperloopTT/HTT), a joint company involving the Hyperloop Transportation Technologies (HTT) and Hamburger Hafen und LogistikAktiengesellschaft (HHLA), a container terminal operator in the Port of Hamburg, is developing a Hyperloop transport system for seaport and inland shipping container operations that will enable movement of ' containers at high speeds using magnetic levitation in a partial vacuum tube to avoid traffic congestion and reduce the environmental impact from transportation'.[74] According to a top functionary of the HHLA, "As a gateway to the future, we want to employ innovative approaches to make a contribution towards relieving the strain on the transport infrastructure in and around the Port of Hamburg and to use the capacities of our terminal facilities in an even more efficient way".[75]

Likewise, India too has shown interest in Hyperloop technology and the Virgin Hyperloop One–DP World Consortium is the Original Project Proponent (OPP) for the Pune-Mumbai Hyperloop Project.[76] Under this project, Jawaharlal Nehru Port in Mumbai would be connected to Pune, a major economic and industrial zone, through a Hyperloop. DP World had announced investment of US$ 500 million for the first phase which could be operational by 2025. This will enable quick and safe movement of cargo thereby reducing transport time to a mere 35 minutes, as compared with the current time which exceeds three-and-a-half hours. Besides, it will help reduce pollution in Mumbai city and could bring 'over US$ 36 billion in wider socio-economic benefits, as well as to create new Hyperloop component and manufacturing opportunities for the region'.[77] Virgin Hyperloop One is confident that the Pune-Mumbai Hyperloop corridor would be a "blueprint for a Hyperloop network spanning the entire nation".[78]

Earlier, in 2017, Hyperloop Transportation Technologies signed a memorandum of understanding with the Andhra Pradesh Development Board (APEDB) to launch Hyperloop between Vijayawada and Amravati that would reduce a one-way trip of more than an hour into a five-minute ride.[79] The company also had plans to move capsules (5 tons and 32 metres long) from Puerto de Santa Maria near Cadiz, Spain, to Toulouse, France.[80]

Blockchain and Supply Chain

Blockchain technology offers a number of usages in the cargo management sector through identity generation/identity authentication. For instance, under the BunkerTrace system, markers can be added to "fuel at every stage of the supply chain and recording each transaction in a Blockchain-based system" thereby creating an "immutable audit trail that follows the fuel, and any changes made to it, recording all activities and sign-offs by actors transacting the fuel".[81] This can potentially assist in IMO 2020 bunker fuel compliance, help owners, suppliers, ports and insurers to track fuels and manage the risk of non-compliance and enhance transparency and traceability in the marine fuels supply chain.

Similarly, Blockchain and Bigdata are central to Smart Container Technology. Traxens, a container shipping service provider, uses digitalized containers and by the end of 2019/early 2020, it is expected to operate over 100,000 smart containers worldwide.[82] According to a top functionary of the company, "Enhanced data will improve visibility and predictability for stakeholders as well as for regulatory agencies that need detailed information on consignments before they arrive at the border". In the Port of Rotterdam, the world's leading shipping companies[83] have come together to test the use of Blockchain technology for a pilot project to "improve the safety and efficiency of the shipping process" and make "port operations smarter, swifter, more efficient, and safer".[84]

Concluding Thoughts

There are numerous practical uses of 4IR technologies in multiple sectors such as shipping, ports, shipbuilding, onboard operational and technical management and automation, maritime supply chains and human resource management. These technologies are at different levels of maturity, i.e., some are just at the conceptual stage and many are at the experimental level or demonstration stage, and some have been developed and are in operational use. These will potentially change the way sea-based commercial operations are conducted and would also have a dramatic impact on future maritime infrastructure. This study now examines the impact of 4IR technologies on naval strategy, doctrines, concept of options, logistic and human resource management and transformation in the civil-military industrial complex.

NOTES

1. See "World's Largest Container Ship Transits Suez Canal", https://www.maritime-executive.com/article/world-s-largest-container-ship-transits-suez-canal (accessed 24 September 2019). *MSC Gulsun, the* largest container ship capable of carrying 23,756-TEU is a technological marvel of shipping in size and automation.
2. "Oil and Gas Forecast to 2050", https://www.ourenergypolicy.org/wp-content/uploads/2017/09/DNV-GL_Energy-Transistion-Outlook-2017_oil-gas_lowres-single_3108_3.pdf (accessed 30 June 2020).
3. Markus Fruth and Frank Teuteberg "Digitization in Maritime Logistics — What is there and what is Missing?", https://www.tandfonline.com/doi/pdf/10.1080/23311975.2017.1411066 (accessed 21 September 2019).
4. "Review of Maritime Transport 2017", http://unctad.org/en/PublicationsLibrary/rmt2017_en.pdf , (accessed 15 December 2017). p.12.
5. The Review of Maritime Transport 2018 compiled by the United Nations Conference on Trade and Development (UNCTAD) has indicated a positive sentiment for the shipping industry. The global seaborne trade grew at 4 per cent, the fastest growth in five years, touching 10.7 billion tons. There was concurrent growth in the world fleet which expanded by 42 million gross tons in 2017 which corresponds to 3.3 per cent growth rate.
6. Source: Ports in the 4th Industrial Revolution – Learning to Think in Circles", https://safety4sea.com/ports-in-the-4th-industrial-revolution-learning-to-think-in-circles/ (accessed 21 September 2019).
7. Kenji Ono1, Masayuki Tanemura and Yasuhiro Akakura, "AI Port Initiatives", http://www.ysk.nilim.go.jp/kakubu/kouwan/system/2018_01.pdf (accessed 21 September 2019).
8. Ibid.
9. Ibid. 'Royal Haskoning (The Netherlands), IBM (USA), ABB (Switzerland), Trelleborg AB (Sweden), Port of Rotterdam (The Netherlands), and Abu Dhabi ports (UAE)'.
10. Matteo Natalucci, "What is a Smart Port?" https://www.porttechnology.org/news/what-is-a-smart-port/ (accessed 2 April 2020).
11. "Smart Ports Market by Technology (IoT, Blockchain, Process Automation, Artificial Intelligence (AI)), Elements (Terminal Automation, PCS, Smart Port Infrastructure, and Others), Throughput Capacity, Port Type, and Region - Global Forecast to 2024", https://www.marketsandmarkets.com/Market-Reports/smart-ports-market-165784113.html (accessed 2 April 2020).
12. "Smart Ports to Become Global Logistics Information Exchange Hubs", https://maritime-executive.com/blog/smart-ports-to-become-global-logistics-information-exchange-hubs (accessed 23 April 2020).
13. "Automation Could Aid Port Operations during Pandemic", https://maritime-executive.com/editorials/automation-could-aid-port-operations-during-pandemic (accessed 11 April 2020).
14. "New Initiatives Contribute to the Drive for Digitization", https://www.maritime-executive.com/article/new-initiatives-contribute-to-the-drive-for-digitizationhttps://www.maritime-executive.com/article/new-initiatives-contribute-to-the-drive-for-digitization (accessed 4 June 2020).
15. "How the Fourth Industrial Revolution is Impacting Ports of the Future", https://www.boldbusiness.com/digital/fourth-industrial-revolution-impacting-ports-future/ (accessed 21 September 2019).

16. "Worldwide Smart Ports Market Insights (2019-2024): Big Data Analytics, IoT, and AI to Transform Port Operations", https://www.globenewswire.com/news-release/2019/08/08/1899479/0/en/Worldwide-Smart-Ports-Market-Insights-2019-2024-Big-Data-Analytics-IoT-and-AI-to-Transform-Port-Operations.html (accessed 21 September 2019).
17. "China Unicom and Huawei Jointly Launch Industry-First 5G Edge-Cloud Smart Port Solution, Trial Already Started", https://www.huawei.com/en/press-events/news/2018/4/Industry-First-5G-Edge-Cloud-Smart-Port-Solution (accessed 21 September 2019).
18. "5G Smart Port System Trialed at Qingdao", https://maritime-executive.com/article/5g-smart-port-system-trialed-at-qingdao (accessed 5 October 2019).
19. Ibid.
20. "The completion of the project under the China-Pakistan Economic Corridor (CPEC) will convert the trade corridor into a digital corridor. The foundation stone of the Pak-China fibre optic cable project was laid in May, 2018". For more details, see https://tribune.com.pk/story/1901975/8-pak-china-fibre-optic-link-activated-commercial-use/(accessed 5 October 2019). Also see "Digital BRI: China and Pakistan Building CPEC Info Expressway with Fiber, 5G", http://www.riazhaq.com/2019/05/digital-bri-china-and-pakistan-building.html (accessed 5 October 2019).
21. The term 'Autonomous ship' is a self-sailing crewless vessel albeit with different degrees of autonomy; a 'Remote ship' is controlled by a human operator ashore; an 'Automated ship' runs on pre-programmed software and can only operate within the scope of the algorithm; the operating system in a 'Fully autonomous ship' can calculate consequences and risks, and make decisions by itself.
22. "Smart Shipping: The Future Of Maritime Shipping?", https://www.lagersmit.com/smart-shipping-future-maritime-shipping/ (accessed 21 September 2019).
23. "Strategic Plan for the Organization", http://www.imo.org/en/About/strategy/Pages/default.aspx (accessed 24 September 2019).
24. "IMO MSC Identifies 4 Degrees of Ship Automation", https://worldmaritimenews.com/archives/266898/imo-msc-identifies-4-degrees-of-ship-automation/ (accessed 24 September 2019).
25. (a) Degree one: A ship that is operated by seafarers with some of the processes automated; (b) Degree two: Remotely controlled ship controlled and operated from a different location with seafarers on board; (c) Degree three: Remotely controlled ship controlled and operated from a different location without seafarers on board; and (d) Degree four: Fully autonomous ship, with an operating system that will make decisions and determine actions by itself.
26. "According to the European Maritime Safety Agency (EMSA), 58 per cent of accidental events and 70 per cent of accidental events were attributed to human error on shipboard operations. For more details see "Autonomous Ships Market - Growth, Trends, and Forecast (2020 - 2025)", https://www.researchandmarkets.com/reports/4897289/autonomous-ships-market-growth-trends-and#rela0-5013080 (accessed 24 April 2020).
27. "Autonomous Ships Market", https://www.marketsandmarkets.com/Market-Reports/autonomous-ships-market-267183224.html (accessed 24 September 2019).
28. "Seafarers and Digital Disruption", https://www.ics-shipping.org/docs/default-source/resources/ics-study-on-seafarers-and-digital-disruption.pdf?sfvrsn=3 (accessed 21 September 2019).
29. For more details see "Autonomous ships equipment/products/systems", https://www.kongsberg.com/maritime/solutions/ship-types/autonomous-ships/?OpenDocument

(accessed 21 September 2019).
30. "World's First Autonomous Shipping Company Established in Norway", https://gcaptain.com/worlds-first-autonomous-shipping-company-coming-to-norway/ (accessed 24 September 2019).
31. "Rolls-Royce publishes vision of the future of remote and autonomous shipping", https://www.rolls-royce.com/media/press-releases/2016/21-06-2016-rr-publishes-vision-of-the-future-of-remote-and-autonomous-shipping.aspxhttps://www.rolls-royce.com/media/press-releases/2016/21-06-2016-rr-publishes-vision-of-the-future-of-remote-and-autonomous-shipping.aspx (accessed 24 September 2019).
32. "Rolls-Royce Demonstrates World's first Remotely Operated Commercial Vessel", https://www.rolls-royce.com/media/press-releases/2017/20-06-2017-rr-demonstrates-worlds-first-remotely-operated-commercial-vessel.aspx (accessed 24 September 2019).
33. Oskar Levander, "Forget Autonomous Cars—Autonomous Ships Are Almost Here", https://spectrum.ieee.org/transportation/marine/forget-autonomous-cars-autonomous-ships-are-almost-here (accessed 24 September 2019). Also see "The maritime IoT landscape in the next decade", https://www.rivieramm.com/opinion/opinion/the-maritime-iot-landscape-in-the-next-decade-23759 (accessed 21 September 2019).
34. "Autonomous Ships Timeline – Comparing Rolls-Royce, Kongsberg, Yara and More", https://emerj.com/ai-adoption-timelines/autonomous-ships-timeline/ (accessed 24 September 2019).
35. "MUNIN Project", http://www.unmanned-ship.org/munin/ (accessed 24 September 2019).
36. "IBM Backs New Autonomous Vessel for Transatlantic Voyage", https://www.maritime-executive.com/article/ibm-backs-new-autonomous-vessel-for-transatlantic-voyage (accessed 18 October 2019).
37. "MOL Launches R & D on Autonomous Ocean Transport System-Selected for Japanese Government Transportation Research Program", https://www.mol.co.jp/en/pr/2017/17031.html (accessed 24 September 2019).
38. "Japan Aims to launch Self-piloting Ships by 2025", https://asia.nikkei.com/Tech-Science/Tech/Japan-aims-to-launch-self-piloting-ships-by-2025(accessed 24 September 2019).
39. "China Starts Building its 1st Autonomous Feeder", https://www.offshore-energy.biz/china-starts-building-its-1st-autonomous-feeder/ (accessed 20 May 2020).
40. "Seafarers and Digital Disruption", https://www.ics-shipping.org/docs/default-source/resources/ics-study-on-seafarers-and-digital-disruption.pdf?sfvrsn=3 (accessed 30 June 2020).
41. "Dutch Maritime Consortium to 3D Print Spare Parts for Ships", https://www.3printr.com/dutch-maritime-consortium-to-3d-print-spare-parts-for-ships-3329871/ (accessed 30 June 2020).
42. "Maritime GUIDE to 3D print", https://greenship.org/wp-content/uploads/2017/01/App-3DP.pdf (accessed 30 June 2020).
43. Ibid.
44. Ibid.
45. "One of the Longest Established Additive Manufacturers in Southeast Asia", http://3dmatters.com.sg/about-us/ (accessed 30 June 2020).
46. "HMI/SCADA Software in the age of Industrial IoT and Evolving Human Machine Interfaces", https://www.i-scoop.eu/industry-4-0/hmi-scada-software/ (accessed 20 June 2020).
47. Priyanka Ann Saini, "Wearable Technology – The Maritime Industry Benefits", https://

seanews.co.uk/features/wearable-technology-the-maritime-industry-benefits/ (accessed 30 September 2019).

48. "Wearable Devices can transform Maritime Operations", *South Asia Defence and Strategy Review*, Vol. 11, Issue 4, Sep-Oct 2017.
49. Priyanka Ann Saini, "Wearable Technology – The Maritime Industry Benefits" https://seanews.co.uk/features/wearable-technology-the-maritime-industry-benefits/ (accessed 30 September 2019).
50. "New App Promises to Digitalize Ship Inspection Paperwork", https://www.maritime-executive.com/features/new-app-promises-to-digitalize-ship-inspection-paperwork (accessed 16 May 2020).
51. "Digital Twinning Explained", https://www.raconteur.net/business-innovation/digital-twinning-explained (accessed 30 September 2019).
52. Vijay Sakhuja, "Maritime Digital Trends in 2018", http://www.ipcs.org/comm_select.php?articleNo=5417 (accessed 30 September 2019).
53. "DNV GL Unveils Concept for Live Asset Risk Assessment Using Digital Twins", https://www.dnvgl.com/news/dnv-gl-unveils-concept-for-live-asset-risk-assessment-using-digital-twins-157142 (accessed 15 March 2020).
54. "Unlock the Hidden Power of Maritime IoT: Actionable Insights Onboard", https://www.maritime-executive.com/features/unlock-the-hidden-power-of-maritime-iot-actionable-insights-onboard-1 (accessed 16 June 2020).
55. "Digital Twins Market by Technology, Solution, Application, and Industry Vertical 2020 – 2025", https://www.researchandmarkets.com/reports/5006128/digital-twins-market-by-technology-solution?utm_code=r84k6x&utm_medium=GN (accessed 15 March 2020).
56. "Unique Cloud-Based Database Now Supports Parts Procurement Contracts", https://maritime-executive.com/features/unique-cloud-based-database-now-supports-parts-procurement-contracts-1 (accessed 30 September 2019).
57. Zvonimir Lušiæ, Mario Bakota, Mirko Èoriæ & Ivica Skoko, "Seafarer Market – Challenges for the Future", https://www.toms.com.hr/index.php/toms/article/download/239/243/ (accessed 1 October 2019).
58. Nah Liang Tuang, "The Fourth Industrial Revolution's Impact on Smaller Militaries: Boon Or Bane? Nah Liang Tuang", RSIS Working Paper No. 8, https://www.rsis.edu.sg/wp-content/uploads/2018/11/WP318.pdf (accessed 5 October 2019).
59. Ibid.
60. "How to Remote-Control Docking Projects during the Pandemic", https://www.maritime-executive.com/corporate/how-to-remote-control-docking-projects-during-the-pandemic (accessed 11 June 2020).
61. "Autonomous Drone Successfully Demonstrates Tank Inspection", https://www.maritime-executive.com/article/autonomous-drone-successfully-demonstrates-tank-inspection (accessed 11 June 2020).
62. "A Magnet for Overseas Talent, US Might Lose AI Race if Restrictive Immigration Policies Remain, Says Report", https://www.scmp.com/tech/policy/article/3027672/magnet-overseas-talent-us-might-lose-ai-race-if-restrictive-immigration (accessed 21 September 2019).
63. S. Bhardwaj: "Technology, and the Up-skilling or Deskilling Conundrum" in *WMU Journal of Maritime Affairs* (Vol. 12, No. 2, Oct. 2013), pp. 245–253. Cited in "Recruitment and retention of seafarers and the promotion of opportunities for women seafarers", https://

www.ilo.org/wcmsp5/groups/public/—ed_dialogue/—sector/documents/meetingdocument/wcms_664163.pdf (accessed 1 October 2019).

64. "Blockchain Ship Registration System under Development", https://www.maritime-executive.com/article/blockchain-ship-registration-system-under-development (accessed 16 October 2019).
65. Ibid.
66. "Container Shipping: The Next 50 Years", https://www.safety4sea.com/wp-content/uploads/2017/10/McKinsey-Container-shipping-The-next-50-years-2017_10.pdf (accessed 21 September 2019).
67. "McKinsey Report on Container Shipping in 2067 Predicts Autonomous 50K TEU Vessels", https://www.supplychainquarterly.com/topics/logistics/20171102-mckinsey-report-on-container-shipping-in-2067-predicts-autonomous-50k-teu-vessels/ (accessed 30 September 2019).
68. Ibid.
69. "Container Shipping: The Next 50 Years", https://www.mckinsey.com/~/media/mckinsey/industries/travel%20transport%20and%20logistics/our%20insights/how%20container%20shipping%20could%20reinvent%20itself%20for%20the%20digital%20age/container-shipping-the-next-50-years-final.ashx (accessed 30 September 2019).
70. Ariet Haxhiaj, "Hyperloop Infrastructure: The Future of Transportation", https://www.morethanshipping.com/hyperloop-infrastructure-future-transportation/ (accessed 30 September 2019).
71. Max Schwerdtfeger, "WATCH: How Hyperloop Can Change the World", https://www.porttechnology.org/news/watch_how_hyperloop_can_change_the_world/ (accessed 30 September 2019).
72. "The Friday Five: Virgin Hyperloop One vs. Current State of the Supply Chain", https://www.slync.io/blog/the-friday-five-virgin-hyperloop-one-vs-current-state-of-the-supply-chain (accessed 30 September 2019).
73. "UAE Hyperloop Opening Date is Revealed", https://www.timeoutdubai.com/travel/394954-uae-hyperloop-opening-date-is-revealed (accessed 30 September 2019).
74. Gary Wollenhaupt, "Hyperloop cargo train pilot set for Hamburg port", https://www.supplychaindive.com/news/hyperloop-cargo-train-hamburg-port/543920/ (accessed 21 September 2019).
75. "Hyperloop Transportation Technologies and Hamburg Port to Explore Hyperloop Possibilities in new Joint Venture", https://www.eft.com/technology/hyperloop-transportation-technologies-and-hamburg-port-explore-hyperloop-possibilities (accessed 21 September 2019).
76. Matteo Natalucci ,"India Chooses DPW-Virgin Hyperloop One", https://www.porttechnology.org/news/india-chooses-dpw-virgin-hyperloop-one/ (accessed 30 September 2019).
77. Ibid.
78. Ibid.
79. "First Hyperloop in India to be Launched Between Amravati and Vijayawada", https://timesofindia.indiatimes.com/city/pune/first-hyperloop-in-india-to-be-launched-between-amravati-and-vijayawada/articleshowprint/60395340.cms (accessed 30 September 2019).
80. Anand Krishnamoorthy, "'1,200 km/hour': World's first Hyperloop Passenger Capsule Unveiled", https://www.livemint.com/Technology/Y8JqALkb9ddeYQ9E2VK3FN/1200-

kmhour-Worlds-first-Hyperloop-passenger-capsule-u.html (accessed 30 September 2019).

81. "Bunker Tracing Test Using Blockchain Successfully Conducted", https://safety4sea.com/bunker-tracing-test-using-blockchain-successfully-conducted/ (accessed 23 March 2020).
82. "Standards for Smart Container Data Exchange Published", https://maritime-executive.com/article/standards-for-smart-container-data-exchange-published (accessed 23 March 2020).
83. CMA-CGM, Hapag-Lloyd, MSC, ONE-Line, Hutchison Ports ECT Rotterdam, Rotterdam Fruit Wharf, Milestone Fresh, VTO, Portmade, and the application developer T-Mining.
84. "Pilot Program Test Blockchain Technology to Improve Container Handling", https://www.maritime-executive.com/article/pilot-program-test-blockchain-technology-to-improve-container-handling (accessed 11 July 2020).

CHAPTER 3

Navies and Fourth Industrial Revolution

Warfare at sea has a rich history of technological revolutions and they have shaped naval development. The earlier revolutions were intimately connected to armies and foot soldiers were carried on ships. Fighting with bows and arrows, they experienced challenges shooting across ships while adjusting for the movement of the ship including 'roll and pitch'. In the 15th century, artillery cannon were the most potent weapon on land, and by the 16th century, cannons were placed on board ships; but had limitations of weight and recoil. Concurrently, there were dangers of carrying gunpowder onboard wooden ships which made them highly susceptible to fire.

In the early 19th century, two notable technological developments transformed the nature of warfare at sea, i.e., the telegraph allowed communication between ships, and guns were now more accurate. By the late 19th century, shipbuilders began cladding vessels with iron, and soon it was the primary material for shipbuilding. Also, there were technological advances in propulsion led by the steam engine and by the 20th century the internal combustion engine made its debut on ships which continues till date along with gas turbines. In current times, some warships and submarines use nuclear propulsion and the majority of ice-breaking vessels deployed in Polar Regions are nuclear propelled.

The revolution in military affairs (RMA), centred on information technology, expanded the communication space, compressed time, enhanced situational awareness and improved decision-making. There are notable changes in the lethality of ordnances and the accuracy in delivery of ordnance is now far superior than it was in earlier decades. Above all, the battlefield C4I2SR (command, control, communications, computers, Intelligence, interoperability, surveillance and reconnaissance) has resulted in a major transformation in the conduct of warfare. Nuclear weapons and their delivery systems are also part of the transformation in warfare in the 21st century and the majority of them are carried on board submarines.

Within the RMA, there is an ongoing Revolution in Maritime Affairs[1] impacting on the shape and size of navies to project maritime power. In the context of the latter, "Technological developments appear to enable modern navies to project maritime power ashore with much more assurance than before. Maritime power projection can now be confidently extended several hundreds of miles behind the shoreline.[2]

Most navies have successfully assimilated the Third Industrial Revolution technologies and a few among them are on the way to harness 4IR technologies which feature AI enabled platforms, equipment, weapons, ordnances, systems and processes. These will benefit naval leadership and warship commanders and operators to be more proficient in taking decisions. The military/naval manufacturing units, laboratories and research institutions are now focused on 4IR-enabled weapons and sensors. They are also joined by industry to help build and acquire more sophisticated weaponry.

4IR technologies present a new form of warfare that can also be labelled as 'neo-digital naval warfare'. Smart, intelligent, predictive and cognitive technologies are being added to the menu of future naval warfare, and technology developers have chosen to name them as autonomous platforms and machines, robots, wearable including person-embedded sensors and human mounted computers. Also, Bigdata, Cloud Computing, Artificial Intelligence, Augmented Intelligence, Cognitive Computing (CC), Internet of Things (IoT) and Internet of Everything (IoE) are gathering momentum and finding reference among military technology developers.

Surface Warfare

Since ancient times, the primary form of warfare at sea has been on the surface of the water and involved close-quarter duels which in subsequent centuries graduated to guns. The guns were replaced by missiles fired from ships, aircraft and submarines to destroy targets at sea and on land. Future surface warfare could be led by unmanned and autonomous vessels that are capable of travelling long distances and also detect and identify targets and fire autonomously. At the heart of this form of warfare are 4IR technologies and these are fast gaining attraction among naval planners.

There are at least three drivers which encourage navies to include 4IR-enabled platforms into their force structure. First is the cost of building such platforms when compared with larger vessels. In this context, there is a paradigm shift in US Navy thinking that it is important to increase the number of vessels in the fleet without additional expenditure. For instance, the Arleigh Burke-class destroyers, one of the most powerful classes of vessels in the world, though "bristling with capabilities, weapons and sensors, are very expensive to build, maintain and upgrade".[3] There is also "a shift in mindset that says, instead of putting as much stuff on the ship for as much money as I have, you start thinking in a different way.... How small can my platform be to get everything I need to be on it?"[4]

Second is the ability of a 4IR-enabled platform to be configured for multiple missions and carry different payloads for an assortment of unmanned missions and 'economies of scale'. A Norwegian defence company, Kongsberg, is building a multirole warship at a commercial yard using commercially available systems for less money when compared with building traditional warships.[5] Labelled as the 'Vanguard' design, the vessel will have plug-and-play capability and carry 'pack containers' for commercial operations as per the International Organization for Standardization's guidelines as also "swap missions as diverse as hydrographic survey to anti-submarine, area-denial, and other roles in a matter of hours".[6]

Third is low human exposure to collision and grounding. Autonomous ships, depending on the level of autonomy,[7] are expected to possess smart systems to prevent accidents and reduce dangers and risks caused by navigational accidents. However, the "extent of consequences resulting particularly from non-navigational accidents (e.g., fire, ship loss due to structural failure) can be expected to be much larger for unmanned ships when compared to the conventional ones".[8]

Fourth is the issue of budget and recurring expenditure for operations. There are numerous advantages arising from reduced crew, maximization of space for weapons, and other expenditure on account of human-related errors and negligence. MUNIN (Maritime Unmanned Navigation through Intelligence in Networks), after a three-year project has "predicted a saving of over $7 million over a 25-year period per autonomous vessel in fuel consumption and crew supplies and salaries".[9]

Underwater Warfare

4IR applications can support a number of underwater operations. These can be categorized into at least four categories; (a) combat operations such as anti-submarine warfare (ASW); mine countermeasures (MCM); underwater domain awareness (UDA); (b) delivery of public goods in the form of search and rescue (SAR); and (c) management and scientific endeavours such as ocean development, marine environment protection and ecology restoration.

In the first category, submarines, mini submarines, tethered drones and Autonomous Underwater Vehicles (AUV) are platforms of choice for navies. These support counter-submarine operations, underwater Intelligence, Surveillance, Reconnaissance (ISR) functions, target identification, designation and battle damage assessment. The latter two categories help reduce human exposure during mine hunting, disposal of underwater munitions, explosives and other types of ordnance, support search, location and recovery of objects, and underwater communications.

Another significant feature of underwater naval operations is the strategic and tactical use of the seabed. Nearly 50 per cent of the oceans are deeper than four kilometres which is a favourable geographical and topographical condition for deployment and concealment of underwater platforms and sensors. These platforms can be with wheels and hidden in the sea trenches, mounds and rocks on the ocean floor. They can be tethered as Blimps and the drones can remain submerged for long durations thus making them most suitable for tracking diesel-electric subs particularly those fitted with Air-independent propulsion (AIP) technology.

Navies can be expected to use drones in swarms and underwater Blimps, and sensors could be deployed floating or moored to the seabed over long durations. These can be positioned at vantage points underwater and can lay in wait until the prey comes to them. Likewise, an autonomous underwater drone or an all-electric ROV fitted with sensors and artificial intelligence features is a useful platform for autonomous anomaly detection on a wide range of sub-sea operations.

For instance, Russia's nuclear delivery vehicle inventory includes an autonomous underwater vehicle (AUV) designated as Ocean Multipurpose

System Status-6.[10] Nicknamed 'Kanyon' by the US Pentagon, this AUV was built by the Russian submarine manufacturers Rubin Design Bureau. It resembles a huge torpedo and has a 'range of 6,200 miles, a top speed in excess of 56 knots and can descend to depths of 3,280 feet below sea level'.[11] Status-6 made its first public appearance in 2015 and its trials were carried out in 2016. It can be launched from different types of cruise missile submarines and one of these is the Oscar-class. According to US officials, Status-6 is "essentially a drone-type device fired underwater that can potentially travel thousands of miles and strike US coastal targets such as military bases or cities"[12] and can also carry "cruise missiles and launch them after hiding for months beneath the water".

Another major concern for modern navies is mine warfare for which 4IR technologies offer reliable and safe solutions. Many of these are 'proven commercial-off-the-shelf (COTS) hardware and software' and can provide 'robust MCM capability to the Navy without waiting for the lengthy planning, programming, budgeting, and execution process to deliver these assets years in the future.'[13]

Aerospace Warfare

4IR technologies have begun to redefine aerospace warfare and the associated aerospace strategy. Unmanned rotary/fixed wing platforms and systems are now challenging the conventional approach to fight wars in air-space zones. There is a strong belief among major and smaller Air Forces that AI and other associated technologies will be at the core of any future aerospace warfare; it will transform the way Air Forces will conduct future operations, manage human resources, and supervise organizations. Consequently, the Military Industrial Complex is transforming and national laboratories, university, research institutions, innovation and incubation centres are reconfiguring. Besides, Air Forces are marshalling private companies and entrepreneurs to help transformation of the force. Perhaps, what is worrisome is that commercially available, cheap yet lethal technologies such as drones, are presenting new challenges for air defence platforms and systems; in particular, non-state actors are now using them with great success with enormous destruction.

Naval Exercises and Interoperability

As part of operational strategy, navies operate in concert and partnerships to respond to crisis through joint operations. In this context, interoperability has been high on the agenda of the navies to counter asymmetric threats and challenges. Likewise, interoperability is critical at the functional operational levels and some navies have taken the lead. For instance, in October 2016, the British Royal Navy along with 18 other navies conducted a Joint Warrior 2016 training exercise which focused on autonomous vessels.

In 2017, the Royal Navy conducted Joint Warrior 2017/1 which addressed five 4IR related themes, i.e., (a) AI: how building an AI 'ship's brain' will enable the fleet to operate faster, better and more effectively; (b) C4: developing the most efficient and comprehensive computer system possible for the Navy; (c) IX: exploiting the information that is out there; (d) CEMA: offensive and defensive cyber operations to protect our nation's interests; and (e) ISR: building the intelligence picture with unmanned systems to further enhance our commander's decisions.[14] The Joint Warrior 2019, the annual Exercise Information Warrior held at Portsdown Technology Park in March-April 2019, tested the Royal Navy's "ability to exploit the information environment and is closely linked to the development and deployment of MAS (Maritime Autonomous System)".[15]

The British Royal Navy also introduced a new Artificial Intelligence system called STARTLE designed to enhance situational awareness of potential threats and response times of various insecurities at sea. The software of the system is designed to perform the way the human brain works and reacts to 'human fear'. One of the important technologies for demonstration during the exercises was Airborne Computer Vision (ACV), a semi-autonomous targeting system aboard a Scan Eagle unmanned aerial vehicle (UAV) and, according to its owners, it can potentially "affect future naval operations significantly".

Joint Warfare

Joint operations have been the mantra of many militaries and have featured in their doctrines, strategy and concept of operations. Joint force commanders determine the kind of platform to be used with a clear understanding of the geographical area of employment, timing and duration of attack and damage constraints. The prime endeavour is to target the centre of gravity of the enemy through coordinated and synchronised actions to match the high speed and tempo of operations. Under the circumstances, present-day conflicts straddle more than one dimension and therefore necessitate a multi-disciplinary approach that features jointmanship.

Jointness is engineered by technology. It helps to transcend the air, land and sea mediums and cuts across operational doctrines and organisational structures in the conduct of warfare.[16] There are numerous examples of fleet engagements on the high seas supported by long-range bombers; operations against enemy land forces involving sea-launched and air-launched standoff missiles; seaward defence involving shore-based cruise missiles; covert special operation forces insertion and recovery; space-based communications for command and control, to name a few.

In contemporary times, expeditionary operations such as the 1982 Falkland War, the 1991 Operation Iraqi Freedom and the 2003 Operation Enduring Freedom are noteworthy and offer major insights into joint operations among the Western militaries. In fact, expeditionary operations are inherently joint in nature and involve pooling of all resources which would result in harnessing maximum potential of available resources.

A number of 4IR technologies can support joint operations and jointmanship at the organisational/functional levels. For instance the US Defence Advanced Research Projects Agency (DARPA) has conceptualized "Mosaic warfare" under which multiple military platforms would be connected through an AI-powered communications network.[17] This envisages "layering a network with AI [which] would enable the war fighter to better decide which asset is most effective in carrying out a specific mission. A good example for this is that if both Air Force and Navy aircraft are in an area to be targeted, AI could suggest which would be the better choice". However, there are limitations with regard to the power/energy needed for such equipment. "While large platforms such as ships and aircraft can carry a lot of power and computing, soldiers on the ground usually cannot. AI could be used to optimize communications in controlling how data and bandwidth are used most effectively".

Maritime Domain Awareness

A robust AI-based maritime domain awareness (MDA) can potentially contribute to transparency across the seas and oceans by integrating multi-source data, analytics and advanced Cloud services. It is a promising technology to track vessels, determine the type of cargo and even the business behaviour of shipping companies including freight forwarders.

An ideal AI-based MDA architecture could be built around numerous diversified technical devices and systems such as radar (ships, aircraft, shore), vessel monitoring systems (VMS), satellite supported systems (AIS and LRIT), UAVs, drones, imagery, open source Intelligence (OSINT), etc., to generate data. Thereafter advanced algorithms fuse data from different sources including data from a vessel profile library developed from stored knowledge and provide automated threat evaluation or early warning on anomalous activities at sea, understand and quantify risks, and provide timely alerts of possible threats or suspicious ships before reaching their destinations. In essence, this helps to minimize the information gap, thus limiting the number of vessels that require investigation.

These new capabilities also help translate MDA into actionable information and offers unprecedented potential to counter crimes at sea. The fishing industry, which has in recent times been under suspicion for engaging in IUU activities, can be monitored and tracked. It is now possible for AI-enabled drones to recognize the identification number of the fishing vessel, count people on board, determine if it is inside a protected area and verify its permit. Google is already using image-recognition technology in conjunction with AI to locate vessels engaged in IUU activity.[18]

As far as search and rescue at sea is concerned, navies and coast guards are often pressed into operations to rescue fishermen during cyclones and hurricanes. It is possible in the future for ships to launch autonomous vehicles to respond to emergencies to help locate and rescue victims that have been left stranded, immobile or are sinking.[19] An interesting application of AI-enabled drones is their use in the safety of beachgoers against sharks. In Australia, a shark detection system powered by Artificial Intelligence will be able to deliver "live-video feed to a drone operator who then uses the shark-spotting software to identify sharks in real time and with more accuracy than the human eye".[20]

Similarly, a technique that uses "an algorithm that analyzes ocean conditions such as the strength and direction of ocean currents, surface winds, and waves" can help first responders to reach the search area quickly. It has been developed by the MIT, the Swiss Federal Institute of Technology (ETH), the Woods Hole Oceanographic Institution (WHOI), and Virginia Tech[21] and it can identify floating objects in real-time.

It is not quite unnatural that unmanned vessels could experience sensor degradation or failures due to adverse sea conditions and would require maintenance or repairs. Machine learning and deep-learning artificial intelligence technology is being applied to ensure that remotely operated and autonomous vehicles can be monitored and kept operational to maintain domain and situational awareness.[22]

Unmanned Aerial Vehicles

The efficacy and successes of UAVs for firepower and in Intelligence, surveillance and reconnaissance (ISR) missions has been demonstrated in a number of conflicts in Afghanistan, Iraq, Syria, and more recently in Yemen. During these operations, UAVs demonstrated accurate targeting and ensured delivery of ordinance with limited collateral damage. UAVs are now being acquired by several militaries to fulfil many ISR tasks and they can remain in the air for long durations. For example, the U-2 or Global Hawk UAV has a very long endurance and a 34–hour-record for continuous flight without refuelling.[23]

A number of navies are investing in AI-enabled aerial and space platforms and the USA, Russia, China, France, Israel and Japan are the leaders. Some smaller navies are also adding such platforms and technologies in their inventories as force multipliers. Perhaps, what is worrisome is that non-state actors now have access to cheap UAVs and drones particularly when they operate drones in swarms which present a new threat for the militaries.

Counter-Drone Warfare

It is now widely acknowledged that as more drones enter the market and deluge the skies, they are turning into a nightmare for militaries. Counter-droning is emerging as an important tool of tactical warfare. The demand for counter-drone technologies is fast catching up among militaries. A series of attacks on energy infrastructure in Saudi Arabia by using drones and the inability to detect them has added to the challenges faced by national air defence.

The possibility of drones themselves serving as weapons in the form of anti-drone platforms is not a stretch of the imagination. This could be by "hijacking and taking control of unidentified drones and marshalling them to collide with other drones or even crashing them by using non-kinetic ways".[24] Furthermore, "counter-drone technologies are also gaining prominence among militaries due to increased 'security breach incidences' and the fear of small and weaponised drone swarms being put to use as tools of warfare".[25] Even smaller navies[26] are keen to acquire them and are scouting for such technologies.

The demand for counter-UAVs (c-UAV) is growing and many players have entered this field. For instance, French Airbus Defence and Space Inc., has developed a c-UAV system that "combines sensor data from different sources with latest data fusion, signal analysis and jamming technologies" and uses "operational radars, infrared cameras and direction finders from Airbus Defence and Space's portfolio".[27] It can detect an incoming drone at a distance of between 5 and 10 kilometres as also determine the potential threat by using "extensive threat library and real time analysis of control signals and then use a jammer that interrupts the link between drone and pilot and/or its navigation".[28]

Drone Defence in the UK is developing Drone Defenders that employ "acoustic, optical, and infrared sensors for real-time detection and identification" and it can "detect, classify, and prosecute unknown UAVs".[29] It also uses a "man-portable Dynopis E1000MP to jam the UAV's controls or Net Gun X1 c-UAV system to capture the aircraft"[30] which adds to flexibility of deployment from both a fixed location and a mobile unit.

The US' Multi-Azimuth Defence Fast Intercept Round Engagement System (MAD-FIRES) developed by the Defence Advanced Research Projects Agency (DARPA) is for countering attacks by unmanned platforms such as small planes, fast attack craft, and other platforms that pose a "perennial, evolving, and potentially lethal threat to ships and other maritime vessels".[31] It also serves as a close-in weapon system (CIWS) and can augment onboard ship defence to target with precision and engage dissimilar targets that may come from different directions. The USA has fielded at least 11 counter-drone technologies; one of them is the 'Ghostbuster looking gun' which uses radio frequencies to disrupt enemy drones instead of kinetic ammunition.[32]

Likewise, Liteye's AUDS non-lethal electronic attack radio-frequency jammer system is paired with an Orbital gun[33] and can fire precision-guided or air-burst ammunition to provide a hard-kill option. The US Central Command deployed it in its area of operation and it proved effective having downed "more than 500 drones with electronic attack".[34]

Israel has also excelled in counter-drone technologies and at least two companies have entered the market.[35] The ReDrone, a counter-drone product that specialises in hacking and diverting drones, has been developed by the Elbit System; and the Israel Aerospace Industries manufactures Drone Guard, a drone detection and disruption system that has been available since 2016.

Drone Mother-ship

Manned and unmanned aviation platforms such as aircraft, helicopters and UAVs, have been part of the inventory of several navies. These are inherently agile and are embarked onboard ships and networked with other geographically dispersed platforms at sea and ashore thus facilitating sustained maritime domain awareness. Current naval trends indicate a move towards reconfiguring surface warships as 'drone mother ships' that can launch and recover unmanned maritime platforms and deploying them at strategic locations.

At the heart of the "Drone Mother-ship" is the idea of 'coordinated and controlled autonomy' under which mother-ships will operate ahead of the fleet and act as the proverbial 'naval' scouts to forewarn the presence of the enemy. They could also function as the Command and Control of multiple sea drones operating in the area. However, in the case of armed drones, human intervention, i.e., humans will decide the use of lethal force.

At least four navies in the West (US, Russian, Belgian and Dutch) are planning to build/repurpose Drone Mother-ships to act as force multipliers. A similar number in Asia (China, Japan, Republic of Korea and Singapore) are experimenting with the 'Drone Mother-ship' concept. The Belgian Naval & Robotics (formed by Naval Group & ECA Group) is building 12 MCM vessels and associated equipment for the Belgian and Dutch navies. According to media reports and published pictures, the MCM mother-ship is fitted with two Inspector 125 unmanned surface vehicles (by ECA Group) which can be launched and recovered by using davits. These can carry a variety of payloads (AUVs and scanners) and conduct operations as far as 12 nautical miles from the mother-ship.[36]

Counter Terrorism and Ship Security

The use of high-speed boats packed with explosives to attack commercial vessels and warships is well documented. In particular, Al Qaeda, a terrorist group, was successful in attacking a US Navy ship *USS Cole* at Aden, Yemen (in 2000) and *MV Limburg*, a French flagged oil tanker, off Yemen (in 2002). To counter these asymmetric threats at sea, navies augmented their surveillance and reconnaissance capabilities with multiple surface and air platforms. Both manned and unmanned aviation platforms such as aircraft, helicopters, UAVs, aerostats and satellites gained priority in the force structure of several navies. Besides being inherently agile, these could be deployed at short notice and networked with other geographically dispersed platforms and systems thus facilitating sustained maritime domain awareness. Among them, the UAVs provided a quantum jump in capabilities for reconnaissance and monitoring of large sea spaces at long distances, a task that can be very tedious for the crew of fixed-wing aircraft or helicopters. The UAVs thus emerged as platforms of choice and began to attract improved funding. Similarly, unmanned vessels became popular among the navies and were meant to reduce human exposure to threats on the surface of the water.

The USA is testing its CUSV (Common Unmanned Surface Vehicle).[37] Textron Systems, the developers of this unmanned platform, claim that this "fourth-generation CUSV is a mature, multi-mission and multi-payload capable vehicle with significant in-water experience" and can be used for 'mine sweeping and neutralization role; Intelligence, surveillance and reconnaissance (ISR); harbour security; monitoring or protection".[38]

Biomimetic Inspired Autonomous Underwater Vehicles

The US Navy started its Silent NEMO program in 2013 and called it developed GhostSwimmer unmanned underwater vehicle (UUV) and was inspired by Tuna. The US Navy Warfare Development Command (NWDC) stated that "its bio-mimicry was intended to provide additional security during low visibility Intelligence, surveillance and reconnaissance (ISR) missions and friendly hull inspections, while quieter than propeller-driven craft of the same size".[39] Similarly, Boston Engineering Corporation's Advanced Systems Group for the US Department of Homeland Security (DHS) Science & Technology (S&T) has developed BIO-Swimmer AUV. This is useful for checking cargo holds, hull inspections and also for search-and-rescue missions.

In 2019, Boya Gongdao Robot Technology, a Chinese technology company, put on display a shark-like, military Autonomous Underwater Vehicle (AUV) at the iOceans China 2019 in Sanya, China. The company claims that Robo-Shark has 'stealth features' and 'high underwater speed and large payload capacity' and can be deployed for Intelligence, surveillance and reconnaissance missions. According to an underwater technology expert, 'fish-tail propulsion' offers a number of advantages such as higher efficiency (up to 80 per cent), improved battery life due to low power consumption and the outer casing which is made of sound-absorbing material reduces its noise signature adding to its stealth. Another Chinese Biomimetics underwater drone (wingspan 0.8 metres and top speed of 1 knot) is based on the Manta Ray fish. It has been designed by the School of Marine Science and Technology at the PRC Northwestern Polytechnical University.

Similarly, the European Defence Agency (EDA) is exploring biomimetic underwater vehicles titled Sabuvis-II. Defendtex, an Australian company engaged in defence production has developed the quid-like Soft Robotic

Cephalopod at DSEI 2019. It can operate in swarms for a number of missions to support anti-submarine warfare, A2/AD operations, and ISR missions.

A number of countries are investing in Biomimetics for applications in the military domain. Future plans envisage developing 'biobots' by replicating humans, wildlife, birds, snakes, marine species and plants and even insects. These 'Biomemetic robots' will be game changers and would shape the nature of future warfare. Also, there is enormous interest in the defence industry which is already developing Biomemetic robots, devices and tools for applications in the civil domain.

At another level, AI-enabled cameras are helping monitor fish. For instance, a system developed by Alphabet's X Development can 'recognise and monitor every individual fish in farms that hold hundreds of thousands'.[40] The system 'pairs underwater cameras with AI techniques such as computer vision to track species'. An up-scaled version of this system could potentially be used for underwater domain awareness.

Near Space Technologies

'Near Space' is virtually a 'space desert' in which aircraft do not fly, no satellite is positioned, and fuel-powered UAVs are unable to operate due to the thin air that hampers functioning of the engine. Understandably, this area has remained underutilized; however, it is now being populated with sub-orbital rockets, high-altitude balloons which can easily jump into and out of near space. The UAVs are now being modified into Solar Powered UAVs (SPUAVs) and they do not need to carry fuel making them relatively lighter. This helps them stay in the air for extended periods and perform a number of tasks currently assigned to satellites or to high-altitude aircraft. They can operate above the weather, are inherently stealthy, and fly above the range of nearly all threats.

There are now plans to use SPUAVs in constellations to undertake seamless ISR operations as also provide stable cellular and internet services. Airbus Defence and Space is a leader in SPUAV technology and successfully landed Zephyr S HAPS (High Altitude Pseudo-Satellite) after nearly 26 days flight.[41] It flies at over 70,000 feet and can be deployed for reconnaissance, surveillance and communications/Internet duties.

Likewise, noteworthy developments have been announced by China and there are plans to position SPUAVs in 'near space', a spatial region between 20 and 99 kilometres altitude from the Earth's surface.[42] Several Chinese companies are working to create a telecommunications network based on SPUAV. The CASTC conducted a test flight of its first solar-powered drone the 'Caihong' (Rainbow) in 2017 and it flew to a height of 65,000 feet. Similarly, in September 2018, AVIC announced that its 'Morning Star' SPUAV cruised at an altitude of more than 20,000 metres.[43]

However, there are a number of constraints and Professor Yang Chunxin from the School of Aeronautic Science and Engineering, Beihang University, in Beijing, has noted that the "biggest headache is the near-vacuum environment, where electric currents can produce a spark. This can lead to shortages and damage electronic equipment.... This is why high-altitude drones are more difficult to build than lower-flying variants. Whether they can play a practical role in military operations remains an open structure question".[44]

New Skills

Artificial intelligence specialists believe that machines will match human intelligence by 2029 and will surpass it by 2045. Further, much of the human tasks will be conducted by robots that would be everywhere, crawling, flying, sailing or swimming. Their numbers would surpass humans living on the Earth and it is plausible that their combined intelligence could be far higher and superior than that of the human population. It is estimated that by 2020, "50 billion objects will be connected to the Internet. This will result in a smart integrated system of sensors, data and Internet-enabled devices that manage our lives. Over the next 25 years, through technological convergence, the 'Internet of Everything' will enable us to manage all aspects of our lives in real time". Amid such predictions, there are fears that humans will be made redundant. Be that as it may, till then, the role of humans in the coming transformation will remain inescapable.

The Royal Navy acknowledges the fact that the "pace and scale of technological change in the world today is breathtaking. The Royal Navy is no less affected than anyone else by the challenges of cheap, smart phone computing power with high-grade encryption. And more is coming in the Internet of Things.... Artificial Intelligence, robotics, automation and quantum computing are all future uncertainties. As a result, the Royal Navy, priding itself on its long history of world-leading innovation, is focused on the implications for maritime and littoral warfare in the Information Age".

Many navies have established Cyber Commands or Cyber Units; however they would soon have to set up specialist units to train for robot-led warfare. It is argued that the developments in AI and related technological developments and advancements must be followed very carefully and it is incumbent on the part of militaries to understand what AI can do and what it cannot. Likewise, the focus should be on building human skills in areas where robots cannot do well, such as strategic thinking, empathy and ethics.

Concluding Remarks

Technological disruptions led by Fourth Industrial Revolution (4IR) technologies are now a common feature among the advanced navies. Smart, intelligent, predictive and cognitive technologies are being added to the menu of naval warfare. At the policy level, departments of defence are encouraging development of 4IR-enabled military hardware. They are allocating some percentage of military budgets for the development of 4IR-enabled weapons and sensors to maintain an edge over their respective adversaries. The ongoing 4IR technological transformation in the naval domain will add to dexterity in naval operations; while that is welcome, it also presents newer challenges for war fighting doctrines, concept of operations and command control. The next chapter offers insights into the policy, practice and assimilation of 4IR technologies among the Western navies.

NOTES

1. Geoffrey Till, "The Navies of the Asia Pacific in a Revolutionary Age" in Dalchoong Kim, Seo-Hang Lee, Jin-Hyun Park (eds.), *Maritime Security and Cooperation in Asia Pacific Towards the 21st Century* (Dooilnet: Seoul, 2000), p. 7.
2. Ibid., p. 20.
3. David B. Larter, "A Classified Pentagon Maritime Drone Program is about to get its Moment in the Sun", https://www.defensenews.com/naval/2019/03/14/a-classified-pentagon-maritime-drone-program-is-about-to-get-its-moment-in-the-sun/ (accessed 4 October 2019).
4. Ibid.
5. "Kongsberg Offers New Warship Design with Plug-and-play Mission Payloads to Rival Commercial Ship Costs", https://www.militaryaerospace.com/power/article/14068078/warships-commercial-plugandplay (accessed 9 October 2019).
6. Ibid.
7. Callum O. Brien, "Key Advantages and Disadvantages of Ship Autonomy", https://safety4sea.com/key-advantages-and-disadvantages-of-ship-autonomy/ (accessed 9 October 2019).
8. Krzysztof Wróbel, Jakub Montewka and Pentti Kujala, "Towards the Assessment of Potential Impact of Unmanned Vessels on Maritime Transportation Safety", https://

www.sciencedirect.com/science/article/pii/S0951832016303337 (accessed 10 October 2019).

9. "Autonomous Ships", https://www.standard-club.com/media/2767846/autonomous-ships.pdf (accessed 5 October 2019); Bernard Marr, "The Incredible Autonomous Ships of The Future: Run By Artificial Intelligence Rather Than a Crew", https://www.forbes.com/sites/bernardmarr/2019/06/05/the-incredible-autonomous-ships-of-the-future-run-by-artificial-intelligence-rather-than-a-crew/#6b4b318e6fbf (accessed 5 October 2019).
10. Valerie Insinna, "Russia's Nuclear Underwater Drone is Real and in the Nuclear Posture Review" https://www.defensenews.com/space/2018/01/12/russias-nuclear-underwater-drone-is-real-and-in-the-nuclear-posture-review/ (accessed 24 October 2919).
11. "Russia Launches Belgorod Nuclear Submarine to Carry Poseidon Underwater Drones", https://medium.com/indrastra/russia-launches-belgorod-nuclear-submarine-to-carry-poseidon-underwater-drones-d49bda5287e3 (accessed 26 October 2919).
12. Daniel Politi, "Pentagon Says Russia Is Building Nuclear Torpedo Described as "Doomsday" Weapon", https://slate.com/news-and-politics/2018/02/pentagon-says-russia-is-building-nuclear-torpedo-described-as-doomsday-weapon.html (accessed 26 October 2919).
13. *U.H. Rowley and Craig Cates,* "Unmanned Solutions for the U.S. Navy's Mine Warfare Renaissance", https://www.maritime-executive.com/editorials/unmanned-solutions-for-the-u-s-navy-s-mine-warfare-renaissance (accessed 24 October 2919).
14. "Royal Navy Pioneers New Age of Information Warfare", https://www.adsgroup.org.uk/news/member-news/royal-navy-pioneers-new-age-of-information-warfare/ (accessed 30 March 2020).
15. "The Royal Navy and Maritime Autonomous Systems – Better Late than Never", https://www.savetheroyalnavy.org/the-royal-navy-and-maritime-autonomous-systems-better-late-than-never/ (accessed 30 March 2020).
16. Vijay Sakhuja, "Future Joint Operations" (ed.) Jasjit Singh, *Air Power and Joint Operations* (New Delhi: CAPS, 2003), pp.182-201.
17. "Artificial Intelligence, Warfighters Form Enhanced Partnership on Battlefield", https://www.defense.gov/Explore/News/Article/Article/2222999/artificial-intelligence-warfighters-form-enhanced-partnership-on-battlefield/ (accessed 17 June 2020).
18. "Google Uses AI to spot Illegal Fishing in seas", https://www.techcircle.in/2018/04/09/google-uses-ai-to-spot-illegal-fishing-in-seas/ (accessed 30 October 20219).
19. "Search and Rescue Robots – Current Applications on Land, Sea, and Air", https://emerj.com/ai-sector-overviews/search-and-rescue-robots-current-applications/ (accessed 30 October 2019).
20. "Shark-detecting drones to patrol Australian beaches", https://www.reuters.com/article/us-australia-sharkdrone/shark-detecting-drones-to-patrol-australian-beaches-idUSKCN1B51KB (accessed 30 October 2019).
21. "Algorithm Aims to Assist Ocean Search and Rescue", https://www.marinetechnologynews.com/news/algorithm-assist-ocean-search-601946 (accessed 29 May 2020).
22. "GMATEK Selected for Sensor Degradation Research by the U.S. Navy", https://dc.citybizlist.com/article/614367/gmatek-selected-for-sensor-degradation-research-by-the-us-navy (accessed 13 June 2020).
23. "U-2 Versus Global Hawk: Why Drones Aren't Always the Best Solution for Warfighters", https://www.forbes.com/sites/lorenthompson/2018/02/05/u-2-versus-global-hawk-why-drones-arent-always-the-best-solution-for-warfighters/#1aa5bbaf4d7e (accessed 30 October 2019).

24. "The Debut of Counter-Drone Technologies", http://www.ipcs.org/comm_select.php?articleNo=5438 (accessed 30 October 2020).
25. Ibid.
26. Rey E. Requejo, "PH Navy Wants Anti-drone Tech", http://manilastandard.net/news/national/306642/ph-navy-wants-anti-drone-tech.html (accessed 6 October 2019).
27. "Counter-UAV System from Airbus Defence and Space protects large installations and events from illicit intrusion", https://www.airbus.com/newsroom/press-releases/en/2015/09/counter-uav-system-from-airbus-defence-and-space-protects-large-installations-and-events-from-illicit-intrusion.html (accessed 15 October 2019).
28. Ibid.
29. "The Dawn of Counter-drone Technologies", https://www.militaryaerospace.com/unmanned/article/16708899/the-dawn-of-counterdrone-technologies (15 October 2019).
30. Ibid.
31. Kate Tringham, "Navy League 2019: Raytheon Tests Rocket Motor for MAD-FIRES Interceptor", https://www.janes.com/article/88345/navy-league-2019-raytheon-tests-rocket-motor-for-mad-fires-interceptor (15 October 2019).
32. "OSD to Recommend Big Budget Increase for Counter-Drone Technologies", https://www.nationaldefensemagazine.org/articles/2017/3/23/osd-to-recommend-big-budget-increase-for-counter-drone-technologies(15 October 2019).
33. "Everything's coming up SHORAD", https://liteye.com/everythings-coming-up-shorad/ (accessed 15 October 2019).
34. "'No Silver Bullet': Pentagon Struggles to Defeat Drones in Cat-and-mouse Game", (accessed 15 October 2019).
35. "As Drones Become Tools of War, Companies Turn to Hacking Them", https://futurism.com/drone-hack-technology (accessed 15 October 2019).
36. "This is What the Future Belgian & Dutch MCM Motherships will Look Like" https://www.navalnews.com/naval-news/2019/05/this-is-what-the-future-belgian-dutch-mcm-motherships-will-look-like/ (accessed 22 May 2020).
37. "The New United States Navy Unmanned Robot Boat To Protect From Terrorist Attacks", http://www.maritimeherald.com/2020/02-24-viral-twitter-video-the-new-united-states-navy-unmanned-robot-boat-to-protect-from-terrorist-attacks-al-qaeda-terrorists-us-ports/#.XlR9csBlcZs.email (accessed 27 February 2020).
38. For more details, see https://www.textronsystems.com/products/cusv (accessed 27 February 2020).
39. H. I. Sutton, "Biomimetic Autonomous Underwater Vehicles", http://www.hisutton.com/Biomimetic_Autonomous_Underwater_Vehicles.html (accessed 19 Frebruary 2020).
40. "Google Parent Alphabet Invents Fish Recognition System", https://fishbio.com/news/google-parent-alphabet-invents-fish-recognition-systemhttps://fishbio.com/news/google-parent-alphabet-invents-fish-recognition-systemhttps://fishbio.com/news/google-parent-alphabet-invents-fish-recognition-system (accessed 5 March 2020).
41. "Solar-Powered "Pseudo-Satellite" Aircraft Logs First Flight of 26 Days", https://www.powerelectronics.com/markets/automotive/article/21864274/solarpowered-pseudosatellite-aircraft-logs-first-flight-of-26-days (accessed 30 October 2019).
42. "China tests new spy drones in near space 'death zone'", https://www.scmp.com/news/china/society/article/2117709/china-tests-new-spy-drones-near-space-death-zone (accessed 30 October 2019).

43. "Chinese solar-powered drone Morning Star Spreads its Wings in Successful Test Flight", https://www.scmp.com/news/china/military/article/2171081/chinese-solar-powered-drone-spreads-its-wings-successful-test (accessed 30 October 2019).
44. "China Tests New Spy Drones in Near Space 'death zone'", https://www.scmp.com/news/china/society/article/2117709/china-tests-new-spy-drones-near-space-death-zone (accessed 30 October 2019).

CHAPTER 4

4IR in Western Navies

The industrial revolution during the 1780s and the 1850s, first centred in Britain and later in Europe, was the 'Age of Enlightenment' and transformed factory production. It introduced coal and iron which enabled the Western world to lead the technology path with strong emphasis on innovations. Its adaptation and absorption in the maritime domain led to major inventions in prime technologies of the time such as steam engines for propulsion, telegraph for communication, and guns for naval war fighting. It also resulted in the setting up of the defence and military industrial infrastructure. Consequently, the Western nations enjoyed technological advantage, took the lead, and set up large-scale networks for production of military hardware.

The two World Wars witnessed a number of scientific innovations and technological developments and these found reference in the military industrial complexes of most of the Western nations[1] including Japan. In the post-World War II period, Revolution in Military Affairs (RMA) driven by information and communication technologies (ICT) was the driver of military transformation. This era of ICT spawned new strategies and there was widespread use of ICT-enabled weapons and sensors in the US-led wars in Iraq, the global war on terror, and the NATO-led war in Bosnia. It was believed that these would have a "far-reaching impact on the concept of future wars, and these militaries began to reorient their tactical military doctrines to deal with information-technology based tactics".[2]

The Western militaries enjoyed distinct advantages through ICT and emerged as the major suppliers of military hardware to the Asian countries including China and India who explored the military markets of Russia, Israel and other European defence industries and developed indigenous technological strengths.

However, there is also the view that "with the beginning of 4IR over the past decade, with its unprecedented democratization of technology, we find ourselves in a world where access to extremely advanced technology is not solely the preserve of the Western alliance. This often puts the average Western, NATO-standard soldier on the same level, qualitatively if not quantitatively, as his or her adversaries".[3] Furthermore, "As more of defence materiel production is devoted to 4IR weapons systems, from missiles to robots to cyber warfare, we will see that the production of that materiel will not only be carried out in the advanced defence manufacturing hubs of the USA or Europe or even Russia; it will be increasingly carried out by a very wide variety of nations, many of which may even be emerging economies".[4]

US Navy

Policy and Strategy

The US Department of Defence announced a pan-military AI Strategy which lays out the imperatives for the integration of Artificial Intelligence across all arms of the US armed forces.[5] It set up the Joint Artificial Intelligence Centre (JAIC) to "preserve and expand military advantage" as also to pursue "AI applications with boldness and alacrity while ensuring strong commitment to military ethics and AI safety".[6] An estimated budget of US$ 1.7 billion is expected to be spent over six years[7] and the JAIC would cooperate with industry, academia and partners and allies[8] in nearly 600 AI projects. It will have oversight over almost all service and defence agency AI efforts. It is also planned to formulate a national strategy for artificial intelligence. The US Army constituted an AI Task Force to identify "specific skill sets that we are going to need to be relevant and to thrive in this environment that will include AI and machine learning".[9]

The US Congressional Research Service released a report in November 2018 detailing the future of military uses of robotics and artificial intelligence. The report notes that Russia and China are "aggressively pursuing" advanced robotic and AI weapons systems "that could be used against US forces".[10] Meanwhile, the US military began planning for introducing robotic tanks and autonomous cargo vehicles. It is also exploring the Fully Autonomous First Wave Concept, which would involve "robotic and autonomous aerial, amphibious and ground platforms ...employed as the first wave of an amphibious assault".[11]

Naval Academia Steps In

In 2017, the US Office of Naval Research (ONR), through an announcement, called for expressions of interest from "Navy, non-Navy, technology, non-technologist gamers to help it prepare for a 'post-Singularity' world that will be shaped by highly capable 'greater-than-human' artificial intelligence.[12] It set up the Massive Multiplayer Online War Game Leveraging the Internet (MMOWGLI) to facilitate exchange of ideas among the players through interaction over the platform and draw upon the intellectual capital of the people to encourage innovation and explore new solutions to complex problems and hypothetical scenarios to develop better strategies and tactics. Eric Gulovsen, director of disruptive technology at the ONR was forthright in noting that "Technology has advanced to the point that we can see the Singularity on the horizon".[13]

The US professional academic institutions such as the Naval War College too have pursued studies concerning the development of 4IR technologies to help naval strategists and practitioners understand the evolving concepts and their use in warfare as also to "talk about the actual applications that AI will bring to the military war fighting world".[14] It is noteworthy that the USA has more than 13,000 top AI researchers, compared with only 5,000 in China.[15]

Naval Budget

There is also an internal debate within the US Navy about having a relook at future plans for surface combatants. The Centre for Strategic and Budgetary Assessments in its study has observed that the "New concepts for surface fleet missions...will increasingly rely on unmanned systems to perform sensing operations because unmanned systems can achieve the proximity or distribution to use passive sensors effectively or employ active sensors at acceptable risk".[16] Furthermore, "Engagements will largely continue to be ordered by a human operator, although that operator may be on a nearby manned platform and the weapon launched by an unmanned vehicle. Unmanned systems would conduct almost all counter-[surveillance and targeting] missions; they can make risk-worthy decoys or employ active countermeasures without exposing a manned platform to detection and attack".[17]

A distinct trend towards unmanned and autonomous vessels and platforms in the future US naval force structure is discernable.[18] The US Navy plans to acquire a variety of large, medium and small unmanned vehicles (UVs) in FY2020 and beyond, and has sought US$ 628.8 million in FY2020 for R&D on three UV programs[19] and the associated enabling technologies.[20]

Platform Choices, Programmes and Development

In 2016, during a House Armed Services Committee hearing, Rear Admiral Michael Jabaley, the US Navy's program executive officer for submarines, made an interesting statement that he would like "some organic means of designing the submarine from the ground up that would seamlessly integrate UUVs".[21] He was inspired by 'remoras', a small fish also called 'shark sucker or sucker fish', that attaches itself to a big fish and free rides along and "when it's time for them to go do something, they do and then come back".[22] It was also his belief this would help to launch and recover UUVs as convenient and would be useful for carrying out operations over a larger area in the oceans.

The Chief of the US Navy submarine arm sees a number of innovations led by 4IR technologies and would transform underwater platforms. "Unmanned systems will play an integral role in the future of undersea warfare. We are working closely with the defence industrial base, academia, and our warfare development centres to study, develop, and field the right mix of unmanned platforms and sensors, as well as how to best employ them. In planning for the future of undersea innovation and dominance, we are also looking for where artificial intelligence, machine learning, and big-data analytics can be used to work more efficiently at fleet scale to improve the speed and quality of our decision-making process".[23]

The US Navy has graduated from conceptual stages of AI-enabled platforms to conducting trials of some of the prototypes. For instance, the US Navy inducted an Anti-Submarine Warfare (ASW) Continuous Trail Unmanned Vessel (ACTUV) designated as Sea Hunter-I.[24] Developed by the Defence Advanced Research Projects Agency (DARPA), the vessel is designed to conduct 'missions spanning thousands of kilometres of range and months of endurance under a sparse remote supervisory control model' as also be compliant with 'maritime laws and conventions for safe navigation, autonomous system management for operational reliability, and autonomous interactions with an intelligent adversary'.[25] Its multi-payload capability was tested during trials; in 2016, it towed a para-kite 'packed with communications equipment from a parachute connected to a vessel' called Towed Airborne Lift of Naval Systems (TALONS), and in 2017 it was put to mine-countermeasure trials.[26]

The US Navy has placed orders with DARPA for Sea Hunter-II.[27] It is developed by Leidos and will incorporate what was learned from Sea Hunter-I to further develop and mature autonomy, both as a stand-alone mission vessel and in cooperation with Sea Hunter-I, which remains an active part of the program, as part of the Navy's goal of deploying collaborative ships, manned and unmanned.[28]

The Sea Hunter programme is now being expanded and DARPA launched the NOMARS "No Manning Required, Ship", which will 'never have a human on board'.[29] Perhaps what is noteworthy that its design "challenge the traditional naval architecture paradigm, designing a sea-frame from the ground up with no provision, allowance, or expectation for humans at sea... By removing the human element from all ship design considerations, NOMARS will demonstrate significant advantages to include size, cost (procurement, operations, and sustainment), at-sea reliability, survivability to sea-state, survivability to adversary actions (stealth considerations, resistance to tampering, etc.), and hydrodynamic efficiency (hull optimization without consideration for crew safety or comfort)".[30] Meanwhile, the US Navy is exploring off-the-shelf technologies for an automated "bridge-to-bridge radio for unmanned surface vehicles" to enable autonomous vessels such as the Sea Hunter to communicate with humans over VHF.[31]

The Mine Warfare Program Office's Hammerhead program is a US Navy-Industry initiative which aims to "deploy from an unmanned underwater vehicle and detect, classify and destroy anti-submarine warfare assets".[32]

An innovative use of drones by the US Navy is about incorporating meteorological data obtained by unmanned platforms for tactical decision-making. The software developed by a US company will collect hydrology data such as "water temperature, humidity, wind speed, and topography" which would be gathered and shared in near real-time "to a command centre where it can be parsed and analyzed rapidly, providing naval officers with a more comprehensive view into conditions in contested areas".[33] Some of the naval platforms that have been identified for such integration are "Teledyne Slocum" autonomous ocean gliders; unmanned surface craft like the "Sea Hunter" and the Common Unmanned Surface Vessel (CUSV); and future platforms like the Ghost Swimmer submersible "shark" and DARPA's "Upward Falling Payload" forward-deployed drones".[34]

The Office of Naval Research (ONR) is also pursuing project CLAWS under which it will be possible for the US Navy to deploy robot submarines fitted with sensors and algorithms and it could "potentially kill without explicit human control". CLAWS is designed to conduct complex missions independently even avoiding anti-submarine warfare systems.[35]

The Defence Advanced Research Projects Agency (DARPA) has commissioned four major US industry giants[36] to develop a new class of unmanned underwater vehicles (UUVs) under the Manta Ray program which would "increase at-sea operational capacity and capabilities for combatant commanders while minimizing disruptions to current operations by remaining independent of crewed vessels and ports once deployed".[37] The US Navy plans to augment the capabilities of its aircraft carriers through "deck-launched drones as part of a strategy aimed at massively increasing the scope of carrier-launched drone missions in coming years".[38] For that, it is re-purposing space to set up a control room called "drone-headquarters" for the command and control of these units.

The USA is focusing on Lockheed Martin's Orca system and the company statement notes that a "critical benefit of Orca is that Navy personnel launch, recover, operate, and communicate with the vehicle from a home base and are never placed in harm's way". Boeing too is developing a prototype based on its Echo Voyager; this 50-ton autonomous submarine (more than 15 metres long and 2.6 metres in diameter) 'can operate for months over a range of 12,000 kilometres, more than enough to sail from San Francisco to Shanghai'. It has a maximum speed of 15 kilometres per hour, can dive to 3 kilometres and carry up to 8 tons of cargo.

The DARPA has a programme called Upward Falling Payload (UFP) and the concept is built around "developing deployable, unmanned, nonlethal distributed systems that lie on the deep-ocean floor in special containers for years at a time. These deep-sea nodes could be remotely activated when needed and recalled to the surface". The US Navy also has an underwater drone fleet comprising smaller platforms which look like torpedoes with fins. The UUVs can be launched from a torpedo tube "to create the same kind of picture of the undersea space that satellites, radars and UAVs can create of airspace".[39] Similarly, the US Naval Undersea Warfare Centre is hoping to receive White Papers outlining potential research for "innovative technological solutions to address current and future security threats in the undersea and maritime environment".[40]

The US Navy is also working with companies such as Bluefin Robotics and Hydroid to develop underwater drones to detect explosive sea mines,[41] a task previously done by sea animals such as dolphins and sea lions.[42]

A demonstrative model of a 3D-printed submersible hull made from carbon fibre composites for the US Navy is a good example of using 3D printer technology. It is not only cheap (US$ 100,000 as against $ 600,000 to $ 800,000) but has been printed (built) in a short period (a few weeks) resulting in savings of cost and time.[43]

Unmanned Maritime Autonomy Architecture is high on the agenda and according to the program manager of the Unmanned Maritime Systems, Naval Sea Systems Command, it involves "integrating autonomy and payloads. Payload integration is allowing us to work out technical challenges and work with technology developers to identify gaps in the experimentation plan".[44] It is testing the Spearhead (T-EPF 1) to serve as a mother-ship (103 metres (338 ft) long and 28.5 metres (94 ft) in beam) for unmanned aerial vehicles (UAVs) and unmanned underwater vehicles (UUVs).[45] This multi-mission vessel is capable of several maritime security functions including humanitarian assistance and disaster relief (HADR) support operations as well as Intelligence, surveillance and reconnaissance. It can launch Scan Eagle unmanned aerial vehicles (UAV) and a VBAT vertical take-off and landing (VTOL) unmanned aerial system (UAS) and, according to reports, it is testing the Knifefish UUV for mine countermeasure missions (MCM).

British Royal Navy

Britain has been one of the leaders in all the earlier technological revolutions and continues to be a major participant and developer of technologies for the evolving 4IR. It is not surprising then that the Royal Navy has a long history of maritime and naval innovation and produced world class warships, submarines and aircraft carriers.

The United Kingdom is embracing 4IR technologies at the national level in various sectors and the British leadership has made reference to the use of Artificial Intelligence and machine learning for activities such as counter-money laundering, fraud, cyber-crime and terrorism, and alluded to using drones for search and rescue operations.[46] The House of Lords Select Committee has announced that "Britain is primed to take on a world-leading role in developing artificial intelligence as we advance into the 21st century"[47] and U.K.'s Ministry of Defence (MoD) revealed its intention to use "AI to make decisions related to national security and warfare".[48]

On behalf of the UK Defence Science and Technology Laboratory (DSTL), the Defence and Security Accelerator (DASA) the research arm of the UK Ministry of Defence which "finds and funds exploitable innovation to support UK defence and security"[49] is leading projects for developing future defence platforms keeping in mind "current and future advances in automation, autonomy, machine learning and AI".[50] The DASA earmarked £ 4 million of which £ 1 million is for nine projects involving development of technology and innovative solutions to support its 'Intelligent Ship programme' a prototype technology demonstrator which adopts an innovative approach for "Human to AI and AI to AI teaming for defence platforms, such as warships, aircraft, and land vehicles in 2040 and beyond".[51] The technical lead for the program at the DSTL has noted that by "harnessing automation, autonomy, machine learning and artificial intelligence with the real-life skill and experience of our men and women, we can revolutionise the way future fleets are put together and operate to keep the UK safe".[52]

Similarly, according to the Chief Technology Officer for the Royal Navy, the Navy aims at a "transition rapidly from what we have now to whatever we want in the future.... We live in an exponential world of technological change and if we can integrate the latest and get it on operations, it will deliver a battle-winning advantage. Specifically, getting that technology onto ships like HMS *Prince of Wales* would be a game-changer".[53]

The Royal Navy operates the ARCIMS, an unmanned minesweeping vessel. It was built by Atlas Elektronik and is designed for countermine operations using acoustic, magnetic and electrical devices that can trigger naval mines at a distance.[54] A three-hull or trimaran named 'Mayflower', a prototype labelled as 'AI Captain' is designed to use "cameras, artificial intelligence and edge computing systems to safely navigate around ships, buoys and other ocean hazards".[55] The vessel is under construction in Gdansk, Poland, and will be deployed onboard the research ship *Plymouth Quest* operated by the Plymouth Marine Laboratory in the U.K. by September 2020.[56]

The BAE Systems and Dassault Aviation-led Anglo-French Taranis armed drone, which is the "most technically advanced demonstration aircraft ever built in the UK,"[57] has been under development since 2014 but its future could be on hold due to Britain's exit from the European Union.[58] The Royal

Navy also uses AM for repairing spare parts. The Royal Navy flight tested a 3-D printed unmanned aerial vehicle (UAV) on board HMS *Mersey* in September 2015.[59]

The Royal Navy has tasked the UK Naval Engineering Science and Technology Forums (UKNEST) to conceptualize a design for a future submarine designated as the Nautilus-100 mother-ship. The platform design is similar to the shape of a "manta ray with a whale shark-styled mouth' and would have the twin features of 'speed and stealth' unmatched by any technology hitherto. The material of the Nautilus-100 would be of super-strong alloys and strong acrylic materials which would be 3D-printed and the 'mother-ship' would be able to operate at depths of over 1,000 metres. The vessel will have 'anechoic coatings' giving it a scale-like skin". Another significant feature of the Nautilus 100 mother-ship is that it would be controlled and operated by using cognitive technology and its 20-member crew 'would use a neuro interface to communicate with multiple systems in the ship's command at once.'

It is well known that the biggest weapon of a submarine is its stealth. It is obtained from the coating applied to the submarine's hull or from other noise-reducing technologies which absorb the noise generated by the engines and other equipment installed on the vessel. It also exploits a variety of seawater properties and conditions such as temperature, salinity and pressure to hide and escape detection by the enemy; vice versa, these are creatively used to carry out attacks on the enemy. Producing a full set of oceanographic data of seas and oceans is a slow process since sea temperature and salinity levels vary according to the seasons. Besides, such data is built up over long periods by the physical presence of scientific research vessels, warships ships or submarines. The navies are well aware of their limitations and constantly endeavour to collect underwater data which helps them plan for a variety of offensive and defensive operations.

Underwater data collection is a challenging exercise and is further compounded by changes in the physical and chemical properties of the seas and oceans due to anthropogenic interventions, climate change and global warming. "Ocean environments are changing–what we knew 20 or 30 years ago doesn't apply now in many areas, particularly the North Atlantic which is our backyard for submarine operations and probably one of the most complicated and challenging bodies of ocean.... Salinity, sound velocity and temperature have all changed. We need to know these accurately as we strive to understand more and more about the undersea environment and how this affects the performance of ship and submarine sensors so we can achieve an operational advantage".[60]

The Royal Navy's Slocum Gliders are capable of obtaining underwater sea conditions and "near real-time information on temperature, depth, salinity, currents, oxygen levels, turbulence and more", which assists in enhancing the efficiency of the sonar and sensors on board the Navy's frigates, maritime patrol aircraft and helicopters for submarine operations. The Royal Navy plans to "eventually deploy gliders continually to high-threat areas to give a clear and constant picture of the underwater battle space, meaning operational decisions will be based on the very latest information. Having this data quickly means sub-hunters will be able to adapt better when they are attempting to detect underwater surface threats".[61]

Another technology development in the UK features the ejectable "autonomous sensor pods which can dissolve on demand when their mission is complete". Based on the eel concept, these are 'soluble micro-drones' and 'could provide a swarm of sensors or drones using 3-D printing. This ability would help them to shield vessels from view while being virtually undetectable themselves.' The "plug in and play" MAPLE system under the Royal Navy's NELSON digital acceleration lab, would help easy integration of autonomous and un-crewed technology.[62]

According to the Royal Navy's Head of Innovation, "The Royal Navy's future success rests on developing the skills and expertise that will keep us one step ahead of the competition.... That's why the Royal Navy has joined with our partners to unveil Nautilus-100. These concepts demonstrate that the UK has the creative foresight to consider the future underwater world, what it might look like, and what role the Royal Navy might play".

Admiral Sir Philip Jones, First Sea Lord, Royal Navy, has observed that the "pace and scale of technological change in the world today is breathtaking. The Royal Navy is no less affected than anyone else by the challenges of cheap, smart phone computing power with high-grade encryption. And more is coming in the Internet of Things...Artificial Intelligence, robotics, automation and quantum computing are all future uncertainties. As a result, the Royal Navy, priding itself on its long history of world-leading innovation, is focused on the implications for maritime and littoral warfare in the Information Age".[63]

French Navy

The French government announced "AI for Humanity"[64] in 2018 and apportioned € 1.5 billion. The strategy notes that AI will be a significant component of the French military's security missions and emphasizes the creation of a "civil-military complex of technological innovation, focused on digital technology and more specifically on artificial intelligence".[65] The government also set up the Defence Innovation Agency (DIA) under the Direction Générale de l'Armement (DGA), the national arms procurement and technology agency, to streamline defence innovation.[66] According to the French Minister for the Armed Forces, Florence Parly, the country has identified three major principles to develop defence artificial intelligence and these are "abiding by international law, maintaining sufficient human control and ensuring the permanent responsibility of the chain of command".[67]

The Naval Group, a French naval defence and innovation industrial house, is leading innovation and its Senior Executive Vice President has observed that "Big Data, Cybersecurity, Artificial Intelligence, automation, drones and anti-drone warfare are now part of the game and we must adopt a technological stance that will allow us to deter threats...and we need to address it in all its forms".[68]

France is a major European power with global interests. It has overseas territories in the Indian and Pacific Ocean and the French Navy has an impressive force structure of nuclear propelled and conventional powered aircraft carriers, submarines and warships. The French Navy is currently experimenting with an embedded additive manufacturing process. In 2018, the French Naval Group along with and its partner, AvenAoProdways Group, is experimenting with a 3D printer onboard the aircraft carrier "Jeanne d'Arc" as part of the Operations Maintenance Engineering (MCO) activities to "better understand the needs of the board and to experiment with remote 3D printing of operational equipment".[69] They are also providing training to the crew in computer-aided design tool (CAD) print parts using a 3D printer. The crew can also seek online assistance.

Russian Federation Navy

In 2018, Russia released its 'National Strategy for the Development of Artificial Intelligence over a period extending up to 2030'.[70] The strategy makes reference to issues of "national security and defence applications" of AI, given that the "Russian defence establishment is pursuing advances in military robotics, unmanned systems, command, control, computers, communications, Intelligence, surveillance, and reconnaissance capabilities where AI applications could have a meaningful impact".[71]

In 2015, the Russian Federation set up the National Centre for the Development of Technology and Basic Elements of Robotics under the Foundation for Advanced Research Projects.[72] In 2018, General of the Army Sergei Shoigu, while speaking at a conference on "Artificial Intelligence: Challenges and Solutions" observed that AI would "lead to favourable conditions for development and extended application of robotics, unmanned systems and new technologies equipped with artificial intelligence".[73] That year, the Ministry of Economic Development also conducted a round-table meeting on "Artificial Intelligence" at the Military-Technical Forum ARMY-2018[74] and "since then, no conference held by the Russian Defence Ministry has avoided this topic".[75]

Russia plans to integrate a variety of platforms (submarines, surface ships supply vessels and robots, and according to the Russian Central Design Bureau for Marine Engineering, Rubin, "The use of network principles of creating complex robotized systems and advanced cutting-edge technical solutions and new methods of programming algorithms will allow for creating systems crucial to the navigation, communication and command of diversified robotized systems operating under the surface of the world ocean and in the air".[76] Furthermore, in the long term, Russia would have a "global network consisting of a large number of deep-diving vessels, autonomous underwater vehicles, gliders, lighting devices, UAVs, and means of communication and other components for conducting large scale research and exploration".[77]

The Russian Navy is developing a 'smart mine complex' with a special command control unit that would identify enemy ships and submarines.[78] The complex could be fitted, albeit modifications, on "practically all classes of warships and submarines, as well as naval, tactical and strategic aviation, and will be able to act as carriers of mines".[79] It was reported that the Russian nuclear delivery vehicle inventory included an autonomous underwater vehicle (AUV) designated as Ocean Multipurpose System Status-6.[80] The AUV, nicknamed 'Kanyon' by the Pentagon, was built by the submarine manufacturers, Rubin Design Bureau. It resembles a huge torpedo and has a 'range of 6,200 miles, a top speed in excess of 56 knots and can descend to depths of 3,280 feet below sea level'. Status-6 made its first public appearance in 2015 and the trials of the platform were carried out in 2016. It 'can be deployed from two types of cruise missile submarine, one being the Oscar-class'. According to US officials, Status-6 is "essentially a drone-type device fired underwater that can potentially travel thousands of miles and strike US coastal targets such as military bases or cities"[81] and can carry "cruise missiles and launch them after hiding for months beneath the water".[82]

Similarly, under Khabarovsk [Project 09852], a submarine would be able to carry six Poseidon nuclear-capable unmanned underwater vehicles (UUVs) and these could operate as an autonomous nuclear torpedo with a nearly unlimited range.[83] Russian companies are exploring India for AI collaboration. The Business Development Director of Zyfra has noted positive prospects for Indo-Russian cooperation in this field[84] and transfer base technology and tools.

The Russian Federation Navy Project 22350 Admiral Gorshkov-class frigate is being re-purposed to serve as the Drone Mother Ship for Mine Warfare. It would host UUVs and USVs and the second ship of this class of ships, i.e., *Admiral Kasatonov*, is reported to test a system named 'Diamond' plugged with Inspector Mk 2 USVs.[85] It is of French origin and three systems were acquired in 2014 for RFN's MCM vessels. Two minesweepers of the project 12700 Alexander Obukhov and Ivan Antonov are already equipped with the system and the third system is now apparently being tested from the *Admiral Kasatonov* frigate. According to Admiral Valentin Selivanov, the former chief of the General Staff of the Russian Navy, the "new robotic systems will seriously increase the combat effectiveness of the ship. It is already known that the frigates of the new series are planned to be equipped with the Orlan-10 UAV and strike boats".

The Russian combat drone program is led by the S-70 Okhotnik ('Hunter' in Russian language) unmanned combat air vehicle. Russian Deputy Prime Minister Yuri Borisov announced that the S-70 would "begin tests in an armed configuration between 2023 and 2024, before the launch of series production in 2025".[86] Okhotnik is big in size with "a hardy landing gear that looks similar to those used on modern Russian tactical jet designs" and apparently, it looks quite similar to UCAVS such as Northrop Grumman's X-47B and Boeing's X-45C Phantom Ray and many other global UCAV designs.[87]

Israeli Navy

Though small in size, Israel packs a huge punch in Industry 4.0 developments and is also referred to as a "start-up nation". Intellectual, financial and technological investments in 4IR continue to surge in Israel[88] and in the last five years the value has jumped from US$ 112 million in 2014 to US$ 650 million at the end of 2019 million.[89]

Israeli innovation spans a wide range of 4IR technologies such as "IoT, big data, and artificial intelligence".[90] In the maritime transportation sector, i.e., ports and shipping operations, Israel's strength are well known and Start-Up Nation Central notes that "54 of the 6,218 start-ups" in Israel are in the maritime sector.[91]

Some of the leading Israeli start-ups are the *Pick-a-Pier* for smart marinas; *AiDock*, uses AI algorithms to sped up Customs clearance processes; *Windward*, is global leader in maritime risk analytics; *Orca AI* offers intelligent tools for navigation; the *DOCK* is an Israeli Navy veterans innovation; hub; *Michnaf* uses drones to inspect merchant vessels; *Totem Plus* offers advanced automation and navigation systems for ports and ships.[92] Similarly, the Haifa Research Centre for Maritime Policy and Strategy and the Inter-University Institute for Marine Sciences undertake "cutting-edge research and symbiotic relationships between the public, private, and academic sectors".[93]

Royal Australian Navy

The Royal Australian Navy's Plan Galileo (to be developed and implemented by 2030), is a navy-industry initiative for a seamless transition from acquisition to sustainment of naval platforms. The programme is built around life-cycle management of platforms and equipment, creation of a skilled workforce and leveraging 4IR technologies such as "digital twinning, augmented reality, master data management, artificial intelligence and machine learning to "improve productivity and promote increased levels of innovation, collaboration and knowledge-sharing in the maritime domain".[94]

At the level of training, a Defence Enterprise Learning Strategy (DELS) 2035 publication notes that the Australian Defence forces (ADF) have plans to augment learning and training through 4IR technologies.[95] Virtual Reality and Augmented Reality products are already in use in a variety of training programs such as "language/cultural training, peacekeeping operations and joint operations" in the three services.

The Royal Australian Navy has conducted trials of SPEE3D's, a Supersonic Deposition 3D metal printer,[96] which will help 'streamline the maintenance of patrol vessels'. The 'AI-Search' algorithm helps to recognise a life raft and other waterborne vessels. It is being developed to be installed onboard any Search and Rescue platform and is being developed by the Air Force's Plan Jericho, Warfare Innovation Navy Branch and Air Mobility Group's 35 Squadron.[97]

The Plan would enable "any aircraft and other defence platforms, including unmanned aerial systems, a low-cost, improvised SAR capability".[98]

Concluding Thoughts

The Western world currently leads 4IR technology development and is all set to field a variety of autonomous and unmanned platforms, equipment and devices for purposes of warfare. One of the key features of the above developments is the ability of their military industrial complexes and research and development laboratories to creatively conceptualize platforms that feature disruptive technologies. Like their Western counterparts, the Asian Navies have captured the transformational 4IR technology momentum based on respective technological and industrial capabilities. This study now attempts to highlight 4IR-related naval developments among the Asian navies.

NOTES

1. Joe Burton and Simona R. Soare, "Understanding the Strategic Implications of the Weaponization of Artificial Intelligence", https://ccdcoe.org/uploads/2019/06/Art_14_Understanding-the-Strategic-Implications.pdf (accessed 28 March 2020).
2. Vijay Sakhuja, *Asian Maritime Power in the 21st Century: Strategic Transactions: China, India and Southeast Asia* (Singapore: ISEAS–Yusof Ishak Institute, 2011), p. 217.
3. Norman M. Ricklefs, "The Fourth Industrial Revolution and the end of the West's brief geopolitical dominance", https://medium.com/@norman.ricklefs/the-fourth-industrial-revolution-and-the-end-of-the-wests-brief-geopolitical-dominance-b973ef28a722 (accessed 28 March 2020).
4. Ibid.
5. "Summary of the 2018 Department of Defence Artificial Intelligence Strategy : Harnessing AI to Advance Our Security and Prosperity", https://media.defense.gov/2019/Feb/12/2002088963/-1/-1/1/SUMMARY-OF-DOD-AI-STRATEGY.PDF (accessed 28 March 2020).
6. "Establishment of the Joint Artificial Intelligence Centre" https://admin.govexec.com/media/establishment_of_the_joint_artificial_intelligence_center_osd008412-18_r....pdf (accessed 28 March 2020).
7. "U.S. Military Declares Mandate on AI: "We Want to Be the Threat"", https://futurism.com/the-byte/jaic-militarys-ai-center (accessed 28 March 2020).
8. "Artificial Intelligence is now a Pentagon Priority. Will Silicon Valley Help?", https://www.nytimes.com/2018/08/26/technology/pentagon-artificial-intelligence.html (accessed 29 March 2020).
9. "Army Considering Artificial Intelligence Task Force", https://www.afcea.org/content/army-considering-artificial-intelligence-task-force (accessed 29 March 2020).
10. "U.S. Ground Forces Robotics and Autonomous Systems (RAS) and Artificial Intelligence (AI): Considerations for Congress", https://digital.library.unt.edu/ark:/67531/metadc1442984/ (accessed 29 March 2020).

11. Ibid.
12. "The Singularity: US Navy calls on Gamers to help it Plan for the Rise of the Machines", https://www.ibtimes.co.uk/singularity-us-navy-calls-gamers-help-it-plan-rise-machines-1612109 (accessed 29 March 2020).
13. Ibid.
14. "U.S. Naval War College Conference on Artificial Intelligence Looks to Move 'Beyond the Hype'", https://usnwc.edu/News-and-Events/News/US-Naval-War-College-Conference-on-Artificial-Intelligence-Looks-to-Move-Beyond-the-Hype (accessed 29 March 2020).
15. Cai Hong, "Japan to Beef up Deploying AI technology in Military Defence", https://www.chinadaily.com.cn/a/201902/12/WS5c6226caa3106c65c34e8dac.html (accessed 4 October 2019).
16. David B. Larter "The surface Navy needs to fundamentally reshape itself to defeat the Chinese threat, study finds", https://www.defensenews.com/digital-show-dailies/surface-navy-association/2020/01/08/the-surface-navy-needs-to-fundamentally-reshape-itself-to-defeat-the-chinese-threat-study-finds/ (accessed 30 March 2020).
17. Ibid.
18. "While the American fleet throughout its history has shifted back and forth between naval concepts favouring fewer large ships or smaller ones, the fleet architecture currently under development for the first time includes large numbers of robotic vessels". See "Yes, the Navy Wants a Lot of Robot Ships to Deter a Rising China", https://nationalinterest.org/blog/buzz/yes-navy-wants-lot-robot-ships-deter-rising-china-115621 (accessed 29 March 2020).
19. Large Unmanned Surface Vehicles (LUSVs), Medium Unmanned Surface Vehicles (MUSVs), and Extra-Large Unmanned Undersea Vehicles (XLUUVs).
20. "Report to Congress on Navy Large Unmanned Surface and Undersea Vehicles", https://news.usni.org/2019/06/11/report-to-congress-on-navy-large-unmanned-surface-and-undersea-vehicles?fbclid=IwAR2COlubN-Eb5HmEvu1vo1ORx-LpsChj9Z7TkfDrgBbhvrX958WdgOJ_0KA (accessed 29 March 2020).
21. Dave Majumdar, "US Navy's Next Submarine: Super Stealthy and Now Underwater Aircraft Carrier?", https://nationalinterest.org/blog/the-buzz/us-navys-next-submarine-super-stealthy-now-underwater-16978 (accessed 15 February 2020).
22. Ibid.
23. "Inside the 'Silent Service': An interview with the Navy's top Submarine Admiral", https://flipboard.com/article/inside-the-silent-service-an-interview-with-the-navy-s-top-submarine-admiral/a-MTr1e4UsTdC2lJpZPQklHA%3Aa%3A48159484-388d11f677%2Fbusiness insider.com (accessed 25 June 2020).
24. Alexander M.G. Walan, "Anti-Submarine Warfare (ASW) Continuous Trail Unmanned Vessel (ACTUV)", https://www.darpa.mil/program/anti-submarine-warfare-continuous-trail-unmanned-vessel (accessed 29 March 2020).
25. Ibid.
26. Ibid.
27. "DSEI: Navy Poised to Order Second Vessel for ACTUV Sea Hunter Test Program", https://news.usni.org/2017/09/15/dsei-navy-poised-order-second-vessel-actuv-sea-hunter-test-program (accessed 29 March 2020).
28. "Artificial intelligence and embedded computing for unmanned vehicles", https://www.militaryaerospace.com/unmanned/article/14175187/artificial-intelligence-and-embedded-computing-for-unmanned-vehicles (accessed 4 May 2020).

29. "DARPA's latest mad science experiment: A ship designed to operate completely without humans", https://www.defensenews.com/naval/2020/01/21/darpas-latest-mad-science-experiment-a-ship-designed-completely-without-humans/ (accessed 14 June 2020).
30. Ibid.
31. "U.S. Navy wants its Unmanned Vessels to Make VHF Calls", https://www.maritime-executive.com/article/u-s-navy-wants-its-unmanned-vessels-to-make-vhf-calls (accessed 29 March 2020).
32. "NAVSEA, PEO USC Host Hammerhead Program Virtual Industry Day", https://www.navsea.navy.mil/Media/News/Article/2146904/navsea-peo-usc-host-hammerhead-program-virtual-industry-day/ (accessed 14 April 2020).
33. "Navy Digitizes its Tactical Weather Data", https://www.maritime-executive.com/article/navy-digitizes-its-tactical-weather-data (accessed 29 March 2020).
34. Ibid.
35. "US Navy robot submarine would be able to kill without human control", https://www.newscientist.com/article/2236638-us-navy-robot-submarine-would-be-able-to-kill-without-human-control/#ixzz6I7ZeJUT8 (accessed 29 March 2020).
36. Lockheed Martin Advanced Technology Laboratories; Northrop Grumman Systems; Coorporation; Navatek, LLC,; and Metron, Inc.
37. "DARPA Awards Contracts for Manta Ray Program", https://www.maritime-executive.com/article/darpa-awards-contracts-for-manta-ray-program (accessed 29 March 2020).
38. Kris Osborn, "How U.S. Navy Aircraft Carriers Are Going all in on Drones", https://nationalinterest.org/blog/buzz/how-us-navy-aircraft-carriers-are-going-all-drones-115366 (accessed 30 March 2020).
39. Brian Wong, "Aircraft and Undersea Drone Carrying Submarines will Disrupt Warfare", https://www.nextbigfuture.com/2018/02/aircraft-and-undersea-drone-carrying-submarines-will-disrupt-warfare.html (accessed 29 March 2020).
40. "Navy Taps Undersea Consortium to Work on 15 Advanced Tech Problems", https://www.nextgov.com/emerging-tech/2020/04/navy-taps-undersea-consortium-work-15-advanced-tech-problems/164807/ (accessed 29 March 2020).
41. Talal Husseini, "Autonomous Underwater Robots: from Swordfish to the Orca", https://www.naval-technology.com/features/autonomous-underwater-robots-navy/ (accessed 29 March 2020).
42. "A Brief History of the US Navy's Dolphins", https://www.technologyreview.com/2019/10/24/306/dolphin-echolocation-us-navy-war/ (accessed 29 March 2020).
43. "3D Printing has Entered the Nuclear Realm", https://www.forbes.com/sites/jamesconca/2020/05/09/3d-printing-has-entered-the-nuclear-realm/#71d4fc4a7d34 (accessed 11 May 2020).
44. "Navy Plans Large new Fleet of 'mothership'-controlled Drone Boats", https://www.foxnews.com/tech/navy-plans-large-new-fleet-of-mothership-controlled-drone-boats (accessed 22 May 2020).
45. "U.S. Navy Testing EPF as Drone Mother Ship", https://www.navalnews.com/naval-news/2019/07/u-s-navy-testing-epf-as-drone-mother-ship/ (accessed 22 May 2020).
46. "Theresa May's Davos address in full", https://www.weforum.org/agenda/2018/01/theresa-may-davos-address/https://www.weforum.org/agenda/2018/01/theresa-may-davos-address/ (accessed 29 March 2020).
47. "Artificial Intelligence – emerging technology, emerging threat", https://

www.contracts.mod.uk/do-features-and-articles/artificial-intelligence-emerging-technology-emerging-threat/ (accessed 29 March 2020).

48. "How Artificial Intelligence Will Make Decisions in Tomorrow's Wars", https://www.forbes.com/sites/simonchandler/2020/01/20/how-artificial-intelligence-will-make-decisions-in-tomorrows-wars/#48869ea4e011 (accessed 29 March 2020).
49. "Defence and Security Accelerator (DASA)", https://www.gov.uk/government/organisations/defence-and-security-accelerator/about (accessed 30 March 2020).
50. "UK Invests in AI Technology for Warships", https://www.maritime-executive.com/article/uk-invests-in-ai-technology-for-warships (accessed 29 March 2020).
51. "Revolutionary Artificial Intelligence Warship Contracts Announced", https://www.gov.uk/government/news/revolutionary-artificial-intelligence-warship-contracts-announced (accessed 29 March 2020).
52. "UK Announces AI Warship Contracts", https://www.infosecurity-magazine.com/news/uk-announces-ai-warship-contracts/https://www.infosecurity-magazine.com/news/uk-announces-ai-warship-contracts/ (accessed 29 March 2020).
53. "Royal Navy Accelerates Adoption of Unmanned Systems", https://www.maritime-executive.com/editorials/photos-royal-navy-accelerates-adoption-of-unmanned-systems (accessed 4 August 2020).
54. "Autonomous Minesweeper set for "Live" Operations", https://www.maritime-executive.com/article/autonomous-minesweeper-set-for-live-operations (accessed 29 March 2020).
55. "Sea Trials Begin for Artificial Intelligence "Captain"", https://maritime-executive.com/article/sea-trials-begin-for-artificial-intelligence-captain (accessed 29 March 2020).
56. Ibid.
57. Kirsten Gronlund, State of AI: Artificial Intelligence, the Military and Increasingly Autonomous Weapons", https://futureoflife.org/2019/05/09/state-of-ai/ (accessed 4 October 2019).
58. "UK was the one to Put the Brakes on Drone Demo Project, Industry Says", https://www.defensenews.com/global/europe/2018/04/12/uk-was-the-one-to-put-the-brakes-on-drone-demo-project-industry-says/ (accessed 29 March 2020).
59. Prakash Panneerselvam (2018), Additive Manufacturing in Aerospace and Defence Sector: Strategy of India, *Journal of Defence Studies*, Vol. 12, No. 1, January-March 2018, pp. 39-60).
60. "Royal Navy Tests Autonomous Gliders to Boost Sub-Hunting Operations", https://www.maritime-executive.com/article/royal-navy-tests-autonomous-gliders-to-boost-sub-hunting-operations (accessed 3 May 2020).
61. "Royal Navy Tests Autonomous Gliders to Boost Sub-Hunting Operations", https://www.maritime-executive.com/article/royal-navy-tests-autonomous-gliders-to-boost-sub-hunting-operations (accessed 3 May 2020).
62. "Royal Navy Accelerates Adoption of Unmanned Systems", https://www.maritime-executive.com/editorials/photos-royal-navy-accelerates-adoption-of-unmanned-systems (accessed 4 August 2020).
63. "Royal Navy Pioneers new age of Information Warfare", https://www.adsgroup.org.uk/news/member-news/royal-navy-pioneers-new-age-of-information-warfare/ (accessed 30 March 2020).
64. "The national French AI strategy Reveals Detailed Research Plans", https://nost-france.org/

2018/12/03/the-national-french-ai-strategy-reveals-detailed-research-plans/ (accessed 30 March 2020).

65. Cited in Kirsten Gronlund, "State of AI: Artificial Intelligence, the Military and Increasingly Autonomous Weapons", https://futureoflife.org/2019/05/09/state-of-ai/ (accessed 30 March 2020).
66. Ibid.
67. Florence Parly, "France's armed forces minister: How AI figures in operational superiority", https://www.defensenews.com/outlook/2019/12/02/frances-armed-forces-minister-how-ai-figures-into-operational-superiority/ (accessed 30 March 2020).
68. "French 'Naval Group' Makes Big Waves in Singapore", https://www.aviation-defence-universe.com/french-naval-group-makes-big-waves-in-singapore/ (accessed 30 March 2020).
69. "Naval Group and Prodways place a 3D printer aboard French Navy vessel" (accessed 30 March 2020).
70. "Decree of the President of the Russian Federation on the Development of Artificial Intelligence in the Russian Federation", Office of the President of the Russian Federation, 10 October 2019. https://cset.georgetown.edu/wp-content/uploads/t0060_Russia_AI_strategy_EN-1.pdf (accessed 30 March 2020).
71. "Thoughts on Russia's AI Strategy", https://cset.georgetown.edu/2019/10/30/russias-ai-strategy/ (accessed 30 March 2020).
72. Ibid.
73. "Russian Minister of Defence Welcomes the Artificial Intelligence Conference", https://www.rusarmyexpo.com/army2020/mediacenter/news/newsmilru/31000.html (accessed 30 March 2020).
74. Vadim B. Kozyulin, "Militarization of AI from a Russian Perspective", July 2019.
75. Ibid.
76. "Is Russia Building a Global Network of Drones?", https://nationalinterest.org/blog/buzz/russia-building-global-network-drones-162536 (accessed 11 June 2020).
77. Ibid.
78. Michael Peck, "Russia Wants to Use AI-Sea Mines to Sink America's Navy", https://nationalinterest.org/blog/buzz/russia-wants-use-ai-sea-mines-sink-americas-navy-120951 (accessed 30 March 2020).
79. Apparently, "after the mines are thrown, the mines will automatically 'line up in battle formation.' In standby mode, they respond to certain characteristics of the magnetic and acoustic fields of ships and submarines. For this, the mine is equipped with special sensors and sensors, and its hardware has a special self-learning algorithm. With it, mines will be able to determine the type of ship and distinguish their ships from strangers. To identify targets, acoustic portraits of their ships and ships of a potential enemy are laid in the software. These peculiar 'passports' make it possible to identify with high probability which ship or submarine is in the affected area. As a result, your ship will move through the minefield in complete safety, and the enemy will be destroyed". Michael Peck, "Russia Wants to Use AI-Sea Mines to Sink America's Navy", https://nationalinterest.org/blog/buzz/russia-wants-use-ai-sea-mines-sink-americas-navy-120951 (accessed 30 March 2020).
80. "Russia's Nuclear Underwater Drone is Real and in the Nuclear Posture Review", https://www.defensenews.com/space/2018/01/12/russias-nuclear-underwater-drone-is-real-and-in-the-nuclear-posture-review/ (accessed 31 March 2020).
81. "Pentagon Says Russia Is Building Nuclear Torpedo Described as "Doomsday" Weapon",

https://slate.com/news-and-politics/2018/02/pentagon-says-russia-is-building-nuclear-torpedo-described-as-doomsday-weapon.html (accessed 31 March 2020).

82. Ibid.
83. "Is Russia Building a Global Network of Drones?", https://nationalinterest.org/blog/buzz/russia-building-global-network-drones-162536 (accessed 11 June 2020).
84. "'Indo-Russian AI coop will Reach Level of Defecse and Nuclear Partnership in Few Years'", https://economictimes.indiatimes.com/news/defence/indo-russian-innovation-cooperation-will-involve-defense-and-nuclear-ties-in-a-few-years/articleshow/74213586.cms?from=mdr (accessed 31 March 2020).
85. "Russian Navy Testing Project 22350 Frigate as Drone Mother Ship for Mine Warfare", https://www.navalnews.com/naval-news/2019/07/russian-navy-testing-project-22350-frigate-as-drone-mother-ship-for-mine-warfare/ (accessed 22 May 2020).
86. "Now Russia Wants its First Okhotnik Combat Drone in Service By 2024", https://www.thedrive.com/the-war-zone/35367/now-russia-wants-its-first-okhotnik-combat-drone-in-service-by-2024 (accessed 5 August 2020).
87. "Is This Russia's 'Hunter' Stealthy Flying Wing Unmanned Combat Air Vehicle?, https://www.thedrive.com/the-war-zone/26139/is-this-russias-hunter-stealthy-flying-wing-unmanned-combat-air-vehicle (accessed 5 August 2020).
88. Éanna Kelly, "Israel Sets out to Become the Next Major Artificial Intelligence Player", https://sciencebusiness.net/news/israel-sets-out-become-next-major-artificial-intelligence-player (accessed 30 March 2020).
89. "Israeli 'smart-industry' Startups Nabbed $650 million from Investors in 2019", https://www.timesofisrael.com/israeli-smart-industry-startups-nabbed-650-million-from-investors-in-2019/ (accessed 30 March 2020).
90. "How Israel Is Becoming a Port of Call for Maritime Innovation", https://itrade.gov.il/belgium-english/how-israel-is-becoming-a-port-of-call-for-maritime-innovation/ (accessed 30 March 2020). Also see "Bringing AI to navigation", https://www.newelectronics.co.uk/electronics-technology/bringing-ai-to-navigation/217775/ (accessed 30 March 2020).
91. Ibid.
92. Ibid.
93. Ibid.
94. "The Royal Australian Navy set up 'Plan Galileo' to Sustain its Growing Fleet", https://www.navalnews.com/naval-news/2020/05/the-royal-australian-navy-set-up-plan-galileo-to-sustain-its-growing-fleet/ (accessed 5 May 2020).
95. "Video Games and Warfighting: The Curious Link", https://www.defenceconnect.com.au/intel-cyber/6237-video-games-and-warfighting-the-curious-link (accessed 9 June 2020).
96. Samira Sarraf, "Royal Australian Navy gets 'world first' 3D Printers", https://www.computerworld.com.au/article/668927/royal-australian-navy-gets-world-first-3d-printers/ (accessed 15 April 2020).
97. Brian Hartigan, "Artificial Intelligence Proves Better than Human in Search and Rescue", https://www.contactairlandandsea.com/2020/04/08/artificial-intelligence-proves-better-than-human-in-search-and-rescue/ (accessed 15 April 2020).
98. "Australian Defence Project Tests Potential of AI at Sea", https://www.naval-technology.com/news/new-project-by-australian-defence-tests-potential-of-ai-at-sea/ (accessed 15 April 2020).

CHAPTER 5

Asian Navies and 4IR Technologies

Few Asian navies were quick to assimilate and exploit 3IR technologies in their force structure, operational concepts and organizational and organisational processes. Similar trends continue and 4IR technologies are beginning to resonate in their strategic and naval tactical thinking. Current trends suggest that the navies of China, India, Japan, Korea and Singapore are moving ahead with 4IR enabled platforms and operations, and this is evident in their strategic thinking and naval orders of battle.

People's Liberation Army (PLA) Navy

The PLA Navy is studying naval applications of 4IR and hopes to harness its potential to make itself a highly sophisticated and capable force. The notable advancements are seen in unmanned surface vessel, drones, UAVs, and robots capable of operating autonomously. "Chinese naval strategists have stated explicitly that they intend to circumvent their long-recognized weakness in submarine warfare by cultivating undersea AI and by developing highly capable UUVs".[1] Furthermore, China now has 'teams of specialist engineers working on development programmes.'[2]

Autonomous Ships

China Aerospace and Science Technology Corporation, a Chinese defence contractor, whose primary strength is in missiles and other aerospace technologies has developed D3000, a 98-foot-long stealthy robotic trimaran warship.[3] The vessel operates in an autonomous mode and can be fitted with guns, anti-ship missiles, torpedoes and can carry mines. It can also act as a mother-vessel for other underwater unmanned vehicles. China has also developed and tested an unmanned 42-foot trimaran High Speed Intercept Boat fitted with machine guns and anti-tank guided missiles with a potential to operate in swarms.

Another similar achievement is the 4.5-tonne SeaFly-01, an unmanned surface vessel (USV) that is capable of 1.5 tons payload comprising electro-optical and infrared (EO/IR) imagers and electronic support measure (ESM) sensors.[4] Perhaps it merits mention that the SeaFly-01 can be "equipped with a retractable unmanned aerial vehicle (UAV) launch and recovery system, which enables it to function as a 'mother-ship' for small vertical take-off and landing UAVs".[5] The other important feature of the SeaFly is its line of sight control for up to 50 kilometres using "shore-based mobile or fixed command-and-control (C2) centre, while beyond-line-of-sight (BLOS) control is supported by the indigenous BeiDou satellite navigation system as well as satellite communication (SATCOM) equipment". In December 2017, Beijing Sifang Automation (Sifang), a research and manufacturing company, announced that it was ready to commence production of its SeaFly.[6]

In October 2019, during the national military parade, China unveiled HSU-001, a large displacement Autonomous Underwater Vehicle (AUV). It is designed for undertaking long range patrols. According to the media, in July 2020[7] Japan discovered a "mini-submarine in a submerged position in the Western sector of the group of islands of Amami in the Ryukyu archipelago in the East China Sea" suspected to be the HSU-001.[8] Similarly, a 7.5-ton unmanned vessel Tianxing-1 is the fastest unmanned vessel with 50 knots speed. According to the Chinese developer of unmanned vessels, it can support naval operations and maritime law enforcement. To support the above initiatives, China is building the world's largest test facility covering an area of 771.6 square kilometres for unmanned vessels called Wanshan Marine Test Field at Zhuhai.[9]

China unveiled a 50-footlong autonomous armed surface vessel with a range of 500 nautical miles. The vessel was developed and built by the state-owned China Shipbuilding Industry Corporation/China State Shipbuilding Corporation (CSSC) and designated 'JARI' USV. Although small in size, it has a full suite of "phased-array radar, a sonar suite, a deck gun, two close-range air defence missiles, two vertical-launch silos for small anti-air/anti-ship missiles and two torpedo launch tubes".[10] It can be loaded onboard an aircraft carrier or amphibious assault ship and could also be "deployed for swarm attacks on enemy surface combatants".

Another noteworthy development has been the production of a drone boat labelled as Marine Lizard for amphibious operations. These 39-foot long boats are armed and suitable for "assist land assault operations and can form a web with other drone ships and airborne drones in order to act in tandem with them".[11]

Drones and Drone Warfare

China is a leader of the commercial drone industry and has invested in a number of swarm drone technologies. It showcased its prowess in this domain by launching hundreds of drones in the air and making them dance before a mesmerized audience. Another example is the video of Yunzhou Tech Corporation, a Chinese company in which a swarm of 56 small unmanned boats were operated. These are good examples that illustrate Chinese capability, and it is not beyond imagination that these anodyne displays of AI-enabled platforms can be quickly armed with ammunitions/explosives and serve as a deterrent against a force with unequal combat advantage. According to a Chinese naval analyst, "Once equipped with weapons, unmanned small combat vessels can attack the enemy in large numbers, similar to drones,"[12] Apparently, the PLA Navy conducted an exercise in the South China Sea using these unmanned assault boats targeted at Taiwan.

The CH-5 drone is a medium-to-high altitude, long-endurance, and large drone system to cope with oceanic conditions.[13] It is capable of carrying a variety of payloads "including photoelectric devices and long-range search radars, and is capable of carrying out various surveillance and monitoring missions at sea".[14]

Great Underwater Wall

The Chinese were unnerved after a PLA Navy ship retrieved and confiscated a US Navy underwater drone capable of sustained underwater operations over months. Since then, China has been making impressive progress in its underwater defences and planed investments on systems to be deployed in the western Pacific Ocean. The PLA Navy sees a number of potential applications of 4IR technology to support a number of underwater operations including anti-submarine warfare (ASW), mine countermeasures (MCM), underwater domain awareness (UDA) and in scientific ocean development, marine environment protection and ecology restoration. As far as warfare is concerned, autonomous underwater drones, sea gliders or the Chinese type-12 Haiyi (Sea Wing) autonomous underwater vehicles to monitor marine environment and track living and non-living activity under the sea are under active consideration.[15]

China's "Blue Ocean Information Network" is designed for monitoring the marine environment but its use by the military for sensing and communications functions merits attention. It involves a network of sensor and communications nodes, i.e., "Ocean E-Stations" ("floating integrated information platforms" (IIFP) and "island reef-based integrated information systems" (IRBIS) and a fixed platform, reportedly deployed at Bombay Reef in the Paracel Islands in mid-2018) in the South China Sea to support similar activity in the East China Sea, and other adjacent ocean areas.[16] By June 2020, China added five floating platforms around Hainan to complement the fixed platform at Bombay Reef. This underwater network of sensors will be capable of obtaining real-time information about bathymetric conditions and seabed activities that are critical for US submarine detection which is known to be forward deployed in the Pacific Ocean.

China also has undersea gliders named Haiyior 'Sea Wing' that are designed to send collected data instantly. According to the project chief scientist, these "autonomous underwater vehicles would roam for one month and collect detailed information in the ocean on a host of topics including temperature, salinity, the cleanness of water, oxygen level and the speed and direction of sea currents".[17]

In the western Pacific Ocean, China has set up a deep-sea communications network comprising sensors deployed at depths of over 400 metres which can 'continuously transmit data to satellites through a grid of solar-powered buoys.'[18] Likewise, the Chinese Institute of Acoustics at the Chinese Academy of Sciences has "developed a long distance communication system for the Jiaolong, China's most powerful operating submersible capable of taking three people down to a depth of 7,000 metres".[19]

Additive Manufacturing and 3D Printing

3D printers have been part of the inventory of the PLA since 2013 and were in operational use for manufacturing some parts for several types of military aircraft.[20] Similarly, the PLA Navy has been using 3D printers onboard its warships and in 2015, the Type 052D destroyer *Harbin* successfully manufactured onboard a wheel gear for its engine "thousands of miles from parts suppliers in the ship's home country".[21] The ship also has a special compartment that is fitted with a computer, 3D printer, casting equipment, and materials.

5G Networks

There have been rapid developments in 5G technology in China and according to a domain expert, it could be the "undisputed leader".[22] Huawei and ZTE are leaders but US security concerns emerge from a report that 'China [had] secretly inserted surveillance microchips into servers used by major technology companies, including Apple and Amazon.com and labelled it an 'audacious military operation'. A top-secret US probe found that motherboards of servers in Department of Defence data centres, the CIA's drone operations, and the onboard networks of Navy warships had a tiny microchip which the above companies had installed without prior approval.[23]

Quantum: Information Science and Technologies

Another feature of Chinese advancements in the 4IR domain is in the field of Quantum information science and associated technological applications. These technologies help sense and measure tiny changes in gravity and other physical effects. Likewise, Quantum encryption (a robust encryption method for data security compared to the public key cryptography in which sender and receiver use a public string of digits which can be cracked by using quantum commuters), sensing, radar (to detect targets that cannot be discerned through conventional radar), and navigation (leverages quantum properties to create a precise form of positioning system that may eventually replace GPS) have seen development in the Chinese context.

In the last few years, Chinese scientists have filed quantum radar-related patents including one related to laser radar. China is also building "unhackable satellites with quantum-based communication systems, building quantum radars, hundreds of kilometres of quantum communication lines, and creating the world's fastest supercomputers".[24]

In the naval domain, the Chinese Academy of Sciences announced the development of quantum-based magnetic detection technology to detect metallic objects hidden deep underground and in the water. Chinese scientists have developed a magnetometer based on a superconducting quantum interference device, or SQUID which will complement the 'Underwater Great Wall', a network of 'submerged sensors, buoys and drone submarines' and make underwater surveillance by China much more effective, particularly against the USA and Japanese submarines.[25]

Near Space Technologies

Solar-powered drones are now a leading technology in the aerospace industry. China is developing solar-powered drones and plans to position them in 'near space', a spatial region between 20 and 99 kilometres altitude from the Earth's surface. Many Chinese companies such as the Aviation Industry Corporation of China (AVIC) are working to create a telecommunication network based on Solar Powered UAVs (SPUAV).[26]

The CASTC conducted test flight of its first solar-powered drone, the 'Caihong' (Rainbow) in June 2017. It flew to a height of 65,000 feet and the company claimed that the drone "would be able to remain in 'near space' for months or even years at a time using only solar power,"[27] It can be used by both civilian authorities and the military.

Similarly, in September 2018, AVIC announced the successful flight of 'Morning Star', a superlight solar-powered UAV (18.9 kilograms) which cruised at an altitude of more than 20,000 metres. The company has noted that "With the development and first flight, in addition to a great number of ground, wind tunnel and scale model tests...a solid foundation has been laid for follow-up development...will move quickly towards large-scale, heavy load and long endurance solar-powered UAVs".[28]

Japanese Maritime Self Defence Force (MSDF)

The Government of Japan is cognizant of the role of 4IR technologies,[29] and has formulated a sophisticated AI strategy[30] and the leadership has emphasized its development.[31] The country has been in the vanguard of robotics and used them in the manufacturing industry particularly in the automobile sectors; however, it faces competition in the software sectors primarily from US technology giants such as Amazon, Microsoft, Apple, Facebook, Google, etc., and now from China where e-commerce giants like Tencent, Alibaba, Baidu and DiDi are the drivers.[32]

This is changing and AI Strategy 2019 promotes 'advancement of industry and society' in "five designated priority areas (manufacturing, transportation and logistics, health and medical care, agriculture and disaster response)".[33] The strategy focuses on practical application of AI across domains and aims to "improve and lower costs of various processes, perform tasks beyond human capabilities and gain insight where human-operated analysis did not reach".[34] Although the strategy does not make reference to the use of AI for military purposes, it is fair to assume the dual-use nature of the technology and its military applications could be explored by the Japanese military.

At another level, Article 9 of the Japanese Constitution forbids aggression and war. It is the guiding principle of the Japanese people and the government and the country's armed forces have been designated as Self Defence Forces (SDF). Yet it has put together a technologically superior military force to respond to the ongoing military modernization by China, Russian naval deployments and air activity in the Far East and missile threats from North Korea.

The Japanese Navy or the Japanese Maritime Self Defence Force (MSDF) has watched with interest the Chinese investments in 4IR technologies for maritime and naval operations and is also exploring its use in tactical and strategic operations. According to media reports, Japan plans to acquire nearly two dozen maritime surveillance drones.[35] The plans also include development of an underwater drone for the MSDF for information collection. The Japanese Air Self Defence Force (ASDF) would "deploy the US-made Global Hawk unmanned aerial vehicle and establish a special unit to handle the drones" during 2021.[36] The latter is particularly important for the US Air Force with whom it conducts regular exercises.

The Japanese Coast Guard (JCG), in partnership with Fujitsu Laboratories, has successfully tested the 'Human Centric AI Zinrai' an AI-enabled safety system at the Tokyo Wan Vessel Traffic Service Centre. The system helps prevent collision or detect near misses between vessels. According to the Japan Transport Safety Board, the JCG, there are 286 marine collision accidents every year in Japan and between 2009 and 2019, a total of 2,863 accidents were recorded.[37]

Japan's Mitsubishi Heavy Industries (MHI) is building the 30FFM next generation multi-mission frigate for the Japan Maritime Self-Defence Force (JMSDF).[38] The warship has a unique circular 360-degreegiant screen combat information centre (CIC) and uses augmented reality (AR) technology for 'displaying key information, such as target tracks and potential hazards, over external views'.[39] The AR can also help 'launch and recovery' of unmanned surface vehicles.

Republic of Korea (RoK) Navy

The Republic of Korea (RoK) has been a front-runner in technology development and has invested in the fields of bioscience, nanotechnology and space technology. In 2014, its R&D budget was 4.29 per cent of GDP, compared to Israel's 4.11 per cent and Japan's at 3.58 per cent.[40] However, in 2016, after the Korean Go Master Lee Sedol was comprehensively defeated by DeepMind's AlphaGo, that South Korea's Ministry of Science and ICT (MSICT) announced US$ 863 million over the next five years for AI research in technology, infrastructure and human resources.[41] In 2018, the RoK military set up its AI Research and Development Centre in partnership with the Korea Advanced Institute of Science and Technology and the Agency for Defence Development. It also announced plans to set up a Combat Readiness & Safety Centre to develop "AI capabilities for the military utility and craft a master plan for trial programs employing AI operations".[42] Simultaneously, South Korea's Defence Acquisition Programme Administration (DAPA), launched a strategy for 'Industry 4.0 technologies' to build up the national military-industrial base focused on artificial intelligence, big data analytics and robotics through two legislations, i.e., the Defence Industry Promotion Act and the Defence Science and Technology Innovation Promotion Act.[43]

A RoK military analyst has argued that "demographic cliff, threats from North Korea and China, and the harsh reality of the need for defence reform, the build-up of a drone and robot system in South Korea becomes a realistic prospect".[44] There are some noteworthy achievements in developing unmanned platforms and the SGR-A1 sentry robot; the latter is deployed in the De-Militarized Zone between North and South Korea.[45] A specialist unit called DronebotJeontudan was constituted in 2017 and is responsible for "command and human resource infrastructure, including a new military occupational specialty, to recruit suitable candidates from within the army or from the private sector".[46]

The RoK Navy plans to acquire unmanned surface and underwater (USV and UUV) platforms.[47] Although not much is known about ROK Navy's plans for building or acquiring unmanned platforms, it has a "vision of a Smart Navy that relies upon a variety of autonomous underwater platforms" and the first such platform could be the Remote Mine-hunting System (RMS).[48] Similarly, the XLUUV project (for command and control of other deep sea assets; ISR missions; and acoustic data collection and antisubmarine warfare) is high on the agenda and is considered "essential to the future of ASW and submarine operations".[49]

The Hyundai Heavy Industries of the Republic of Korea has showcased its HCX-19 concept ship and offers a glimpse of what "surface combatants will look like in the 2030s".[50] This concept ship of a 'drone mother-ship' should be able to "deploy unmanned systems in all domains: Air (UAV), Surface (USV), Sub-surface (UUV) and that these vessels will even need to be able to deploy remotely operated vehicles (ROVs)".

Hyundai Heavy Industries Co., a major shipbuilding company, in partnership with the Korea Institute of Machinery and Materials (KIMM), has drawn plans to develop "AI-based emergency prediction and response technology". The companies are optimistic about using 4IR technologies for national defence.[51] The RoK government has allocated US$ 150 million for the development of commercial-military 4IR technologies in 2020 to support national military modernization.[52]

Republic of Singapore Navy (RSN)

Among the smaller navies of Asia, the Republic of Singapore Navy (RSN) is perhaps the most modern. It has harnessed 4IR-enabled platforms, systems and devices in many of the operational tasks such as homeland security, maritime safety in the Strait of Singapore, and maritime domain awareness. It has in its inventory a variety of autonomous and unmanned air, surface and subsurface platforms to undertake the above missions and tasks. Most of the 4IR requirements of the RSN are met by the Defence Science and Technology Agency (DSTA), the national agency under the Ministry of Defence (MINDEF), for 'acquisitions management, systems management, systems development' for the Singapore Armed Forces.

The DSTA is engaged in "virtual scenario-based experiments to build ships", smart systems by using data analytics to "swiftly identify suspicious vessels sailing near its waters" and in its labs navy officials can simulate operating a ship even before building it.[53] The Digital Hub, which is part of the DSTA, used cognitive task analysis in building ships and augmented reality to help in running maintenance checks on naval equipment.[54]

The RSN plans to conduct maritime patrols by unmanned surface vessels by the end of 2020 and in this context, Rear-Admiral Lew Chuen Hong, Chief of RSN, has noted that while referring to unmanned technology, "We can also put ships and boats to do operations without putting men and women in harm's way" and that unmanned vehicles controlled by a single operator would be significant force multipliers.[55]

Singapore's ST Engineering has chosen the Vanguard 130 Multi-Role

Combatant and its modular design helps it to reconfigure and serve as a "mother-ship to deploy and recover a wide array of unmanned systems such as UAV, USV and UUV".[56]

The company has developed and patented an in-house system called Q-LARS 2.0 which can handle wide range of small crafts and unmanned surface vehicles.

Concluding Thoughts

Asian navies acknowledge the disruptive nature of 4IR technologies and have begun to assimilate it into their strategic thinking, albeit at varying levels. China's naval inventory is a variety of autonomous and unmanned air, surface and subsurface platforms to undertake the above missions and tasks. The Japanese Navy has responded to the Chinese naval developments concerning 4IR technologies and is working towards a new naval strategy and exploring 4IR use in tactical and strategic operations. Likewise, the RoK Navy too is building capacities and capabilities to be relevant in the new naval environment led by disruptive technologies. Singapore is investing in national laboratories, universities, research institutions, innovation and incubation centres, private companies and entrepreneurs in 4IR and related technologies and platforms. The study now moves to examine the Indian Navy's policy and roadmap to embrace and integrate these disruptive technologies.

NOTES

1. "New UUVs: China's Plan to 'Attack from the Sea Floor'", https://nationalinterest.org/blog/buzz/new-uuvs-chinas-plan-attack-sea-floor-131067 (accessed 26 March 2020).
2. "Xiangshan Forum in Beijing asks Whether Military AI will make War more Acceptable", https://www.scmp.com/news/china/diplomacy/article/3034094/xiangshan-forum-beijing-asks-whether-military-ai-will-make-war (accessed 23 October 2019).
3. Brian Wang, "China Touts Vaporware Robotic Military Ship", https://www.nextbigfuture.com/2017/09/china-touts-vaporware-robotic-military-ship.html (accessed on 28 February 2020).
4. For more details see "South China Sea: Unmanned Vessels and Future Operations", http://ipcs.org/comm_select.php?articleNo=5433 (accessed 28 February 2020).
5. "South China Sea: Unmanned Vessels and Future Operations", http://www.indiandefencereview.com/spotlights/south-china-sea-unmanned-vessels-and-future-operations/ (accessed 28 February 2020).
6. "SeaFly USV", http://defenseph.net/drp/index.php?PHPSESSID=49d3u4ljpi64iums80li7nj0s4&topic=2964.msg9386#msg9386 (accessed 28 February 2020).
7. "China just Unveiled an Underwater Drone that could one day even the Odds Against the US and its Top Allies", https://www.businessinsider.co.za/chinas-underwater-drone-allies-

in-pacific-2019-10 (accessed 11 July 2020).

8. "The Japanese Navy intend to deal with Unmanned Submarines China", https://webcache.googleusercontent.com/search?q=cache:WkuuY7WK5mEJ:https://thetimeshub.in/the-japanese-navy-intend-to-deal-with-unmanned-submarines-china/45550/+&cd=1&hl=en&ct=clnk&gl=in (accessed 11 July 2020).
9. Kristin Huang, "China starts work on World's biggest test site for Drone Ships at gateway to South China Sea", https://www.scmp.com/news/china/diplomacy-defence/article/2133076/china-starts-work-worlds-biggest-test-site-drone-ships (accessed 4 March 2019).
10. "China's Unmanned "Mini-Destroyer" Out on Sea Trials", https://www.maritime-executive.com/article/china-s-unmanned-mini-destroyer-out-on-sea-trials (accessed 5 March 2020).
11. "China's Military Built an Autonomous Amphibious Landing Vehicle", https://futurism.com/the-byte/china-autonomous-amphibious-boat (accessed 23 March 2020).
12. "Unmanned 'shark swarm' to be used in Sea Battles, Military Patrols", http://www.globaltimes.cn/content/1105736.shtml (accessed 5 March 2020).
13. "China Conducts First Flight of CH-5 Maritime Drone", https://usadefensenews.com/2020/07/19/china-conducts-first-flight-of-ch-5-maritime-drone/ (accessed 20 July 2020).
14. Ibid.
15. Vijay Sakhuja, "China Leaps into Artificial Intelligence", *South Asia Defence and Strategic Review*, Vol. 11, Issue, 6, Jan-Feb 2018, p. 31.
16. "Exploring China's Unmanned Ocean Network" https://amti.csis.org/exploring-chinas-unmanned-ocean-network/ (accessed 17 June 2020).
17. "Underwater Gliders to Help China Track Foreign Submarines", http://www.defenseworld.net/news/20048/Underwater_Gliders_to_Help_China_Track_Foreign_Submarines#.XJcIZlUzZ0w (accessed 4 March 2020).
18. Vijay Sakhuja, "The Fourth Industrial Revolution and Underwater Warfare" *South Asia Defence and Strategic Review*, Vol. 2, Issue 1, Mar-Apr 2018, p. 47.
19. "Why Beijing is Speeding up Underwater Drone Tests in the South China Sea", https://www.todayonline.com/chinaindia/china/why-beijing-speeding-underwater-drone-tests-south-china-sea (accessed 2 March 2020).
20. "China shows off world largest 3D printed titanium fighter component", https://www.3ders.org/articles/20130529-china-shows-off-world-largest-3d-printed-titanium-fighter-component.html (accessed 2 March 2020).
21. "China's PLA Navy Deploys 3D Printers Onboard Warships to Replace Small Parts", https://3dprint.com/35981/china-pla-navy-3d-printing/ (accessed 2 March 2020).
22. Ibid.
23. "China Snuck A Tiny Microchip Inside US Top Secret Servers Used By The DoD And CIA — NSA Struggles To Assess Risk", https://www.bgp4.com/2018/10/05/china-snuck-a-tiny-microchip-inside-us-top-secret-servers-used-by-the-dod-and-cia-nsa-struggles-to-assess-risk/ (accessed 23 February 2019).
24. Wang Wei, "Chinese Quantum Satellite Sends First 'Unhackable' Data to Earth", https://thehackernews.com/2017/08/quantum-satellite-data.htmlhttps://thehackernews.com/2017/08/quantum-satellite-data.html (accessed 23 February 2019).
25. "China's Quantum Submarine Detector could Seal South China Sea", https://www.newscientist.com/article/2144721-chinas-quantum-submarine-detector-could-seal-south-china-sea/#ixzz6TyBuASA6 (accessed 23 February 2019).

26. "Chinese Solar-powered Drone Morning Star Spreads its Wings in Successful Test Flight" https://www.scmp.com/news/china/military/article/2171081/chinese-solar-powered-drone-spreads-its-wings-successful-test (accessed 23 February 2019).
27. Jeffrey Lin and P.W. Singer, "China just Flew a 130-foot, Solar-powered Drone Designed to Stay in the air for Months", https://webcache.googleusercontent.com/search?q=cache:bVENAR6RChMJ:https://www.popsci.com/china-solar-powered-drone+&cd=9&hl=en&ct=clnk&gl=in (accessed 23 February 2019).
28. "China Tests Solar-Powered Drone That Flies for Months", https://dronebelow.com/2018/11/06/china-tests-solar-powered-drone-that-flies-for-months/(accessed 27 March 2020).
29. The Japanese government announced the 5th Science and Technology Basic Plan1 in 2016 which lists goals for Japan to be "Society 5.0". Cited in "Artificial Intelligence in Japan: Industrial Cooperation and Business Opportunities for European Companies", https://www.eu-japan.eu/sites/default/files/publications/docs/artificial_intelligence_in_japan_-_guillermo_garcia_-_0511.pdf (accessed 27 March 2020).
30. "Artificial Intelligence Technology Strategy", Strategic Council for AI Technology, March 31, 2017, https://www.nedo.go.jp/content/100865202.pdf (accessed 23 March 2020).
31. Ibid. According to Prime Minister Shinzo Abe, "The key of the second stage of Japan's growth strategy is in realization of the fourth industrial revolution. Individualized services and new business models tailored to each individual will be created as a result of IoT and robots. All factories and shops will be connected through IoT, enabling zero inventory and instantaneous order-made production. This could represent a game-changer for industry as we know it".
32. "How Japan can win in the ongoing AI War", https://www.japantimes.co.jp/opinion/2019/09/09/commentary/japan-commentary/japan-can-win-ongoing-ai-war/#.Xn7U84hKg2w (accessed 27 March 2020).
33. "The Rapid Growth in Artificial Intelligence in Japan", https://www.openaccessgovernment.org/artificial-intelligence-in-japan/80985/https://www.openaccessgovernment.org/artificial-intelligence-in-japan/80985/ (accessed 23 March 2020).
34. Ibid.
35. "Japan to Beef up Deploying AI technology in Military Defence", http://www.china.org.cn/world/2019-02/12/content_74456776.htm (accessed 23 March 2020).
36. Ibid.
37. "AI System Tested by Tokyo Bay Vessel Traffic Controllers", https://maritime-executive.com/article/ai-system-tested-by-tokyo-bay-vessel-traffic-controllers (accessed 16 April 2020).
38. "JMSDF Future Frigate to Feature Futuristic 360° Augmented Reality Wall", https://www.navalnews.com/event-news/sas-2019/2019/05/jmsdf-future-frigate-to-feature-futuristic-360-augmented-reality-wall/ (accessed 22 May 2020).
39. Ibid.
40. "South Korea Aims High on AI, Pumps $2 Billion into R&D", https://medium.com/syncedreview/south-korea-aims-high-on-ai-pumps-2-billion-into-r-d-de8e5c0c8ac5#:~:text=Eager%20to%20kickstart%20its%20AI,strengthen%20its%20AI%20R%26D%20capability (accessed 22 March 2020).
41. Ibid.
42. "South Korean Army to Launch New Artificial Intelligence Research Institute", https://www.defenseworld.net/news/23972/South_Korean_Army_to_Launch_New_ Artificial_Intelligence_Research_Institute#.X6voHWgzY2w (accessed 23 March 2020).

43. State of AI: Artificial Intelligence, the Military and Increasingly Autonomous Weapons" https://www.paxforpeace.nl/media/files/state-of-artificial-intelligence—pax-report.pdf (accessed 23 March 2020).
44. "The South Korean Military is Catching up with a new Drone Army", https://www.the-security-times.com/the-south-korean-military-is-catching-up-with-a-new-drone-army/ (accessed 27 March 2020).
45. "These Insane Robot Machine Guns Guard the Korean DMZ", https://www.wearethemighty.com/gear-tech/robot-machine-guns-guard-dmzhttps://www.wearethemighty.com/gear-tech/robot-machine-guns-guard-dmz (accessed 27 March 2020).
46. "High Readiness Remains", https://asianmilitaryreview.com/2019/12/high-readiness-remains/ (accessed 27 March 2020).
47. "Make Way for South Korea's Underwater Drones", https://thediplomat.com/2020/02/make-way-for-south-koreas-underwater-drones/ (accessed 6 June 2020).
48. Ibid.
49. Ibid.
50. "MADEX 2019: HHI Unveils HCX-19 Concept Ship", https://defence.pk/pdf/threads/madex-2019-hhi-unveils-hcx-19-concept-ship.640467/ (accessed 22 May 2020).
51. "South Korean Navy Touts Future AI Technology", http://koreabizwire.com/south-korean-navy-touts-future-ai-technology/136523 (accessed 27 March 2020).
52. Jon Grevatt, "Seoul Boosts Funding for 4IR Projects", https://www.janes.com/article/94792/seoul-boosts-funding-for-4ir-projects (accessed 27 March 2020).
53. "Singapore's new 'soldiers': AI, Augmented Reality, and Data Analytics", https://govinsider.asia/security/singapore-defence-dsta-mindef-ai-ar-data-analytics/ (accessed 27 March 2020).
54. "How Exports inspired Singapore's digital military lab", https://govinsider.asia/digital-gov/esports-mmorpg-dsta-digital-hub-lena-lim/ (accessed 9 April 2020).
55. "Singaporeans must Guard against 'sea blindness': Chief of Navy", https://www.straitstimes.com/singapore/singaporeans-must-guard-against-sea-blindness-chief-of-navy (accessed 27 March 2020).
56. "IMDEX 2019: ST Engineering Unveils Vanguard 130 Multi-Role Combatant" https://www.navalnews.com/event-news/imdex-asia-2019/2019/05/imdex-2019-st-engineering-unveils-vanguard-130-multi-role-combatant/ (accessed 22 May 2020).

CHAPTER 6

4IR and Indian Navy

High-technology growth with strong accents on information and communication technologies (ICT) has been quite impressive in India. Similarly, ICT expansion in the defence industrial complex is noteworthy and a number of public sector undertakings (PSUs) are engaged in the production of military-related electronic equipment, products and services. At another level, the military successes of the USA and NATO in the Persian Gulf War (1991), the war in Bosnia (1992-95), the war in Kosovo (1999), the U.S. led war on Terror (2001) and the War on Iraq (2003) encouraged India to build an ICT-enabled military.[1] Although not as grandiose as that of the USA/NATO, Indian military transformation features IT-enabled concepts of operations, logistic supply chains management, maintenance procedures and human resource management.

During the last three decades, globalisation and opening up of the naval industrial complex created ambient conditions for the hybridisation of warships based on imported and home-grown designs, technologies, weapons and sensors. This has been the feature of the Indian Navy's technology enrichment. Also, Indian naval planners have developed comprehensive strategies with emphasis on ICT and introduced network-centric warfare (NCW) in their strategic thought and practice.

The Indian Navy was perhaps the first among the Indian fighting forces to internalize NCW[2] and published the Indian Naval Doctrine for Information Warfare (INDIW). The Doctrine emphasizes 'Network Centric Operations enable exchange of information amongst a large number of heterogeneous nodes in a network' and ' is crucial for gaining competitive edge in a naval warfare by generating information and exploiting information superiority'.[3] Furthermore, the Ministry of Defence in its Annual Report for 2006-07 recorded that 'networking and e-enabled solutions are the two key thrust areas of the Indian Navy and several IT applications have been initiated across a wide spectrum of naval activities'.[4]

The Indian Navy established an IT-enabled network among its shore command centres, ships and other support establishments including logistic hubs. Naval operations, particularly with foreign navies such as the USA, Britain, France and Japan were synchronized with international ICT practices to facilitate interoperability. Importantly, ICT-enabled operations moved from the periphery of naval planning to the centrestage including the process of absorbing technical skills. The thrust was on C_4I_2SR (command, control, communications, computers, Intelligence, interoperability, surveillance and reconnaissance) capability and seamless integrated networks to meet the transformed battle space.

The Indian Naval Doctrine for Information Warfare (INDIW) was perhaps the highlight of the new paradigm of warfare and was internalized at all levels. Under the doctrine, the Navy shifted from platform-centric to network centric operations for seamless integration of various platforms including space-based assets for real-time-navy-wide exchange of information and operations and directions among the joint command centres.

4IR in Indian Military Lexicon

While the Indian defence establishment has assimilated ICT, it has also taken note of the ongoing proliferation of 4IR technologies among many militaries of the world. The "Indian Naval Indigenisation Plan (INIP) 2015-2030" notes that "future wars will be characterised by deployment of unmanned weapon systems, robotic soldiers and sophisticated machines which can operate in all environments. Space, cyber space and asymmetric dimensions are likely to assume greater importance and advancement in critical technologies, sensors, robotics, communication and electronics are paving the way for future warfare".[5] The plan highlights the need for developing 4IR technology-enabled systems, devices and platforms and calls for "a need to infuse state-of-the art technologies in partnership with Indian industry and prepare our human capital to optimally exploit them to generate maximum combat power".[6]

A modest beginning was made in 2018 after the government set up a

17-member multi-stakeholder taskforce for Strategic Implementation of Artificial Intelligence for National Security and Defence with a mandate to explore the use of AI in offensive and defensive operations concerning aviation, naval, land systems, cyber, nuclear and biological warfare arenas.[7] The task force made several recommendations on how to make India a significant AI power and the government called for open tenders or RFIs (requests for information) on dual-use AI technologies to equip the military with autonomous and unmanned platforms and robotic weaponry.

This was followed by setting up a high-level Defence AI Council (DAIC) (under Minister of Defence) in 2019 which was tasked to advise on the strategic directions for the adoption of AI in defence. The DAIC is expected to serve as the central executive body of a Defence AI Project Agency (DAIPA).[8] The government also allocated Rs. 100 crore to each of the service arms for AI-specific application developments from the Defence Budget.

The Indian Ministry of Defence has noted that the "use of AI would add more teeth to the military and it would be a big area considering the requirements of future warfare";[9] it also emphasized that AI would be part of future Indian military strategy. Furthermore, multiple stakeholders such as the defence PSUs, the armed forces, IT industry, start-ups, and academia would lead the initiative as also define the roadmap aimed at "creating a situation where we [India] are going to increasingly see AI in our country's defence setup".[10]

Addressing a stakeholders' workshop on 'Artificial Intelligence in National Security and Defence', Defence Minister Nirmala Sitharaman stated that the "task force should be able to tell us where the defence forces are today, such as bridging with the private sector. The task force should be able to tell us what is it that will encourage, yet regulate the use of the AI in defence forces. The challenges identified are the lack of infrastructure to enable the use of AI. I would place cyber, nuclear and space high on this agenda".[11]

This was further reinforced by the political leadership at the apex level. Prime Minister Modi, while speaking at DEFEXPO-2018 stressed the need to develop AI and noted "New and emerging technologies like Artificial Intelligence and Robotics are perhaps the most important determinant of defensive and offensive capabilities for any defence force in the future. India, with its leadership in the Information Technology domain, would strive to use this technology tilt to its advantage".[12]

In 2018, the Indian Ministry of Defence started Innovations for Defence

Excellence (iDex) aimed at developing an "ecosystem to foster innovation and technology development in Defence and Aerospace by engaging with innovators and start-ups to deliver technologically advanced solutions for modernizing the Indian Military".[13]

India has drawn up plans to set up five laboratories for futuristic technologies under the Defence Research and Development Organisation (DRDO) and these will specialize in artificial intelligence, quantum technologies, cognitive technologies, asymmetric technologies and smart materials.[14] According to a DRDO statement, "the impact of science and technology on defence systems remains undisputed. Edge in technology continues to define the directions of operational, tactical and strategic warfare paradigms.... The pace of innovation is such that today's technology needs to be evaluated and its future potential ascertained with unimaginable".[15]

In 2019, the DRDO also set up a Young Scientists' Lab (DYSL) for developing cutting-edge technologies such as Artificial Intelligence (AI) and associated technologies and as part of its expansion, a "global centre of research" to "build products for the military and those that impact the lives of people in general".[16] It is useful to mention that there are a number of non-governmental AI research centres across the country; and the top ten are in Bengaluru and an important source for talent in this domain.[17]

Indian Navy AI Roadmap

The Indian Navy chief, during an interview to an Indian defence magazine, has stated that "the incorporation of AI into our weapons and sensors is being undertaken in accordance with the 'IN-AI Roadmap'. Several projects are being progressed by the Indian Navy through PSUs and industry. The Proof of Concept of AI projects in the field of Predictive Maintenance, Information Retrieval, Database Management, etc., are in advanced stages of implementation. The Indian Navy envisages leveraging AI to enhance the combat edge by imbibing it in operations, maintenance as well as logistics, and further into support verticals, such as physical security, medical diagnostics, etc".[18]

Significantly, the Naval Commanders' Conference of 2019 focused on "acquisition of new capabilities, harnessing niche technologies like 'Artificial Intelligence' (AI) and 'Big Data Analytics' for solutions in the domains of naval combat, convergence of networks/information, administration, logistics and equipment health monitoring for sustained operations".[19]

According to a naval expert, the Indian Navy requires "secure and robust high end Naval Data Server network infrastructure spread over the country. The data collected is further crucial as a unique building block for Big Data and Artificial Intelligence engines (like Deep Learning Neural Networks), to be exploited via Cloud Computing concepts. Due to lack of in-house knowledge, the precious information generated during naval exercises like TROPEX (Theatre Level Readiness and Operational Exercise), etc., is not being recorded as per Big Data concept for AI engine precision".[20] Similarly, "A common Cloud-sharing platform across all the Navy's shore-based establishments will enable seamless data-sharing between organisations".[21]

The Indian Navy's roadmap is at two levels. First is a collaborative arrangement with the Council of Scientific and Industrial Research (CSIR) and Indian industry, under which it signed a MoU for joint research and development of advanced technologies for the force.[22] The MoU envisages projects such as (a) development of alternative desalination technologies; (b) installation of wireless MEMS-based sensors for remote operation; and (c) residual life assessment studies of gas turbine generator blades to improve reliability. Besides, the MoU would facilitate a "formal framework for interaction between the Indian Navy and CSIR' and 'joint R&D activities in diverse fields of mechanical, electronics, communication, computer science, propulsion systems, metallurgy and nanotechnology".[23]

Closely associated is the Naval Science & Technological Laboratory (NSTL) initiative called 'NSTL-Academia Meet on Artificial Intelligence for Naval Systems'. It was set up in 2019 and during the meeting, AI and its applications in the defence-military systems, with specific emphasis on naval systems, was discussed.[24] Researchers and faculty from 18 universities, technologists and system developers of six labs of the DRDO[25] actively participated in the meeting and exchanged views and ideas in the exciting area of research.[26] This endeavour, it is hoped, would "bridge the gap between academia and R&D institutes and bring out a roadmap for futuristic research in respect of AI-enabled naval systems" as also help in "identifying potential threats unambiguously and immediately. It will also help the command team to make informed decisions faster and rapidly detect and evaluate potential threats removing anomalies".[27] It was also noted that "AI is inherently designed to integrate itself into existing warship equipment suits to optimise their exploitation" but "there are things that can stand in the way of technical progress in the Indian Navy such as

(a) Lack of data science talent internally; (b) Lack of AI initiatives for the Navy; and (c) Undeveloped eco-system for enterprise-level exploitation".[28]

At the second level, the Indian Navy set up a 'state-of-the-art' Virtual Reality Centre (VRC) at the Directorate of Naval Design (Surface Ship Group) which would 'provide a major boost to the indigenous warship design capabilities of the Indian Navy, providing impetus to self-reliance and greater fillip to warship construction under the "Make in India" initiative of the Indian government.'[29] Under the project, "collaborative design reviews will be conducted for continuous interaction between the designers and end users to improve design and ergonomics onboard warships".[30] It is worth mentioning that indigenous warship design capabilities of the Indian Navy have been improving over the last several decades and feature self-reliance for warship design and construction and 19 warship designs have led to construction of nearly 100 platforms.

Similarly, the Indian Navy's training establishments such as INS *Valsura* have augmented technical infrastructure "in the field of Electrical, Electronics and Information Technology' particularly in the context of the emerging trends in 'Machine Learning, Artificial Intelligence (AI) and Big Data Analytics (BDA) Labs' and the latter would serve as the 'Centre of Excellence (CoE) to promote the Navy's fundamental research and development efforts in AI and BDA'.[31]

Perhaps one of the most significant developments is the setting up of the Naval Innovation and Indigenisation Organisation (NIIO). It builds on the Indian Navy's existing Directorate of Indigenisation and facilitates "end users to interact with academia and industry towards fostering innovation and indigenisation for self-reliance in defence in keeping with the vision of Atmanirbhar Bharat".[32] One of its agencies, i.e., Naval Technology Acceleration Council (N-TAC) "will bring together the twin aspects of innovation and indigenisation and provide apex level directives" and a working group under it will implement the projects. Under the N-TAC, is the Technology Development Acceleration Cell (TDAC) which is specifically meant for "induction of emerging disruptive technology in an accelerated time frame".[33] During the launch of the NIIO, the Indian Ministry of Defence also announced the setting up of the Maritime Innovation Forum (Security and Scientific Technical Research Agency - SASTRA), a platform for deliberations on defence manufacturing in India.[34]

At the tri-Services level, the Military Institute of Technology (MILIT) has begun to take note of 4IR-related developments and the first ever capsule course on 'Military robotics, autonomous systems and artificial intelligence' was conducted in 2019.[35] This would bring "greater awareness of contemporary and futuristic technologies for military applications particularly in the context of cryptography algorithms, cyber forensic, enhancing combat effectiveness, and national strategy on cyber security, etc".[36]

The Centre for Artificial Intelligence and Robotics (CAIR) set up at the DRDO for military-related AI merits attention. The Centre is reported to have developed numerous robots such as the Multi-Agent Robotics Framework (MARF) which is capable of functioning as a human soldier.[37] It is also engaged in developing different kinds of intelligent systems, devices and platforms including robots for the Indian Navy. For instance, the Trigun System is designed for enhancing the Maritime Domain Awareness for 'battle space transparency with better network-centric warfare tools riding on high-speed data communication systems and their integration'.[38] It can "collect data about all kinds of civil and military vessels, submarines and aircraft and then the information is collated in special nodes. The outcome of analysed information and the observations can then be shared with the Indian Navy's warships, submarines and aircraft through the indigenous satellite, aid the scientist working on the system. The development of the Trigun began during the first decade of 2000 and by 2012 the first phase was completed. The second phase was to be operational by March 2020 and the third phase is planned for 2020-2024 during which 'Artificial Intelligence and Data Analytics' helps provide an integrated naval common operational picture.[39]

In the context of maritime domain awareness (MDA), it has been noted that it is a "near-ideal candidate for the adoption of AI/ML models. The inputs are diverse and numerous, the environment affects the presence or absence of other units, and there is a variety of sensors that provide information. The inputs could come from shore, ship or space-based sensors, various ship tracking and monitoring systems (AIS, VMS, LRIT, to name three), and open-source information. AI/ML algorithms could then fuse this data to present a single coherent picture of the area of interest. The benefits that could accrue from its adoption could be in the form of enhanced visibility of activities of units at sea, determining patterns of deployment, the determination of risks arising from anomalous behaviour of ships, particularly small craft, and so forth".[40]

Encouraged by the Innovations for Defence Excellence (iDex) initiative of the Indian Ministry of Defence, the IROV Technologies, a start-up, developed a "remotely operated underwater drone, which can send real-time videos of ships and other underwater structures to help with their repair and maintenance". It can "navigate up to a depth of 50 metres to take real-time HD video images to examine underwater, thus eliminating the need for costly and riskier manual inspection by divers,"[41] It also uses sonar technology and is particularly effective for survey and inspection of submerged structures up to 100 metres.

Similarly, another start-up dealing with underwater robots is the Bangalore Robotics is known for developing innovative and low-cost Underwater Swarm AUVs, UAVs, AGVs and similar Unmanned Systems.[42] It plans to "Swarm the Seafloor with Intelligent AUVs to map, monitor and maintain systems to conserve the deep sea ecosystem; detect chemicals, plastic in the ocean depths and oil-spill for ocean eco-system health monitoring and clean the oceans of plastic". Besides, many other start-ups like Dataval Analytics, Innefu Labs, and ChironX. AI, Grobomac and SatSure are working with the government to develop innovative technologies.[43]

Additive Manufacturing Technologies, Spare Parts and Warship Building

In the absence of in-house Additive Manufacturing (AM)/3D printing capacity, the Indian Navy has contracted Think3D, an Indian company, to supply 3D printed spare parts which were 'successfully tested and incorporated into several machines.'[44] The company uses HP's multi-jet fusion technology and manufactures 3D printed parts for centrifugal pump impellers. This encouraged the Indian Navy to consider installing a 3D printer onboard its ships with the 'CAD designs of spare parts pre-loaded into the machine so that the operator can 3D Print the parts on-demand'.[45]

Indian shipyards have entered into partnership with foreign and Indian technology suppliers to build Unmanned Surface Vessels (USVs) for the Indian Navy. Garden Reach Shipbuilders & Engineers Ltd (GRSE) and Bharat Electronics Limited (BEL) entered into an MoU with Elbit Systems, an Israeli firm, to develop and customize the vessels to meet the specifications of the Indian Navy.[46] However, there are no success stories with regard to Indian warship building shipyards using Additive Manufacturing (3D printing) technologies in shipbuilding.[47]

UAVs and Drones

The Indian Naval Indigenisation Plan (INIP) 2015-2030 acknowledges that the "UAVs will act as a force multiplier and represent the 'eyes' of naval units in the future, providing them with the possibility to see in real-time-over-the-horizon. They may in future be used in lieu of helicopters for certain roles".[48] Currently, the Indian Navy operates two variants of the Searcher Mk II and these are launched from shore bases. There are reports to suggest that the USA has "offered to sell 30 Sea Guardians (unarmed naval variant, or UAV, of the Predator-B made by General Atomics) for over $ 4 billion".[49]

It also plans to deploy drones from ships and has issued a Request for Information to acquire five Naval Shipborne Unmanned Aerial Systems (NSUAS) for surveillance and reconnaissance tasks in support of 'Sea lines of Communication (SLOC) monitoring and Coastal /Exclusive Economic Zone (EEZ) surveillance, anti-piracy and anti-terrorism, assistance in Search-and-Rescue and assistance in Maritime Domain Awareness'.[50] Besides, "these drones will be deployed on warships enabling them to detect Chinese movement as well as any other activities in and around Indian territorial waters".[51]

Bigdata, Analytics and Modelling

As far as the underwater domain is concerned, the Indian Navy signed a MoU with the Geological Survey of India (GSI) for 'Sharing of seabed sediments data, products and expertise for Naval Application in Meteorology and Oceanography'.[52] India claims nearly 2.1 million square kilometres of EEZ and the Marine and Coastal Survey Division of the GSI has "mapped most of India's (coastline) and has a vast repository of offshore data". India also possesses "state-of-the-art oceanic research vessels, *Samudra Manthan*, *Samudra Kaustubh*, *Samudra Shaudhikama* and *Samudra Ratnakar*" that have over the decades collected data and is held by the GSI. The Indian Navy could use 4IR technologies such as AI and Bigdata for oceanographic modelling to be used in maritime operations.

Challenges posed by 4IR-enabled PLA Navy

The PLA Navy is studying naval applications of 4IR in command and control, decision-making and intelligent military systems and platforms, and hopes to harness its potential to make itself a highly sophisticated and capable force. The notable advancements in the naval domain are in UAVs, drones, robots and warships that are capable of operating autonomously. These and such other platforms can potentially help the PLA Navy to adapt to a new form of warfare that can be labelled as 'remote naval warfare'.

In the short term, the PLA can be expected to closely follow AI-related developments and integrate them in its military strategy. In the long term, there will be a robust civil-military integration of AI built around indigenously/copied systems and platforms. This will surely add to the war fighting tool kit of the PLA and provide a lethal mix of cutting-edge technologies with conventional forces that could encourage dangerous escalation of a new kind resulting in destabilization, and adversely affect regional security.

The likely thrust areas could be integrated autonomous unmanned vehicles, drones, modern ships, submarines and projectiles such as missiles and torpedoes to support 'remote warfare'. It is quite plausible that the PLA Navy may have already begun to conduct exercises based on AI and ML and assimilated commonly used and commercially available communication devices such as smart phones, tablets and hybrid devices into its naval strategy.

The above-mentioned Chinese investments are indeed transformative and the PLA Navy may reconstitute the composition of future task forces bound for the Indian Ocean. These would seek naval dominance and upset the force advantage enjoyed by the Indian Navy. It is quite plausible that in the future, the PLA Navy may even conduct UAV/drone swarm-led exercises operated and supported from friendly Indian Ocean military facilities. This will only add to the increasing challenges already posed by the Chinese advantages in space and cyber capability. Indian naval planners may have to develop new strategies and fleet architecture that integrate emerging technologies of the kind discussed above. These plans are sure to impact ship design, budgets and concept of operations.

Pakistan and China have a robust civilian space cooperation programme. In 2010, China agreed to provide RMB 86.5 million concessional loan for setting up two ground stations in Karachi and Lahore for the Chinese-built Paksat-1R communication satellite. More recently, in 2018, China provided launch services at the Jiuquan Satellite Launch Centre for Pakistan's first Remote Sensing Satellite (PRSS-1) and Pakistan's indigenous Technology Evaluation Satellite (PakTES-1A) that became fully operational on 14 August.[53]

At another level, China and Pakistan have a military space cooperation arrangement signed in 2011 under which 'Pakistan has full access to Beidou's military grade secure navigation signal, which is more fool-proof, resistant to jamming and spoofing and more accurate than the civilian grade signal available to all in the satellite coverage area".[54] The Beidou satellite tracking station in Karachi is run by Pakistan.

Concluding Thoughts

The Indian Navy is fervently exploring acquisition of transformative weaponry and is seeking intelligent and autonomous robotic platforms and cyber defence systems from the domestic market. It has a roadmap and a plan to build a 4IR-enabled force to meet the challenges of the evolving naval environment that will increasingly feature disruptive technologies. It is exploring ways to leverage 4IR for advancing operational training and war-gaming. These plans are sure to impact ship design, budgets and concept of operations. At the tri-Services level, 4IR-related developments are also taking shape including training and capsule courses on 4IR related issues. The Indian Navy is also keen to marshal the private sector to meet its 4IR needs and fill critical gaps. The next chapter is focused on the role of 4IR technologies on the development of the Blue Economy which is resonating across the globe and, in India, the Prime Minister has linked it to the mantra of Security and Growth for all (SAGAR).

NOTES

1. Vijay Sakhuja, *Asian Maritime Power in the 21st Century: Strategic Transactions: China, India and Southeast Asia*, (Singapore: Institute of South East Asian Studies, 2015), pp. 215-250.
2. Ibid., pp. 234-238.
3. *Indian Naval Doctrine for Information Warfare*, Information Warfare Cell, Naval Headquarters, New Delhi, 2001, p. 45.
4. *Annual Report 2006-07*, Ministry of Defence, Government of India, p. 28.
5. "Indian Naval Indigenisation Plan (INIP) 2015-2030", https://ddpmod.gov.in/sites/default/files/INIP%20(2015-2030).pdf (accessed 2 November 2019).
6. Ibid.
7. "Artificial Intelligence" https://pib.gov.in/Pressreleaseshare.aspx?PRID=1541023 (accessed 2 November 2019).
8. Brig P. Binura, "Digitalisation is an Imperative to Improve Operational Readiness and Combat Efficiency", "*South Asia Defence and Strategic Review*", Vol. 13, Issue 6A, Jan/Feb 2020, p.19.
9. "India to equip Defence Forces with Autonomous Tanks Aerial Vehicles Robotic Weaponry", https://analyticsindiamag.com/india-to-equip-defence-forces-with-autonomous-tanks-aerial-vehicles-robotic-weaponry/ (accessed 2 November 2019).
10. Ibid.
11. "Use of AI in Defence Forces a Key Challenge: Sitharaman", https://www.business-standard.com/article/news-ani/use-of-ai-in-defence-forces-a-key-challenge-sitharaman-118052100450_1.html (accessed 3 November 2019).

12. "India now wants Artificial Intelligence-based Weapon Systems", https://timesofindia.indiatimes.com/india/india-moves-to-develop-ai-based-military-systems/articleshow/64250232.cms (accessed 3 November 2019).
13. Pranbihanga Borpuzari & Geetha Jayaraman, "From DRDO to BPCL, India's first Underwater Drone, EyeROV Tuna, finds many Takers" (accessed 23 March 2020).
14. "DRDO to set up five new labs to prepare Indian armed forces for future high-tech warfare", //economictimes.indiatimes.com/articleshow/73072702.cms?utm_source=contentofinterest&utm_medium=text&utm_campaign=cppst (accessed 4 January 2020).
15. Ibid.
16. "A new Defence Lab aims to Embed AI into the Military", https://www.deccanherald.com/national/a-new-defence-lab-aims-to-embed-ai-into-the-military-819482.html (accessed 31 March 2020).
17. "Top 10 Artificial Intelligence Research Centres in Bengaluru", https://analyticsindiamag.com/top-10-ai-analytics-research-centres-in-bengaluru/ (accessed 23 March 23020).
18. "Interview with the CNS", https://www.defstrat.com/magazine_articles/interview-with-the-cns/(accessed 4 January 2020).
19. Huma Siddiqui, "Naval Commanders Conference to Focus on Niche Technologies like AI and Big Data Analytics", "https://www.financialexpress.com/defence/naval-commanders-conference-to-focus-on-niche-technologies-like-ai-and-big-data-analytics/1556569/ (accessed 4 January 2020).
20. Ibid.
21. "AI & Machine Learning For The Indian Navy", Paper No. 21, April 2020.
22. "Indian Navy signs MoU with Council of Scientific and Industrial Research (CSIR)", https://pib.gov.in/PressReleasePage.aspx?PRID=1570091(accessed 20 January 2020).
23. Ibid.
24. "NSTL - Academia Meet (NAM 2019) @ NSTL on 19.01.2019" , https://pib.gov.in/PressReleasePage.aspx?PRID=1560623 (accessed 20 January 2020).
25. Naval Science & Technological Laboratory (NSTL); Naval Materials Research Laboratory (NMRL); Centre for Artificial Intelligence and Robotics (CAIR); Naval Physical & Oceanographic Laboratory (NPOL); Defence Metallurgical Research Laboratory (DMRL), & Defence Electronics Application Laboratory (DEAL); and the Centre for Military Airworthiness & Certification (CEMILAC).
26. Ibid.
27. Ibid.
28. Ibid.
29. "Virtual Reality Centre" a Reality - shall Boost Indigenous Warship Design Capabilities", https://pib.gov.in/PressReleasePage.aspx?PRID=1570481(accessed 4 January 2020).
30. Ibid.
31. "AI, Data Analytics Research Lab Opens at INS Valsura", https://timesofindia.indiatimes.com/city/rajkot/ai-data-analytics-research-lab-opens-at-ins-valsura/articleshow/73091584.cms (accessed 4 January 2020).
32. "Raksha Mantri Shri Rajnath Singh Launches Naval Innovation and Indigenisation Organisation (NIIO)", https://pib.gov.in/PressReleseDetailm.aspx?PRID=1645549 (accessed 13 August 2020).
33. Ibid.

34. "RSU inks MoU with Indian Navy for Capacity Building, Research Projects", https://timesofindia.indiatimes.com/india/rsu-inks-mou-with-indian-navy-for-capacity-building-research-projects/articleshowprint/77532161.cms (accessed 14 August 2020).
35. "Military Institute to conduct Lectures on Robotics, Autonomous Systems and AI for Officers in Pune", https://realtime.rediff.com/news/india/Military-institute-to-conduct-lectures-on-robotics-autonomous-systems-and-AI-for-officers-in-Pune/a5ef1141497b5a87 (accessed 4 November 2019).
36. Ibid.
37. Chethan Kumar, "Army to get Self-reliant, Autonomous Robots soon", https://economictimes.indiatimes.com/news/defence/army-to-get-self-reliant-autonomous-robots-soon/articleshow/57466543.cms?from=mdr (accessed 10 February 2020).
38. Mayank Singh, "New System with AI to Boost Maritime Security", https://www.newindianexpress.com/thesundaystandard/2020/feb/09/new-system-with-ai-to-boost-maritime-security-2100873.html (accessed 10 February 2020).
39. Ibid.
40. Subhash Dutta, "Artificial Intelligence and Machine Learning for the Indian Navy", https://maritimeindia.org/artificial-intelligence-and-machine-learning-for-the-indian-navy/ (accessed 4 May 2020).
41. Pranbihanga Borpuzari & Geetha Jayaraman, "From DRDO to BPCL, India's First Underwater Drone, EyeROV Tuna, Finds Many Takers" (accessed 23 March 2020).
42. "BangaloreRobotics", https://bangalorerobotics.org/ (accessed 23 March 2020).
43. "AI Has Now Reached the Battlefield with Killer Robots, Automated Weapons & UAVs" https://analyticsindiamag.com/ai-has-now-reached-the-battlefield-with-killer-robots-automated-weapons-uavs/ (accessed 23 March 2020).
44. "Think3D to Provide Expertise and 3D Printed Spare Parts to the Indian Navy", https://www.3dprintingmedia.network/3d-printed-spare-parts-indian-navy/ (accessed 11 March 2020).
45. Ibid.
46. "BEL, GRSE to Customize Elbit's Unmanned Surface Vessels for Indian Navy", https://www.defenseworld.net/news/26292/BEL__GRSE_to_Customize_Elbit_s_Unmanned_Surface_Vessels_for_Indian_Navy#.XkJGpVUzZ0w (accessed 12 February 2020).
47. "Goa Shipyard should explore Artificial Intelligence to Build Warships: Defence Ministry", http://www.defenceindia.com/news/goa-shipyard-should-explore-artificial-intelligence-to-build-warships-defence-ministry/ (accessed 12 February 2020). The Secretary for Defence Production, Government of India, "while lauding the Goa Shipyard Limited's performance in exporting warships to friendly nations, urged the defence public sector shipyard to focus on artificial intelligence-driven technologies for shipbuilding".
48. "Indian Naval Indigenisation Plan (INIP) 2015-2030", https://ddpmod.gov.in/sites/default/files/INIP%20(2015-2030).pdf (accessed 15 August 2020).
49. "India Eyes Acquisition of Predator-B drones from US", https://www.hindustantimes.com/india-news/india-eyes-acquisition-of-predator-drones-from-us/story-nVOOMnUWNh7KokbqE9uVYM.html (accessed 30 July 2020). Also see "Indian Govt Seals Sea Guardian Drones Procurement Deal With US", https://www.thequint.com/news/india/india-to-get-sea-guardian-drones-procurement-deal-with-us (accessed 30 July 2020). The platform "travels at 300 kilometers per hour at 50,000 feet. It has the capacity to fly 14-hour missions to survey waters 1,800 km from the base. According to the report, a Sea Guardian

sends the 'imagery in real time to a ground control room on base, which flies the drone through a two-way data link."

50. "India Navy to buy 15 Ship-borne Drones to Enhance Surveillance". https://defence.capital/2020/03/05/india-navy-to-buy-15-ship-borne-drones-to-enhance-surveillance/?fbclid=IwAR1d45lBvJLBX-UucguF_eakMF5F9dCVcBS-2fmUntqYYEbLeSp7rjzULSo (accessed 5 March 2020).
51. "Indian Navy to Upgrade Existing UAVs, Purchase 10 new Drones to Monitor Chinese Movement", https://www.indiatoday.in/india/story/indian-navy-to-upgrade-existing-drones-purchase-10-new-to-monitor-chinese-movement-1711230-2020-08-14(accessed 15 August 2020).
52. "Indian Navy Signs MoU for offshore Data with Geological Survey of India", https://pib.gov.in/newsite/PrintRelease.aspx?relid=197541 (accessed 20 March 2020).
53. "Karachi + Lahore Ground Stations", https://www.globalsecurity.org/space/world/china/karachi.htm (accessed 14 April 2019).
54. Ibid.

CHAPTER 7

4IR and Blue Economy

There is a long and well-established relationship between mankind and the sea. It has been an important source of food, a medium for trade and commerce, and facilitator for the movement of people, transmission of culture, religion and ideas and, in modern times, the harbinger for globalization, human development and integration of the global economy.

However, little is known about the value of the goods and services accrued from the oceans and seas. According to the United Nations, the economic value of the oceans is between US$ 3 trillion and US$ 6 trillion.[1] The goods include "food (fisheries and aquaculture feed 4.3 billion people with more than 15 per cent of annual consumption of animal protein), oil and gas (over 30 per cent is produced from offshore), and services such as marine transport (90 per cent of global trade moves over the seas), global telecommunications (submarine cables carry 95 per cent of all digital data across the globe), marine tourism (5 per cent of the global Gross Domestic Product (GDP) and 6-7 per cent of global employment), shore-based commercial activity (13 of the world's top 20 megacities and over 40 per cent, or 3.1 billion, of the world population lives within 100 km of the sea in about 150 cities located along the coast and in island nations)".[2]

While the above indicators are very promising, human knowledge about the oceans is still poor and the manifold capabilities of 4IR technologies offer enormous opportunities to gain a deeper knowledge of the oceans so that this last 'reservoir of resource wealth' can be used sustainably. Significantly, the underwater domain is the least explored and little is known about organisms and plant life that live, thrive and flourish on the seabed. 4IR technologies can help understand the marine eco-system services provided by the seas and oceans, its role as a 'carbon sink' and importantly provide real-time data of physical, chemical and biological conditions of the oceans and seas. In this context, this chapter illustrates the role of 4IR technologies in the development of the Blue Economy.

What is Blue Economy?

In the past, concepts related to the seas and the oceans such as 'Sea Power' and 'Maritime Power' have been debated, discussed and theorized; the new understanding of the oceans is led by the idea of Blue Economy. Gunter Pauli was the first to coin the term 'Blue Economy' in his book, *Blue Economy - 10 Years, 100 Innovations, 100 Million Jobs.*[3] However, his understanding of the Blue Economy has undergone mutation and transformation leading to a number of terms such as 'ocean economy', 'coastal economy', 'Blue Economy' and 'Greening the Blue Economy'.

Among these terms, 'Blue Economy' is more popular and is finding reference and relevance in international relations, geopolitics, geostrategic issues, safety and security discourses, environment and ecological debates, financing, legal implications and in entrepreneurship and technological innovation. Some countries have appointed ministers for Blue Economy[4] and some states have announced Blue Bonds, a financial instrument.[5] Further, Blue Economy is also finds reference in Goal 14 of the Sustainable Development Goals (SDG) 2030 which focuses on the oceans and calls for sustainable development of the sea based resources.[6]

The World Bank defines 'Blue Economy' as "sustainable use of ocean resources for economic growth, improved livelihoods, and jobs while preserving the health of ocean ecosystem";[7] and the Centre for Blue Economy makes a distinction between 'ocean economy' and 'coastal economy' and states that "it is now a widely-used term around the world with three related but distinct meanings, the overall contribution of the oceans to economies, the need to address the environmental and ecological sustainability of the oceans, and the ocean economy as a growth opportunity for both developed and developing countries".[8]

In India, the FICCI Taskforce Report titled "Blue Economy Vision 2025: Harnessing Business Potential for India Inc. and International Partners", a pioneering effort, defines 'Blue Economy' as one that "encompasses a wide range of economic activities pertaining to sustainable development of resources and assets in the oceans, related rivers, water bodies and coastal regions—in a manner that ensures equity, inclusion, innovation and modern technology".[9]

4IR Technologies for Blue Economy

There is strong evidence of digitalisation through information communication technologies in all sectors of the Blue Economy and features automation, smart sensors, data transfer, unmanned and remote-controlled devices and platforms and semi or fully autonomous operations. These have transformed the way the marine and maritime sectors operate. Marine and maritime industries and businesses are harnessing a variety of 4IR technologies to harness the seas as also support offshore and shore-based static and mobile marine-maritime infrastructure. These technologies are the frontrunners of the future of the Blue Economy.

Big Data

Oceans and seas are a source of a large amount of data generated by "ships, oceans, wave stations, observations from environmental conditions, fishing and maritime biodiversity, routes and trajectories, and incidental or voluntary oil spill events", etc.[10] This data is both structured and unstructured, obtained-generated by humans and machines, and as noted in Chapter 1, it is characterized by the 5Vs, i.e., Volume scale (data generated and collected); Velocity (rapidity and time); Variety (heterogeneity in data types, formats, structure and data generation); Veracity (quality of the data) and Value (value obtained from processing and mining big data).[11] The maritime Bigdata information system compromises marine Cloud platform, integrated database, Bigdata standardization, and data processing and analysis. According to a report, the maritime industry "generates roughly 100-120 million data points every day from different sources such as ports and vessel movements".[12]

Similarly, with the advent of ICT, ocean science has witnessed an exponential growth in data and this has been further supplemented by growth in ocean observatories-platforms fitted with sensors.[13] These generate "huge volume, diverse types, sustained measurement, and potential uses of ocean observing data and is a typical kind of big data, namely, marine big data. The traditional data-centric infrastructure is insufficient to deal with new challenges arising in ocean science"[14] and is urgently required.

At the organisational and structural levels, there are now trends in convergences among institutions with similar mandates and responsibilities to contribute to ocean governance. For instance, Global Fishing Watch (GFW) and Ocean Data Foundation (ODF) have come together for a common mission to "harness, and openly share, new data and technology to advance understanding and stewardship of our ocean and its resources" and develop "new methods for combining and visualizing big ocean data, and develop complementary technology solutions that make open data sources easy to use and share, in support of better science and management of our ocean".[15] GFW's vessel detection capability and ODF's ability to collect ocean environmental data and generate actionable information to help in ocean governance.

AI and Machine Learning

Ocean and seas have deluged marine scientists, data analysts, maritime practitioners and economists with data, and posed a major challenge for harnessing the potential of the Blue Economy. Artificial intelligence is a useful analysis tool for the management and streamlining of various uses of the oceans and seas in a sustainable manner. Nature Conservancy in partnership with Microsoft's Environmental Sustainability and AI for Earth have incorporated tools such as AI, machine learning, Cloud computing and data crunching to "better understand the state of the world's natural resources—and how they can better protect the planet".[16]

A number of scientific instruments fitted with 4IR technologies are being developed for studying organisms and plant life. For instance VR/AR/AI-enabled microscopes help in understanding how the ecosystem operates to manage the health of the environment.[17] AI and ML are also proving useful to understand life in the oceans. The Charles Stark Draper Laboratory and the New England Aquarium are counting whales by developing a probability model through a machine-learning algorithm that would integrate data obtained from satellites, sonar, radar, human sightings, ocean currents, etc. This would help "federal, state and local authorities could make decisions about shipping lanes and speeds and fishing more quickly, helping them to better protect the whales".[18]

Interestingly, machine learning can help penetrate "dark data" used for organized crime on the web. The DeepDive tool "extracts value from the universe of data buried in text, tables, images and other sources that are unable to be processed by existing software".

Blockchain and IUU Fishing

Sea-based fishing is a major source of livelihood for coastal communities and fish is an important protein supplement for people's dietary needs. Illegal, Unreported and Unregulated (IUU) fishing,[19] also referred to as 'pirate fishing' is a crime and has been high on the agenda for debate and discussions at the level of the United Nations, regional fishery management organizations, and regional maritime security arrangements. According to the FAO, IUU fishing is rampant and the situation is alarming and "one out of every five fish is caught illegally in the western Indian Ocean region".[20]

Blockchain technology has the potential to secure the supply chain against a number of illegal activity and frauds. It can potentially help in transparency and traceability through verification and validation and prevent IUU fishing by "tracking the journey of a single fish, recording information regarding where it was caught and how it was processed".[21] The technology helps obtain 'an immutable record of provenance and building confidence in the quality and freshness of the catch'; it also helps to track data concerning the place where it was caught, when it was landed portside, graded, selected, packed and shipped to its final destination.[22]

Underwater Robots

Scientists have developed several types of robots inspired by octopuses and are designed to move tentacles made of flexible material like the real thing.[23] The arms are moved by electrical motors and have 'computer-controlled air chambers in its tentacles, which are opened and closed by pneumatic valves to change the direction'. Made from soft material, the octopus robot uses a "novel fluidic actuation mechanism that allows the robot to advance forward, change direction and rotate around its primary axis".[24] Further, 'soft robots have an edge over the traditional "rigid" robots in terms of elasticity and flexibility as the technology is inspired by the way in Jellyfish, a ubiquitous marine invertebrate, is believed to be the oldest and has been in existence for over 500 million years. The 'body structure has remained largely unchanged' and scientists plan to mimic these creatures and explore underwater life. They have developed 'bionic jellyfish by embedding microelectronics' and 'deploy them to monitor and explore the world's oceans'.

A small sized 'prosthetic' embedded bionic can swim 'three times faster and more efficiently without causing any apparent stress to the animals, which have no brain, central nervous system or pain receptors'.[25] Scientists plan to embed miniaturized sensors and cameras to undertake "long-term measurements of ocean conditions such as temperature, salinity, acidity, oxygen levels, nutrients and microbial communities" and "to monitor signs of climate change or observe natural phenomena".[26]

Fish are very sensitive to human intervention and in that context, underwater robots are ideal for aquaculture farming. These platforms help in observing the health and growth of fish, including monitoring cage cleanliness. The turtle robot, as the name suggests, is a small device and makes slow manoeuvres without disturbing the fish.

A French start-up has developed a device that can measure 24/7 the water quality and provide water quality parameters such as "temperature, dissolved oxygen, pH, salinity, turbidity and chlorophyll" and these help in forecasting the condition of the water. It is a completely autonomous device with "plug and play" and is powered by a solar panel and equipped with long-range communication technology (LoRaWan).[27]

Biometetics

NASA scientists successfully copied the "microscopic patterns of dentricles" of shark skin, to create a 'riblets' film which "reduces drag and deters microorganisms (such as algae) attaching to the surface".[28] This can be used on the hull of sailboats adding to speed and for marine vessels to good advantage by 'reducing friction' and saving fuel. Its use in the development and utilisation as "coatings for ship hulls, submarines, aircraft, and even swimwear for humans" are being explored.[29]

Concluding Thoughts

4IR technologies are impacting the development of the Blue Economy and all its sectors are taking advantage of these disruptive technologies. These are also transforming and helping in strengthening Marine Spatial Planning (MSP), bio-remediation, bio-prospecting, and a variety of other marine sectors. Big data applications are helping improve fish domain awareness, including countering illegal and unauthorised fishing. Similarly, autonomous platforms and robots can potentially improve overall sustainable use, help in improving efficiency and add value to the Blue Economy. This study would discuss two significant issues concerning ethics and international law connected with 4IR technologies in the next chapter.

NOTES

1. "Ocean Assets Valued at $ 24 Trillion, but Dwindling Fast", http://www.worldwildlife.org/stories/ocean-assets-valued-at-24- trillion-but-dwindling-fast (accessed 10 November 2020).
2. Cited in Vijay Sakhuja and Kapil Narula, *Perspectives on the Blue Economy* (New Delhi: Vij Publication, 2015). Also see "Goal 14—Conserve and Sustainably Use Oceans, Seas and Marine Resources for Sustainable Development", https://unchronicle.un.org/article/goal-14-conserve-and-sustainably-use-oceans-seas-and-marine-resources-sustainable (accessed 20 January 2020).
3. Gunter Pauli, "*Blue Economy-10 Years, 100 Innovations, 100 Million Jobs*", (New Mexico: Paradigm Publications, 2010).
4. For details, see http://newenergyevents.com/blue-economy-caribbean/speakers/hon-kirk-humphrey/ (accessed 12 January 2020).
5, Vijay Sakhuja, "Blue Bonds for Bay of Bengal", http://www.kalingainternational.com/Vijay-Sakhuja17.html (accessed 26 March 2020). Also see "Seychelles launches World's First Sovereign Blue Bond", https://www.worldbank.org/en/news/press-release/2018/10/29/seychelles-launches-worlds-first-sovereign-blue-bond (accessed 12 January 2020).
6. "Sustainable Development Goal 14 : Conserve and Sustainably use the Oceans, Seas and Marine Resources for Sustainable Development", https://sustainabledevelopment.un.org/sdg14 (accessed 12 January 2020).
7. "What is Blue Economy", http://www.worldbank.org/en/news/infographic/2017/06/06/blue-economy (accessed 12 January 2020).
8. "Our History and Methodology", https://www.middlebury.edu/institute/academics/centers-initiatives/center-blue-economy/about/history (accessed 12 January 2020).
9. "Blue Economy Vision 2025: Harnessing Business Potential for India Inc. and International Partners", http://ficci.in/spdocument/20896/Blue-Economy-Vision-2025.pdf (accessed 12 January 2020).
10. Ioanna Lytra , Maria-Esther Vidal, Fabrizio Orlandi and Judie Attard, "A Big Data Architecture for Managing Oceans of Data and Maritime Applications", https://www.researchgate.net/publication/322997369_A_big_data_architecture_for_managing_oceans_of_ data_and_maritime_applications (accessed 10 April 2020).
11. Ibid.
12. "Use of Big Data in the Maritime Industry", https://www.patersonsimons.com/wp-content/uploads/2018/06/TMS_SmartPort_InsightBee_Report-to-GUIDE_01.02.18.pdf (accessed 10 April 2020).
13. Yingjian Liu, Meng Qiu, Chao Liu and Zhongwen Guo, "Big Data Challenges in Ocean Observation: a Survey", https://www.researchgate.net/publication/309962243_Big_data_challenges_in_ocean_observation_a_survey (accessed 10 April 2020).
14. Ibid.
15. "New Partnership Aims to Build a better Understanding of the Ocean", https://globalfishingwatch.org/news-views/new-partnership/ (accessed 25 April 2020).
16. "Cloud Computing and AI help the Nature Conservancy Dive Deeper into Conservation", https://blogs.microsoft.com/green/2018/04/19/the-nature-conservancy-case-study/ (accessed 10 April 2020).
17. "Pioneering Microscopic Reality with New AI-powered Microscopes", https://www.ibm.com/blogs/research/2018/03/microscopic-reality-ai-microscopes/ (accessed 10 April 2020).

18. Tatiana Schlossberg , "A.I. Is Helping Scientists Understand an Ocean's Worth of Data", https://www.nytimes.com/2020/04/08/science/ai-ocean-whales-study.html?auth=login-facebook (accessed 11 April 2020).
19. "IUU fishing is illegal fishing and usually refers to fishing without a licence, fishing in a closed area, fishing with prohibited gear, fishing over a quota, or the fishing of prohibited species." See "Illegal, Unreported, and Unregulated Fishing", https://www.pewtrusts.org/en/research-and-analysis/fact-sheets/2013/08/27/faq-illegal-unreported-and-unregulated-fishing (accessed 10 April 2020).
20. Cited in "Harbouring Information: Combating Illegal Fishing", https://geographical.co.uk/nature/oceans/item/2542-harbouring-information(accessed 10 April 2020).
21. "Blockchain could Police the Fishing Industry - Here's how", https://www.weforum.org/agenda/2020/02/blockchain-tuna-sustainability-fisheries-food-security/ (accessed 26 March 2020).
22. "IBM Blockchain Solution Provides Seafood Traceability", https://www.maritime-executive.com/article/ibm-blockchain-solution-provides-seafood-traceability (accessed 18 October 2019).
23. J. Fras, Y. Noh, M. Macias, H. Wurdemann and K. Althoefer, "Bio-Inspired Octopus Robot Based on Novel Soft Fluidic Actuator," *2018 IEEE International Conference on Robotics and Automation (ICRA)*, Brisbane, QLD, 2018, pp. 1583-1588.
24. "Robots that Move like Octopuses? Scientists Have Developed Bots Inspired by Biology", https://www.news18.com/news/buzz/robots-that-move-like-octopuses-scientists-have-developed-bots-inspired-by-biology-2244527.html (accessed 15 February 2020).
25. "Scientists Create Bionic Jellyfish to Explore World's Oceans", https://nypost.com/2020/01/31/scientists-create-bionic-jellyfish-to-explore-worlds-oceans/ (accessed 15 February 2020).
26. Ibid.
27. "Underwater Weather Station nets € 1.5m Funding", https://thefishsite.com/articles/under water-weather-station-nets-1-5m-funding (accessed 10 June 2020).
28. "Skin Reduces Biofouling", https://asknature.org/strategy/skin-reduces-biofouling/#.Xk5Jl5UzZ0w (accessed 15 February 2020).
29. "Biomimicry: 9 Ways Engineers Have Been 'Inspired' by Nature", https://interestingengineer ing.com/biomimicry-9-ways-engineers-have-been-inspired-by-nature (accessed 12 January 2020).

CHAPTER 8

4IR, Ethics and International Law

Since ages, warfare has witnessed changes and, in contemporary times, 4IR technology is offering immense opportunities to produce smart, intelligent and autonomous systems and devices for use across the spectrum of warfare from offensive to defensive operations. It is also freeing human operators from dangerous and sometimes fatal tasks and missions such as bomb disposal and mine clearance and protecting them from exposure to lethal ordnances. These systems and devices can also make emergency responses more effective and accurate thereby reducing collateral damage, liberate humans from any inner guilt, moral costs of killing or using them in self-defence.

However, fully autonomous weapon systems can have potentially "frightening outcomes amid fears that humans are being pushed to the secondary level or even sidelined in the decision-making process".[1] Furthermore, "delegating complex tasks including decision-making to devices, sensors and algorithms could potentially engender severe complications.[2] Besides, there are several other issues concerning assurance, trustworthiness and quality of 4IR-enabled equipment and parts".[3]

At another level, 4IR-enabled maritime operations bring with them attendant legal issues that span the entire domain from the definition of autonomous ships, accountability during accidents, supply chain management and crew qualifications. In the above contexts, three important issues merit attention, i.e., ethics and morality in warfare; legal issues concerning platforms; and trustworthiness of the parts/equipment produced by Additive Manufacturing/3D printing.

Conscience, Morality, and Ethics

While there is visible euphoria concerning 4IR technologies, "every technology since fire has intertwined promise and peril".[4] Militaries are keen to harness the benefits of the ongoing transformation and add these technologies in their war fighting menu. However, "legal and ethical issues are beginning to gain greater salience, particularly in the context of warfare where surrendering unbridled control to machines to take decisions to kill, injure, or destroy could challenge international law, ethics of war fighting, and human values".[5] This belief has attracted a number of issues including conscience, morals and ethics in warfare, particularly in the context of International Humanitarian Law given that some militaries are now exploring weaponisation of autonomous technologies.

In 2017, the Group of Governmental Experts (GGE) on lethal autonomous weapon systems (LAWS) met in Geneva to "exchange and examine the various dimensions of emerging technologies" particularly in the area of LAWS in the context of the "objectives and purposes of the Convention on Prohibitions or Restrictions on the Use of Certain CCW/GGE.1/2017/3 5 Conventional Weapons".[6]

The International Committee of the Red Cross (ICRC) has been spearheading the global debate on ethics and conscience in the context of the use of fully autonomous weapon systems and has upheld and promoted the "rules governing the conduct of hostilities under international humanitarian law and the use of force under international human rights law" which "require a minimum level of human control to be retained over weapon systems and the use of force, variously characterized as 'meaningful' or 'effective' 'human control' or 'appropriate human involvement'. As such, these rules demand limits on autonomy in weapon systems".[7]

Besides, a number of Non-Governmental Organisations (NGOs) have joined the ICRC chorus and are demanding a global ban on 'killer robots', including a treaty for emerging weapons.[8] For instance, Professor Noel Sharkey of the University of Sheffield, who is leading the "Coalition to Stop Killer Robots" campaign, has "expressed concerns over the growing competition among companies and militaries to build and acquire autonomous and smarter weapons, and labelled this trend as 'a new arms race'".[9]

The International Committee for Robot Arms Control (ICRAC) has been actively engaged in the issues concerning LAWS.[10] Likewise, the issue caught the attention of Google, the global technology giant who, under pressures from its staff, announced suspension of a US military project involving drones and artificial intelligence capability.[11] The company however clarified that it will work with governments to "keep service members and civilians safe" and pursue AI-based technologies for the military in "cyber security, training, military recruitment, veterans' healthcare, and search and rescue".[12]

Meanwhile, Elon Musk, the owner of Tesla, which has been a pioneer in revolutionary technologies, robotics and AI, and is leading a group of 116 specialists from across 26 countries, urged the United Nations to ban the development and use of 'killer robots'.

Sundar Pichai, CEO of Google said, "As a leader in AI, we feel a deep responsibility to get this right" and the company would withdraw from Project Maven and not develop in future "technologies that cause or are likely to cause overall harm", those which "violate internationally accepted norms," and "widely accepted principles of international law and human rights",[13] He listed seven principles that would guide Google's future research and product development and business decisions. Furthermore, four 'No's have been listed: (a) Technologies that cause or are likely to cause overall harm; (b) Weapons or other technologies whose principal purpose or implementation is to cause or directly facilitate injury to people; (c) Technologies that gather or use information for surveillance violating internationally accepted norms; and (d) Technologies whose purpose contravenes widely accepted principles of international law and human rights.

IBM too announced that it would not pursue research and development of facial recognition technology for "mass surveillance, racial profiling, violations of basic human rights and freedom". The IBM CEO has called for a "national dialogue on whether and how facial recognition technology should be employed by domestic law enforcement agencies".[14]

Similarly, Korea Advanced Institute of Science and Technology (KAIST) decided to shelve projects associated with autonomous weapons systems after its scientists and academics engaged in the project announced boycotting the project.[15]

Although no country has openly declared that they are pursuing LAWS, states have made public their views on the issue. For instance, China has argued that LAWS merits the attention of the international community but it has not been clearly defined. Further, it supports, along with other States, prohibiting fully autonomous weapons on the battlefield but not their development.[16] This dichotomy has raised concerns about China's policy with regards to LAWS and has invited sharp reaction: "They're simultaneously working on the technology while trying to use international law as a limit against their competitors".[17]

The UK has endorsed and made public its policy not to "develop and use fully autonomous weapons, or weapons that can make decisions independent from human oversight".[18] In 2017, the British Minister of State for the Armed Forces had observed the issue from a doctrinal perspective and stated that it is "absolutely right that our weapons are operated by real people capable of making incredibly important decisions, and we are guaranteeing that vital oversight".[19]

Unlike China and the UK, the Russian submission to the GGE notes that the "preventive, prohibitive or restrictive measures against LAWS" are complex, and given the limited human understanding of these technologies, such a ban may not serve the purpose.[20] Although it is difficult to distinguish between civilian and military developments in autonomous systems, a ban on LAWS can preclude peaceful uses of these technologies.

The USA, according to a memo issued by US Defence Secretary, Mark Esper, has issued five guidelines and the Pentagon has pledged that military use by the USA of Artificial Intelligence will be (a) responsible; (b) equitable; (c) traceable; (d) reliable' and (e) governable.[21] Recalling Project Maven that was secretively launched, the head of the Joint Artificial Intelligence Centre has been reported saying that "We would be doing these AI ethics principles regardless of the angst in the tech industry....And sometimes I think the angst is a little hyped, but we do have people who have serious concerns about working with the Department of Defence".[22] Furthermore, "If we would have had the AI ethics principles three years ago...and our starting point with one of the big tech companies was that—and we were transparent about what we were trying to do and why we were trying to do it—maybe we would have had a different outcome".[23]

In India, the NITI Aayog has recommended setting up a "consortium of Ethics Councils at each Centre of Excellence...to define the standard practice (on the lines of Open AI charter). It would be expected that all Centres of Excellence adhere to standard practices while developing AI technology and products".[24]

International experts are of the view that a "legally binding instrument is the optimal framework for dealing with the many serious challenges raised by fully autonomous weapons" and a "new international ban treaty could lay down explicit rules to ensure appropriate constraints on autonomy in weapons systems and resolve differing views on human control over the use of force" which should impress upon States the "urgency to this existential threat to humanity".[25]

Autonomous Vessels

Industry experts believe that in the next five to ten years, remotely operated vessels will be out in the open sea, and unmanned ocean-going vessels could soon become a common sight. In this context, it has been observed that "the legal framework for unmanned shipping is still unprepared for this evolution and a large part of maritime laws and regulations are still dating back from the 19th century"[26] which necessitates a deeper understanding of the regulatory mechanism, particularly for remote controlled and autonomous shipping.[27] This may necessitate adjustments in the manning requirements contained in Article 94 (4b), 1982 UN Convention on the Law of the Sea to allow the vessel to sail without a human master.[28]

There are a number of important conventions for shipping such as (a) International Convention for the Safety of Life at Sea (SOLAS); (b) International Convention for the Prevention of Pollution from ships (MARPOL); (c) International Convention on Standards of Training, Certification and Watch-keeping for Seafarers (STCW); and (d) Convention on the International Regulations for Preventing Collisions at Sea (COLREGS). These cover numerous aspects of ships, crew, navigation, safety, and a host of other issues that regulate international shipping, and therefore would have to address the arrival of autonomous and unmanned types of vessels.

Debate: 'vessel' or 'ship'

One of the major issues for debate is whether an autonomous platform at sea is to be considered a vessel or a ship which is critical for the "determination of legal significance, as craft that so qualify have certain entitlements"[29] including registration and flying a civilian ensign. Currently, there is nothing in international law indicating that an autonomous platform cannot be considered a vessel or a ship and as a corollary, "there is also nothing that says they can, or must, be so considered".[30]

The terms 'ship' and 'vessel' appear to be synonymous in international law and the 1982 LoS uses them interchangeably giving an impression that the terms are synonymous. However, the International Convention for the Prevention of Pollution from Ships, 1973, as modified by the Protocol of 1978 (MARPOL), and was negotiated under the auspices of the International Maritime Organization (IMO), defines 'ship' to mean "a vessel of any type whatsoever operating in the marine environment and includes hydrofoil boats, air-cushion vehicles, submersibles, floating craft and fixed or floating platforms".[31] The Convention on the International Regulations for Preventing Collisions at Sea (1972) defines 'vessel' in Rule 3 as "every description of water craft, including non-displacement craft and sea-planes, used or capable of being used as a means of transportation on water".[32] Meanwhile, the Convention on Registration of Ships, defines "ship" to mean "any self-propelled sea-going vessel used in international seaborne trade for the transport of goods, passengers, or both with the exception of vessels of less than 500 gross registered tons".[33]

Article 94 poses a number of challenges to Unmanned Maritime Systems (UMSs) in the context of flying a flag, master and officers, training, qualifications, maintenance of communications ,etc., and therefore merits attention. For the USA, 'vessel' "includes every description of watercraft or other artificial contrivance used, or capable of being used, as a means of transportation on water".[34] In November 2017, the UK Ship Register signed its first ever unmanned vessel to the flag. The vessel can be used under direct control, semi-manned or completely unmanned and is designed for "subsea positioning, surveying and environmental monitoring"[35] and should trigger a number of debates on its legal status. For instance, "there is no uniform definition of the term vessel or ship in international maritime conventions but unmanned vessels will in most cases fall within the scope of the definitions used. Even if the unmanned vessel is covered by scope of the various conventions, the fact remains that most international conventions are drafted without consideration to unmanned vessels".[36]

In June 2017, nine countries (Denmark, Estonia, Finland, Japan, the Netherlands, Norway, South Korea, the United Kingdom and the USA) had raised with the IMO the issue of regulating autonomous shipping,[37] and had started the process of "mapping out how existing international regulations should be applied to the rapidly emerging field of self-driving ships and autonomous maritime technologies".[38]

However, in June 2020, it was noted that "international rules on the deployment and requirements are unlikely to be in force for more than 15 years despite rapid advances in robotics and a growing number of large vessel projects propelling the industry forward" and that "it was not likely that rule changes at the International Maritime Organization would appear until 2030', probably late 2030's", which should "allow the test beds to be developed to demonstrate the robustness of the technologies at the same time as the rule makers look at the regulations".[39]

Concluding Thoughts

It is evident that 4IR transformations can potentially challenge natural human values of fellow feeling, empathy and kindness. Before these technologies are welcomed, it is important to fully understand the value of human life and address the ethical issues. It is equally important that Artificial Intelligence should not become an 'unfettered and unbridled' destructive force of destruction, and therefore demands and necessitates a deeper understanding of regulatory mechanisms for 'killer robots' or similar platforms and technologies. As far as autonomous ships are concerned, as technology matures, they will be a common sight in the immediate future and would require regulatory and legal frameworks to facilitate safe and secure operations at sea.

NOTES

1. "New Technologies Demand New Laws and Ethics", http://www.ipcs.org/comm_select.php?articleNo=5457 (accessed 30 June 2020).
2. "Autonomous Weapon Systems: An Ethical Basis for Human Control?", https://blogs.icrc.org/law-and-policy/2018/04/03/autonomous-weapon-systems-ethical-basis-human-control/ (accessed 10 March 2020).
3. Ibid. Also see "Ethical Analysis of AI and Robotics Technologies", https://www.sienna-project.eu/digitalAssets/801/c_801912-l_1-k_d4.4_ethical-analysis--ai-and-r--with-acknowledgements.pdf (accessed 30 June 2020).
4. "Ray Kurzweil on the Promise and Peril of Technology in the 21st Century", https://www.cio.com/article/2441963/ray-kurzweil-on-the-promise-and-peril-of-technology-in-the-21st-century.html (accessed 30 June 2020).
5. "New Technologies Demand New Laws and Ethics", http://www.ipcs.org/comm_select.php?articleNo=5457 (accessed 10 April 2020).
6. "Group of Governmental Experts of the High Contracting Parties to the Convention on Prohibitions or Restrictions on the Use of Certain Conventional Weapons Which May Be Deemed to Be Excessively Injurious or to Have Indiscriminate Effects", https://undocs.org/CCW/GGE.1/2017/3 (accessed 10 April 2020).
7. "Autonomous Weapon Systems: An Ethical Basis for Human Control?", https://blogs.icrc.org/law-and-policy/2018/04/03/autonomous-weapon-systems-ethical-basis-human-control/ (accessed 10 April 2020).
8. Stopping Killer Robots: Country Positions on Banning Fully Autonomous Weapons and Retaining Human Control", https://www.hrw.org/report/2020/08/10/stopping-killer-

robots/country-positions-banning-fully-autonomous-weapons-and (accessed 10 August 2020).

9. Vijay Sakhuja, "New Technologies Demand New Laws and Ethics", http://www.ipcs.org/comm_select.php?articleNo=5457 (accessed 10 April 2020).
10. "ICRAC Statement at Informal Consultations of the August 2019 CCW GGE on LAWS"https://www.icrac.net/icrac-statement-at-informal-consultations-of-the-ccw-gge-on-laws/(accessed 10 April 2020).
11. "Google to Scrub US Military Deal Protested by Employees: Source", https://www.financialexpress.com/industry/google-to-scrub-us-military-deal-protested-by-employees-source/1190716/ (accessed 6 June 2020).
12. "AI at Google: our principles", https://blog.google/topics/ai/ai-principles/ (accessed 6 June 2020).
13. Ibid.
14. "IBM Will no Longer Offer or Develop Facial Recognition Software in Pursuit of Racial Justice Reform", https://www.forbes.com/sites/isabeltogoh/2020/06/09/ibm-will-no-longer-offer-or-develop-facial-recognition-software-in-pursuit-of-racial-justice-reform/?utm_campaign=forbes&utm_source=facebook&utm_medium=social&utm_term=Gordie/#20e7c6b11192 (accessed 9 June 2020).
15. "South Korean university's AI work for Defence Contractor Draws Boycott", https://www.bbc.com/news/technology-43653648 (accessed 27 February 2020).
16. "Group of Governmental Experts of the High Contracting Parties to the Convention on Prohibitions or Restrictions on the Use of Certain Conventional Weapons Which May Be Deemed to Be Excessively Injurious or to Have Indiscriminate Effects".
17. "China and the U.S. Are Fighting a Major Battle over Killer Robots and the Future of AI", https://time.com/5673240/china-killer-robots-weapons/ (accessed 06 June 2020).
18. "Following Elon Musk Letter, UK Government Plans to Ban Fully Autonomous Weapons", https://futurism.com/following-elon-musk-letter-uk-government-plans-to-ban-fully-autonomous-weapons (accessed 6 June 2020).
19. Ibid.
20. "Examination of Various Dimensions of Emerging technologies in the area of Lethal Autonomous Weapons Systems, in the context of the Objectives and Purposes of the Convention", https://www.unog.ch/80256EDD006B8954/(httpAssets)/2C67D752B299E6A7C12581D400661C98/$file/2017_GGEonLAWS_WP8_RussianFederation.pdf (accessed 6 June 2020).
21. Meghann Myers, "The Pentagon Promises to use Artificial Intelligence for Good, not Evil", https://www.militarytimes.com/news/your-military/2020/02/25/the-pentagon-promises-to-use-artificial-intelligence-for-good-not-evil/?utm_source=facebook.com&utm_campaign=Socialflow+MIL&utm_medium=social (accessed 27 February 2020).
22. "DoD Adopts AI Ethics Principles—But How Will They Be Enforced?", https://breakingdefense.com/2020/02/dod-adopts-ai-ethics-principles-but-how-will-they-be-enforced/ (accessed 28 February 2020).
23. Ibid.
24. "Discussion Paper: National Strategy for Artificial Intelligence", https://niti.gov.in/writereaddata/files/document_publication/NationalStrategy-for-AI-Discussion-Paper.pdf (accessed 11 June 2020).
25. Stopping Killer Robots: Country Positions on Banning Fully Autonomous Weapons and

Retaining Human Control", https://www.hrw.org/report/2020/08/10/stopping-killer-robots/country-positions-banning-fully-autonomous-weapons-and (accessed 10 August 2020).

26. Pol Deketelaere, "The Legal Challenges of Unmanned Vessels Student", https://lib.ugent.be/fulltxt/RUG01/002/349/671/RUG01-002349671_2017_0001_AC.pdf (accessed 15 December 2017).
27. "Disruptive Technologies Drive Sustainable Shipping", https://www.huffingtonpost.com/entry/disruptive-technologies-drive-sustainable-shipping_us_5924278ce4b07617ae4cbf6a (accessed 19 December 2017).
28. "Denmark Calls for IMO Rules for Autonomous Ships", https://maritime-executive.com/article/denmark-calls-for-imo-rules-for-autonomous-ships (accessed 26 December 2017).
29. Andrew Norris, "Legal Issues Relating to Unmanned Maritime Systems" , http://maritimeinside.com/2016/11/12/unmanned-vessels-is-the-current-legal-framework-adequate/(accessed 15 December 2017).
30. Ibid.
31. Andrew H. Henderson, "Murky Waters: The Legal Status of Unmanned Undersea Vehicles", http://www.sevenhorizons.org/docs/HendersonMurkyWaters.pdf (accessed 15 December 2017).
32. Llana and Wisneskey, *Handbook of the Nautical Rules of the Road,* http://navrules handbook.com/Rule3.html (accessed 15 December 2017).
33. United Nations Convention on Conditions for Registration of Ships, Geneva, 7 February 1986, http://www.admiraltylawguide.com/conven/registration1986.html(accessed 15 December 2019).
34. "General Provisions: Chapter 1 - Rules of Construction", https://www.law.cornell.edu/uscode/pdf/uscode01/lii_usc_TI_01_CH_1_SE_3.pdf (accessed 15 December 2019).
35. "First Unmanned Vessel Joins UK Ship Register", https://worldmaritimenews.com/archives/235207/first-unmanned-vessel-joins-uk-ship-register/(accessed 15 December 2019).
36. "Maritime Law in the Wake of the Unmanned Vessel", https://www.hellenicshippingnews.com/wp-content/uploads/2017/08/svw_maritime-law-in-the-wake-of-the-unmanned-vessel.pdf (accessed 15 December 2019).
37. "Unmanned Ships added to IMO Agenda", https://www.thedigitalship.com/news/maritime-satellite-communications/item/5014-unmanned-ships-added-to-imo-agenda (accessed 15 December 2020).
38. "IMO to Establish Legal Framework for Safe Operation of Autonomous Vessels", https://www.freightwaves.com/news/imo-to-establish-legal-framework-for-safe-operation-of-autonomous-vessels (accessed 15 December 2019); https://www.americanshipper.com/main/news/imo-to-establish-legal-framework-for-safe-operatio-67861.aspx (accessed 19 December 2019).
39. "No rules on Autonomous Ships for another 10 years – at least", https://fathom.world/no-rules-on-autonomous-ships-for-another-10-years-at-least/ (accessed 10 August 2020).

CHAPTER 9

Conclusion

This study has analysed the role of 4IR technologies in the maritime-commercial and military-naval domains. There is strong evidence that 4IR technologies will transform future operations at sea and ashore necessitating disruption of conventional understandings and formulations. Systematic incorporation of 4IR technologies in strategy processes, acquisition choices and human skill development would become increasingly imperative. It is therefore not surprising then that major shipping companies of the world are now investing financial and technological capital to respond to a new era of 4IR-enabled commercial operations. Similarly, many advanced navies are planning to invest in 4IR tools, tactics and methodologies for warfare as also to build up a highly skilled human resource to assimilate these technologies.

Maritime-Commercial

The discussions in the preceding chapters have clearly illustrated that 4IR is making several inroads into the ship-shore supply chain continuum and it will potentially shape the future of movement of goods across the oceans and the heartland. The maritime trading ecosystem built around ships, ports, freight vehicles (rail and road), industries, production houses and human will not only embrace 4IR technologies and maximise efficiency, but integrate 4IR as a 'way of life'.

There will be widespread use of the autonomous platform and equipment in port operations for loading and discharging of cargo, and movement of ships in harbour would be by autonomous tugs. Besides, there will be rapid data exchange between ships, terminals, shore-based transportation network and the end user for an efficient movement of transportation of goods with greater transparency and authenticity. Introduction of intelligent systems in ports, ships, rail and road networks and smart containers would eliminate paperwork and reduce processing times and smart business models and contracts will unlock huge advantages. The shipbuilding industry will also witness transformative changes resulting in low construction periods supported by robots and AI-enabled machines.

At the operational level, 4IR will empower merchant ships to attain higher levels of autonomy and improved decision making across operations and functions. 4IR-enabled maintenance tools will provide early warning of malfunctions for timely response, thereby reducing downtime and prevent disruption in supply chains.

The crew will be better equipped with requisite tools to optimize vessel operation and enable safe navigation to avoid accidents. 4IR-enabled operations would also help crews in obtaining improved visibility and interpretation of their surroundings in difficult weather conditions and reduce human error. Cloud-based operations and communications would transform shipping companies and enable them to maintain centralized data management systems in a highly efficient manner across global locations with multiple stakeholders.

Further, much of the human tasks will be conducted by Bots and Robots which would be a common sight—crawling, flying, sailing or swimming. Their numbers would surpass humans living on the Earth and it is plausible that their combined intelligence could be far higher and superior than that of the human population. Billions of machineries, equipment and sensors will be connected to the Internet. This will result in a smart integrated maritime ecosystem of sensors, data and Internet-enabled devices. Over the next 25 years, 'Internet of Everything' will emerge and enable us to manage commercial maritime operations in real time. Amid such predictions, there are fears that many tasks performed by humans will become redundant. Be that as it may, till then, the role of humans in the coming transformation will remain inescapable.

Naval Operations

Artificial Intelligence has already made its debut in the naval domain and its usage by modern militaries can be seen in combat, reconnaissance and surveillance, engineering, electrical operations and logistics management including supply chains. All this is rapidly increasing. In this context, Artificial Intelligence will fundamentally transform naval warfare from 'informatized' to 'intelligentized' and future warfare at sea will witness smart platforms take centre stage.

Swarm drones would gain popularity and their use will grow rapidly to perform numerous tasks and supporting operations such as reconnaissance, surveillance, strikes against enemy targets, electronic warfare through jamming, and other such missions. It is plausible that these can be targeted against major combat platforms at sea such as aircraft carriers through dive-bombing, much like the 'Kamikaze attacks' of the October 1944 Battle of Leyte Gulf, thus offering cheap options for attacking a powerful enemy. Likewise, underwater drones including swarm formations would operate autonomously and intelligently navigate to avoid obstacles to carry out reconnaissance and combat missions. Besides they can be used as decoys against submarines and act as scouts for submarines by gathering data, carrying out reconnaissance for submarines and carry explosives to detonate near enemy underwater platforms.

Future missiles will possess a high degree of artificial intelligence for a number of functions such as mission control, flight management, and target designation. It will be possible to overcome the limitations of 'fire and forget' and control them in real-time and redirect them to other tasks while in flight.

Similarly, 4IR will help in data fusion, synthesis of multi-source data and images, automated target recognition based on machine learning and intelligent sensing in a complex electromagnetic environment. Closely associated with it is the challenge of abundance of data and its retrieval and use. For this purpose, Bigdata analytics are important enablers that would be able to retrieve massive information, and, by using advanced computational capacity, make intelligent decisions. While it will be possible to achieve information and data superiority, human physical and psychological shortcomings could be compensated by an external and intelligent brain thereby augmenting battle space awareness for quick decision making and hasten the command-cycle by presenting recommendations to the commander.

There are also options to leverage Artificial Intelligence for advancing operational training and war-gaming. Innovative and challenging scenarios can be created which can offer unexpected tactics. These can be supplemented with augmented reality and virtual reality to overcome actual battlefield experience.

In essence, future warfare at sea will be highly 'intelligentized' and led by an integrated command platform that will draw on artificial intelligence, big data, machine learning, Cloud computing, etc. However, there are clear indications that human cognition will not be able to remain abreast of the speed of operations and would necessitate a new model of operations at sea in which artificial intelligence will have a greater role.

Furthermore, super-intelligent artificial intelligence can be expected to improve upon itself continuously and create another improved version of it. This will result in an 'intelligence explosion' and the 'simple, biological machines' that humans are will be left far behind. Whenever that happens, Singularity in naval warfare would have arrived and become a reality and would pose severe challenges to human power to micromanage and exercise authority.

Similarly, there will also be a major transformation in force structure choices. There are now clear trends among major navies to acquire 4IR-enabled unmanned and autonomous ships and craft that are capable of travelling long distances and detect and identify targets and open fire autonomously. Parallel developments are underway in the underwater and air-space domains featuring unmanned and autonomous platforms paving the way for contactless-remote warfare adding to complexity in offensive and defensive operations.

Many navies have established Cyber Commands or Cyber Units; however, they would soon have to set up specialist units to train and operate robots. This will give rise to a Drone Mothership that would act as the 'eyes and ears' of the fleet. It is also not farfetched to imagine specialist Robot Control Officers onboard ships.

However, 4IR technological developments and advancements must be followed very carefully. Artificial intelligence specialists believe that machines will match human intelligence by 2029 and will surpass it by 2045. It is therefore incumbent on the part of militaries to understand what Artificial Intelligence 'can do' as also how much it 'must do'. It is a complex issue and would require building human skills in strategic thinking, tactical planning and, importantly, having a deeper understanding of morals, empathy and ethics.

A '4IR technology rivalry' among the navies is already underway. Though competition is welcomed in the hope that it would generate a new product, 4IR competition is mired in geopolitical and geostrategic contestations. There is a sense of urgency among the navies to gain ascendency in the field of artificial intelligence and machine learning to obtain a favourable naval balance of power.

Finally, disruption would be the key feature of the future success of the commercial maritime ecosystem and navies will need to seek innovative technologies, evolve creative tactics and develop a new concept of operations to support disruption caused by the Fourth Industrial Revolution.

A large number of navies across the globe have internalized the concept of Sea Power and the writings of Rear Admiral Alfred Thayer Mahan, United States Navy, through his most famous work, *The Influence of Sea Power Upon History 1660-1783*, are frequently recalled. His thesis was that no nation could aspire to be a great power unless it effectively used the sea for both commercial and military purposes. The Mahanian thought on Sea Power was a product of the First Industrial Revolution (18th century-Steam power) and over the last three centuries, three industrial revolutions have impacted mankind, i.e., the Second Industrial Revolution (19th century—Electricity); the Third Industrial Revolution (20th century—Electronics) and now in the 21st century we are experiencing extreme automation led by microchips and super computation led by artificial intelligence with impending 'superhuman intelligence'.

In this context, 21st century Sea Power could be led by Singularity when super-intelligent artificial intelligence can be expected to improve upon itself continuously and create another improved version of it. Masayosi Son believes that "Those who rule chips will rule the entire world. Those who rule data will rule the entire world. That's what people of the future will say."

It is fair to argue that disruptive thinking challenges dogmas, promotes unconventional thinking, moves us from 'out of the box' to 'without the box' approaches, for which the maritime and the naval sectors must 'first unwire, and then retool and re-skill' to emerge as better placed for operational and organisational successes in the 4IR environment.

Policy Recommendations

Flowing from the discussions and analysis contained in this study, a set of recommendations is offered. These have been placed in two baskets and can potentially trigger proactive and facilitative policy prescriptions for the growth of a number of vectors in the commercial-maritime and military-naval domains.

Commercial-Maritime Operations

India is a maritime state and 90 per cent of its external trade by volume and 70 per cent by value are carried on ships. Over 200 ports (12 major ports and approximately 200 non-major ports) spread along the 7,516 kilometre-long coastline handle a variety of vessels such as dry cargo, oil and gas, containers, fishing vessels and cruise liners. The maritime trade has been expanding and the focus is on infrastructure development and capacity enhancement of the maritime ecosystem. The Sagarmala Programme (2015-2035) is a flagship initiative of the current government and features port-led development. Furthermore, India's ranking in 'Ease of Doing Business' is noteworthy and it is currently 77th among 190 countries.

Ports

Many major ports across the globe are designing innovative business models not only to lower operational costs but also to add efficiency through real-time tracking and tracing of shipments using 4IR tools and technologies. Lloyd's List, a major maritime conglomerate, is of the view that there would be trade expansion through port infrastructure investment in the South Asia, Middle East and Africa (SAMEA) region and smaller ports would be the 'game-changer' for trade. Further, new global Blockchain initiatives by major shipping companies necessitate data synchronization within the maritime ecosystem and across the value chain which is becoming critical. Some industry experts believe that "smart ports are the only ports that will survive." At least three ports (Colombo Port in Sri Lanka, Jebel Ali, Dubai in UAE and one in Singapore) in the Indian Ocean region are among the top 20 container ports and have plans to graduate towards 'Smart Ports'.

The Indian Government has promoted 'digital India' and a few Indian ports are pursuing this objective in full earnest. The Jawaharlal Nehru Port Trust (JNPT) ranks 32nd among the top 50 ports in the world. It has adopted reforms and pursued innovations through digital technologies and there is a push towards "AI-led restructuring of the ports-logistics sector" for automated management of cargo movements, and vessel-port-vehicle traffic management through data based analytics, GPS and image-recognition technologies.

Another significant move towards digitalization is that India has moved towards electronic Port Community System (PCS) under which bills of lading and other trade documentation workflows will use a Blockchain platform for document transfer. Its 'Portall Infosystems' is functional at 19 ports and connects 16,000 corporate stakeholders, including India's 13 major ports.

(a) Indian ports would have to quickly adapt to the ongoing transformation in the port ecosystem that is rapidly absorbing 4IR technologies to enable them to remain competitive at national and international levels.

(b) Logistic corridors based on an e-commerce model merit attention and must be encouraged.

Shipbuilding

There are 28 shipyards in the county capable of building ocean-going and coastal vessels and warships for the Indian Navy and the Coast Guard. The largest, Cochin Shipyard Ltd., is capable of building ships up to 110,000 DWT and repairing vessels up to 125,00) DWT. Also, a number of private shipyards have made their debut in the domestic shipbuilding market and ABG Shipyard, Pipavav Shipyard, and Bharati Shipyard are ranked in the global Top 150. There are plans to set up two international quality shipyards and the National Ship Design Research Centre (NSDRC) is the backbone for design and research.

(a) China, Japan and Korea are leading the Smart Ship segment in Asia and NSRDC can explore joint shipbuilding projects with the last two.
(b) Use of Robots to improve efficiency, reduce errors, and perform dangerous tasks such as welding, painting, and heavy lifting are critical for improving the output of shipyards.
(c) Innovative technologies such as 3D printing would add to the efficiency of the shipbuilding ancillary industry.
(d) Indian shipyards will have to rely on skilled human resources which is not only proficient in various tasks related to shipbuilding but conversant with 4IR-enabled tools and devices.

Shipping

Indian shipping accounts for 1,019 vessels (1.27 per cent of the world's total) of which 854 vessels were under the national flag and 165 are foreign-flagged vessels (UNCTAD, 2019). However, no Indian shipping company is listed among the top 30 global liner companies.

(a) Use 4IR technologies such as artificial intelligence, Blockchain and Bigdata for managing shipping operations to remain globally competitive.
(b) Encourage stakeholders such as freight forwarders, shipping agents and supply chain managers to familiarize and train in 4IR technologies concerning shipping operations.

Inland Water Transport

Inland waterway transport (IWT) provides an efficient, flexible and cost-effective network of transportation. The Government has encouraged States to optimally utilize the natural geography and build up the IWT sector. The annual requirement is of nearly 200 inland vessels for inland waterways.

(a) IWT sector offers unique opportunities for operating AI-enabled unmanned and autonomous vessels.
(b) Blockchain and IoT network of sensors is a useful tool to monitor and track river water systems.
(c) Remote sensing devices, static sensors and remotely controlled or autonomous piloted platforms can help measure, record and transmit in real time a variety of data concerning vessels and the river.

Marine Awareness and Skill Development

(a) Vocational institutions are critical for promoting, training and skilling workers with 4IR tool kits to support maritime industry.
(b) Sector-specific 4IR technology talent development is imperative for a number of white (administrative and institutional) and blue (products and services) collar jobs.
(c) 4IR technologies can potentially plug the gap between demand and supply of the new generation of marine professionals and technicians.
(d) The role of entrepreneurs, start-ups and medium and small enterprises cannot be underestimated. In this context, a national agenda of '4IR skill development' dovetailed into 'make in India' and 'digital India' would support the development of a smart commercial maritime ecosystem.

Military-Naval Operations

Prime Minister Narendra Modi has made a clarion call for 'Make in India' and 'Atma Nirbhar Bharat' (self-reliant India) and called on the Indian armed forces to internalize these as the twin mantras in defence technology development and production of military hardware. Defence Minister Rajnath Singh and General Bipin Rawat, the Chief of the Defence Staff, have reiterated Prime Minister Modi's thoughts and urged the Indian military to internalize them. The Finance Minister too has echoed the above guidance, and announced policy reforms in the defence sector by raising the Foreign Direct Investment (FDI) cap through the automatic route from 49 per cent to 74 per cent. The Ministry of Defence has also announced INR 400 crore for Defence Testing Infrastructure Scheme (DTIS) under which six to eight testing facilities for domestic defence and aerospace equipment will be set up.

Policy

(a) The Department of Military Affairs (DMA), Integrated Defence Staff (IDS) of the Ministry of Defence and the Defence Research and Development Organisation (DRDO) should formulate a 'Strategic 4IR Technology Vision for Defence' and prepare a road map for development and integration of 4IR technologies across the Indian armed forces. This would necessitate a policy framework to integrate existing structures and institutions engaged in developing strategic 4IR technologies to support the national Vision. A consistent dialogue between policy makers and the military is essential that would help in distinctive policies for the planning, development and budgeting for 4IR technologies, platforms and devices including autonomous weapons systems and for cyber warfare.

(b) The DRDO and industry would have to internalize 'disruption' as the 'way to go' and engage in innovative thinking to ensure development and 'delivery of enablers' for a 4IR-driven warfare. A DRDO-Industry-4IR interconnection through the Confederation of Indian Industry (CII), Federation of Indian Chambers of Commerce and Industry (FICCI), and the Associated Chambers of Commerce of India (ASSOCHAM) would be a useful initiative that would help identify numerous Micro, Small and Medium Enterprises (MSME), start-ups, entrepreneurs and technology-related educational and research institutions including designers and engineers from civil sources with appropriate knowledge and expertise in the field of 4IR to provide support.

Civil-Military Interface

(c) Financial incentives are a must to engage specialist companies, start-ups and research institutions to ensure targeted capacity development. This is critical and becomes particularly important given that the DRDO does not possess a large capacity and necessary resources to undertake all 4IR-related requirements of the Indian armed forces for developing advanced capabilities.

(d) With defence budgets taking a hit, most advanced militaries are prioritizing investments in Artificial Intelligence and robotics research and development. The Integrated Defence Staff (IDS) of the Ministry of Defence could pursue crowd sourcing of ideas and technology by organizing hakathon/hackfest/codefest and 3D printer competitions. This would help identify skilled human resources to support the military requirements of 4IR technology.

(e) 'Test basin' and 'platforms for testing' 4IR-enabled prototypes are critical for the Indian Navy. The government has allocated Rs. 400 crore for the Defence Testing Infrastructure Scheme (DTIS). Further, the government plans to set up six to eight test facilities in partnership with private industry in two Defence Industrial Corridors (DICs), one each in Tamil Nadu and Uttar Pradesh. The Indian Navy may require its own specialist test basin; likewise, it would require a "dedicated platform" for testing devices or it may explore to repurpose an existing platform to serve as a Mother Ship.

Force Planning, Operations and Training

(f) The unmanned arms race has already begun and the Indian Navy would have to reassess its future requirements of conventional assets. The remedy lies in both rethinking priorities as also the design of future ship classes focused on 4IR, i.e., explore transitioning from manned fleet infrastructure (large manned platforms to smaller platforms) to a mix of both manned and unmanned platforms.

(g) At the operational level, a sample deployment (manned and unmanned) vessels could be attempted under the Mission Based Deployment of the Indian Navy and these could be equipped with 'mission modules' for tasks such as ISR and EW. Future platforms would be of a unique modular architecture and highly automated. Naval plans for acquisition should allow for new capabilities to ensure a cutting edge naval force.

(h) AR/VR/MR is a revolutionary technology and has enormous potential for a variety of naval functions that span tactical operations, training, maintenance and supply chain management. At the operational level it can be a game changer for situational awareness and improve decision-making in complex battle environments. Adopting AR can also help achieve information superiority over opponents.

(i) The use of wearable technologies (smart watches, smart glasses, health monitors, and activity trackers) will soon become a reality to perform a number of tasks and the Indian Navy must begin to socialize them as part of special gear. There are algorithms that integrate signal detection, data processing and sensor fusion. With wearable devices, it is possible to send data to a command post for analysis and augment decision-making in complex environments.

(j) It would also require training and preparing personnel with the skills needed to become habituated to 4IR technologies and succeed in this new age of 4IR-enabled warfare. The initiative calls for prioritizing training programs in Science, Technology, Engineering, and Math (STEM) and computer science.

Defence Budget

(k) Budgetary allocation for the Indian Navy has been declining and the leadership has often argued for a "long time fiscal support to build a Navy" given that warship building is a capital-intensive activity. Given that naval allocations in the defence budget are unlikely to register a major jump, prudence necessitates a disruptive approach in force structure plans, operations and organisation.

(l) The austerity could be an opportunity for the Indian Navy to explore an in-house "Naval Innovation Fund" to quickly enable a transition of technology from the private sector under a novel programme which can be labelled as a "great naval idea" which will encourage SMEs and MSMEs to pursue maritime/naval projects

(m) Future naval budget submissions should include allocations for research and development and acquisition of deployable prototypes of unmanned vessels directly from the industry.

Bilateral Naval Engagements

(n) The Indian Navy should explore the possibility of studying the use of 4IR technologies during the Malabar series of joint naval exercises with the US Navy. For instance, US Defence Secretary Mark Esper announced that the USA "together with our allies and partners, must accelerate the adoption of AI and lead in its national security applications to maintain our strategic position, prevail on future battlefields, and safeguard the rule-based international order." Similarly, the other institutionalized naval engagements with the British Royal Navy and the French Navy merit attention.

Finally, the Indian Navy must plan a superior integrated naval force for the next decade and beyond. It would have to be necessarily 'lightly manned', yet brisling with '4IR technologies', that would serve both as the 'ordnance' and tool of 'deterrence'. This would require an imaginative yet powerful matrix of naval requirements, costs and military industrial complex that can produce/ support 4IR-enabled naval platforms.

Under the circumstances, the 'status quo' would have to be discarded and replaced by disruptive thinking. It can be achieved by overcoming bureaucratic constraints through smarter processes of decision making, clearer thinking by the Indian Navy of the future 4IR-led naval environment, and importantly a sustained support from industry.

APPENDIX

4IR Technology Industry Markets and Trends

Industry 4.0

"The Industry 4.0 market is estimated to be valued at USD 71.7 billion in 2019 and is expected to reach USD 156.6 billion by 2024, at a CAGR of 16.9 per cent from 2019 to 2024. Increasing adoption of the industrial Internet worldwide in manufacturing units, growing focus on enhanced efficiency of machinery and systems, and reduced production costs play a significant role in the growth of the market worldwide. Also, the growing demand for industrial robotics is expected to fuel the growth of the Industry 4.0 market".[1]

Artificial Intelligence

The market size of AI in the military domain is expected to reach US$ 18.82 billion by 2025, at a CAGR of 14.75 per cent from 2017 to 2025.[2]

Machine Learning

"The global machine learning market is expected to grow from USD 1.41 billion in 2017 to USD 8.81 billion by 2022, at a Compound Annual Growth Rate (CAGR) of 44.1 per cent. The main driving factors for the market are proliferation in data generation and technological advancement".[3]

Bigdata

"The global big data market size is set to grow from USD 138.9 billion in 2020 to USD 229.4 billion by 2025, at a Compound Annual Growth Rate (CAGR) of 10.6 per cent during the forecast period".[4]

Maritime Analytics

"The maritime analytics market is expected to register a CAGR of 16.82 per cent over the forecast period (2020-2025). The continuously evolving nature of the shipping industry is making the global economy and technical innovations pose new challenges and opportunities".[5]

Blockchain

The militaries too see several uses and it will become an important technology for a number of other naval activities and operations. The current trends in the use of Blockchain technology are indeed very promising and the Blockchain market is estimated to grow to over US$ 23.3 billion in size by 2023.[6]

Virtual Reality and Augmented Reality

"The virtual reality market was valued at USD 5.12 billion in 2017 and is expected to reach USD 34.08 billion by 2023, at a CAGR of 33.95 per cent, between 2018 and 2023".[7] The Augmented Reality Market is estimated to grow from USD 10.7 billion in 2019 and projected to reach USD 72.7 billion by 2024; it is expected to grow at a CAGR of 46.6 per cent from 2019 to 2024.[8]

Additive Manufacturing or 3D Printing Technology

According to a survey of manufacturers of 3D printers in 2014, the market share of printer sales in the industrial sector was 12 per cent for aerospace and 5 per cent for the maritime sector. The global aerospace 3D printing market size is projected to reach USD 6.74 billion by 2026, exhibiting a CAGR of 22.17 per cent during the forecast period.[9] The growing interest in 3D printing for space applications is expected to generate new avenues of expansion in this market, according to Fortune Business Insights™.[10] The report states that the market value was at USD 1.35 billion in 2018.

5G or Fifth Generation Wireless Communications Technologies

The number of IoT-connected devices across the globe will grow from 7.6 billion in 2019 to 24.1 billion in 2030.[11] Experts are of the view that future networks could be transmitting zettabytes (ZB) of data and by 2025 the "storage industry will ship 42 ZB of capacity over the next seven years (beginning 2018); 90 ZB of data will be created on IoT devices by 2025; 49 per cent of data will be stored in public Cloud environments; and nearly 30 per cent of the data generated will be consumed in real-time by 2025".[12] "The global market for

5G technology is projected to reach USD 5.53 billion in 2020, reaching USD 667.90 billion by 2026, showing a CAGR of 122.3 per cent from 2021 to 2026".[13]

Submarine Fibre Optic Cables

The global demand for cable networks is growing and, according to a market report, the submarine cable system market will touch US$ 22.0 billion by 2025 from US$ 10.3 billion in 2019; it is expected to grow at a CAGR of 11.1 per cent from 2020 to 2025" due to "surge in global bandwidth demand, increasing Internet connection worldwide, increasing new offshore wind capacity additions, and growing demand for inter-country and island connections are the key factors driving the growth of the submarine cable system market".[14]

Data Storage

"The global next-generation data storage market size was valued at USD 53.1 billion in 2018 and is expected to grow at a compound annual growth rate (CAGR) of 12.5 per cent from 2019 to 2025".[15]

Wearable Technologies

According to market data, the wearable (smart watches, smart clothing, eyewear, headwear, and footwear) market is expected to grow by US$ 35.48 billion during 2020-2024, progressing at a CAGR of 13 per cent during the forecast period.[16]

Quantum Computing

"The overall quantum computing market is expected to grow from USD 93 million by 2019 to USD 283 million by 2024 at a CAGR of 24.9 per cent.[17]

Global Military UAV Market

The global military UAV market is set to grow from US$ 10.9 billion in 2019 to US$ 14.8 billion in 2029 at a compound annual growth rate (CAGR) of 3.14 per cent.[18] Similarly, the drone market is set to grow in value from US$ 7.93 billion in 2018 to US$ 21.76 billion by 2026 at a CAGR of 12.4 per cent during the forecast period.[19]

The anti-drone market is expected to grow from US$ 342.6 million in 2016 to US$ 1,571.3 million by 2023, at a compound annual growth rate (CAGR) of 25.9 per cent between 2017 and 2023.[20]

Autonomous Ships

By 2020, there could be nearly 100 autonomously-operated vessels[21] and by 2025 the number could be of the order of nearly 1,000 autonomous vessels and as many as 2,000 semi-autonomous vessels. The market trends for autonomous ships are indeed very encouraging and according to an estimate, this segment is "estimated to be USD 6.1 billion in 2018 and is projected to reach USD 13.8 billion by 2030, at a CAGR of 7.00 per cent from 2018 to 2030".[22]

Automatic Weapons

The adoption of automatic weapons by land and marine forces is growing with rising cross-border activities globally. The Global Automatic Weapons Market is estimated to account for US$ 6.61 billion in 2018 and is expected to grow at a CAGR of 9.9 per cent during the forecast period 2018 – 2027, to account to US$ 14.95 billion by 2027".[23]

Biomimetics

There has been a surge in the number of patents for biomimetic technologies and from fewer than 500 in 1997 these have grown almost 7,000 by 2017.[24]

Digital Twinning

The market trends for Digital Twinning are very promising and according to a report, "Up to 89 per cent of all IoT platforms will contain some form of Digital Twinning capability by 2025".

Cloud Computing

"The global Cloud computing market size is expected to grow from USD 371.4 billion in 2020 to USD 832.1 billion by 2025 at a Compound Annual Growth Rate (CAGR) of 17.5 per cent during the forecast period".[25]

Chatbots

The global market for automated navigation is expected to grow to $78.8 billion in 2025, according to the British firm, Credence Research, or more than 25 times the 2018 figure. About 2,000 accidents occur at sea each year, with 70 per cent caused by human error.[26]

Smart Ports

The future global market for the smart port segment is very encouraging and is projected to touch US$ 5.3 billion by 2024 from an estimated US$ 1.7 billion in 2019, at a CAGR of 25 per cent; in this, the Blockchain segment (control over the information, privacy of the user and prevention of manipulation of data) is expected to be the fastest-growing market during this period.[27]

Global Shipbuilding

In 2018, the global shipbuilding market size amounted to roughly 114.3 billion US dollars. By 2025, this market is expected to exceed 175 billion US dollars, increasing at a compound annual growth rate of 5.7 per cent.[28]

Indian Shipbuilding

The Indian shipbuilding industry would grow at a CAGR of 30 per cent through 2020, achieving a total value of $22.1 billion. This represents 4.6 per cent of the global order book. Further, job opportunities within the Indian shipbuilding industry are forecast to rise at 20 per cent, with the potential of employing more than 171,000 people by 2020. Besides, the 34 dry docks for ship repair in the public and private sectors add to business opportunities.

NOTES

1. "Industry 4.0 Market by Technology (IoT, Artificial Intelligence, Industrial Metrology, Industrial Robotics, AR & VR, Blockchain, 3D Printing, Digital Twin, and 5G – Offering, Application, and End Users) and Geography- Global Forecast to 2024", https://www.marketsandmarkets.com/Market-Reports/industry-4-market-102536746.html (accessed 4 August 2020).
2. "8 Key Military Applications for Artificial Intelligence in 2018", https://blog.marketresearch.com/8-key-military-applications-for-artificial-intelligence-in-2018 (accessed 24 February 2020).
3. "Machine Learning Market by Vertical (BFSI, Healthcare and Life Sciences, Retail, Telecommunication, Government and Defence, Manufacturing, Energy and Utilities), Deployment Mode, Service, Organization Size, and Region - Global Forecast to 2022", https://www.marketsandmarkets.com/Market-Reports/machine-learning-market-263397704.html#:~:text=Available%20Customizations&text=The%20global%20machine%20learning%20market,data%20generation%20and%20technological%20advancement. (accessed 4 August 2020).
4. "Big Data Market by Component, Deployment Mode, Organization Size, Business Function (Operations, Finance, and Marketing and Sales), Industry Vertical (BFSI, Manufacturing, and Healthcare and Life Sciences), and Region - Global Forecast to 2025", https://www.marketsandmarkets.com/Market-Reports/big-data-market-1068.html#:~:text=Big%20Data%20market%3F-,The%20global%20big%20data%20market%20size%20 to

%20grow%20from%20USD,10.6%25%20during%20the%20forecast%20period. (accessed 4 August 2020).

5. "Maritime Analytics Market - Growth, Trends, And Forecast (2020 - 2025)", https://www.mordorintelligence.com/industry-reports/maritime-analytics-market (accessed 4 August 2020).
6. "Size of the Blockchain Technology Market Worldwide from 2018 to 2023", https://www.statista.com/statistics/647231/worldwide-blockchain-technology-market-size/ (accessed 23 November 2019).
7. "Augmented Reality and Virtual Reality Market by Offering (Hardware & Software), Device Type (HMD, HUD, Handheld Device, Gesture Tracking), Application (Enterprise, Consumer, Commercial, Healthcare, Automotive), and Geography - Global Forecast to 2023", https://www.marketsandmarkets.com/Market-Reports/augmented-reality-virtual-reality-market-1185.html#:~:text=%5B249%20Pages%20Report%5D%20 Augmented %20 Reality,objects%20accurately%20in %20real%2Dtime.&text=The%20virtual%20 reality%20market%20was,%25%2C%20between%202018%20and%202023 (accessed 4 August 2020).
8. "Augmented Reality Market by Offering (Hardware (Sensor, Displays & Projectors, Cameras), Software), Device Type (Head-mounted, Head-up), Application (Enterprise, Consumer, Commercial, Healthcare, Automotive), and Region - Global Forecast to 2024", https://www.google.com/search?sxsrf=ALeKk03ndMiNlOVYYUyk WPqGMmBREHNJNw%3 A1596516125168&ei=HecoX6nrCdre9QPns6-4Aw&q=augmented+reality+ market+ report&oq= augmented+ reality+ market+report&gs_lcp=CgZwc3ktYWIQA RgBMgYIA BAH EB4yAggAOgcIABBHELADUJVCWJVCYI5ZaAFwAHgAgAGHAYgBhwGSAQ MwLjGYAQCgAQGqAQdnd3Mtd2l6wAEB&sclient=psy-ab(accessed 4 August 2020).
9. "Aerospace-3d-printing-market", https://www.fortunebusinessinsights.com/industry-reports/infographics/aerospace-3d-printing-market-101613 (accessed 4 August 2020).
10. "Aerospace 3D Printing Market Size, COVID19 Impact Analysis, Industry Growth Forecast, 2019-2026, Says Fortune Business Insights™", https://www.globenewswire.com/news-release/2020/06/04/2043879/0/en/Aerospace-3D-Printing-Market-Size-COVID19-Impact-Analysis-Industry-Growth-Forecast-2019-2026-Says-Fortune-Business-Insights.html (accessed 6 June 2020).
11. "The IoT in 2030: 24 billion Connected Things Generating $1.5 trillion", https://iotbusinessnews.com/2020/05/20/03177-the-iot-in-2030-24-billion-connected-things-generating-1-5-trillion/#:~:text=The%20IoT%20in%202030%3A%2024%20 billion%20 connected %20things%20generating%20%241.5%20trillion,-Posted%20by%20IoT& text=By%20Matt%20Hatton%2C%20Founding%20Partner,USD465 %20billion%20 to%20over%20USD1. (accessed 6 June 2020).
12. "IDC: Expect 175 zettabytes of data worldwide by 2025", https://www.networkworld.com/article/3325397/idc-expect-175-zettabytes-of-data-worldwide-by-2025.html (accessed 21 April 2020).
13. "5G Technology Market Size is Expected to Reach USD 667.90 billion by 2026, Valuates Reports", https://www.prnewswire.com/news-releases/5g-technology-market-size-is-expected-to-reach-usd-667-90-billion-by-2026--valuates-reports-301007406.html (accessed 4 August 2020).
14. "Submarine Cable System Market by Application (Communication (Component, Offering (Installation & Commissioning, Upgrades)), Power (Type, Voltage, End User (Offshore

Wind Power Generation, Offshore Oil & Gas), and Region - Global Forecast to 2025", https://www.businesswire.com/news/home/20200317005632/en/Global-Submarine-Cable-System-Market-2020-2025

15. "Next-generation Data Storage Market Size, Share & Trends Analysis Report By Technology, By Technique (Direct-attached Storage, Network-attached Storage), By Type, By End User, By Region, And Segment Forecasts, 2019 – 2025", https://www.grandviewresearch.com/industry-analysis/next-generation-data-storage-market (accessed 4 August 2020).
16. "Wearable Technology Market 2020-2024", https://www.businesswire.com/news/home/20200207005233/en/Wearable-Technology-Market-2020-2024-Popularity-Wearable-Devices (accessed 21 April 2020).
17. "Quantum Computing Market by Offering (Systems and Consulting Solutions), End-User Industry, and Geography; QCaaS Market by Application (Optimization, Machine Learning, and Material Simulation) and Geography - Global Forecast to 2024", https://www.marketsandmarkets.com/Market-Reports/quantum-computing-market-144888301.html (accessed 4 August 2020).
18. "The Global Military UAV Market 2019-2029", https://www.globenewswire.com/news-release/2019/10/22/1933394/0/en/The-Global-Military-UAV-Market-2019-2029.html (accessed 24 March 2020).
19. "Military Drone Market Size to Reach USD 21.76 billion by 2026; Introduction to Advanced Technology Will Boost Growth, says Fortune Business Insights", https://www.globenewswire.com/news-release/2020/02/17/1985673/0/en/Military-Drone-Market-Size-to-Reach-USD-21-76-Billion-by-2026-Introduction-to-Advanced-Technology-Will-Boost-Growth-says-Fortune-Business-Insights.html (accessed 24 March 2020).
20. "Anti-drone Market", https://www.marketsandmarkets.com/PressReleases/anti-drone.asp (accessed 24 February 2020).
21. "Seafarers and Digital Disruption", https://www.ics-shipping.org/docs/default-source/resources/ics-study-on-seafarers-and-digital-disruption.pdf?sfvrsn=3(accessed 21 September 2019).
22. "Autonomous Ships Market", https://www.marketsandmarkets.com/Market-Reports/autonomous-ships-market-267183224.html (accessed 24 September 2019).
23. "Automatic Weapons Market Trends, Business Growth, Leading Players and Forecast 2027", https://3wnews.org/news/1371677/automatic-weapons-market-trends-business-growth-leading-players-and-forecast-2027/ (accessed 16 June 2020).
24. "Can Biomimicry Save The Planet? This Exhibition Shows The Green Side Of Tech—And Exposes The Greenwashing", https://www.forbes.com/sites/jonathonkeats/2020/07/28/biomimicry-moda/#4921ec525887 (accessed 30 July 2020).
25. "Cloud Computing Market by Service Model (Infrastructure as a Service (IaaS), Platform as a Service (PaaS), and Software as a Service (SaaS)), Deployment Model (Public and Private), Organization Size, Vertical, and Region - Global Forecast to 2025", https://www.marketsandmarkets.com/Market-Reports/cloud-computing-market-234.html#:~:text=cloud%20computing%20market%3F-,The%20global%20cloud%20computing%20market%20size%20is%20 expected%20to%20grow,17.5%25%20during%20the%20forecast%20period. (accessed 4 August 2020).
26. "Mitsui OSK Charts Course to Remote Ship Navigation with Big Data", https://asia.nikkei.com/Business/Transportation/Mitsui-OSK-charts-course-to-remote-ship-navigation-with-big-data (accessed 4 June 2020).

27. "Worldwide Smart Ports Market Insights (2019-2024): Big Data Analytics, IoT, and AI to Transform Port Operations", https://www.globenewswire.com/news-release/2019/08/08/1899479/0/en/Worldwide-Smart-Ports-Market-Insights-2019-2024-Big-Data-Analytics-IoT-and-AI-to-Transform-Port-Operations.html (accessed 21 September 2019).
28. "Size of the Global Shipbuilding Market in 2018 with a Forecast for 2019 to 2025", https://www.statista.com/statistics/1102252/size-of-the-global-shipbuilding-market/ (accessed 4 August 2020).

Selected Bibliography

Primary Sources

The White House, Executive Order 13859, Executive Order on Maintaining American,

Leadership in Artificial Intelligence, February 11, 2019.

Indian Naval Doctrine for Information Warfare, Information Warfare Cell, Naval Headquarters, New Delhi, 2001,

United Nations, "Review of Maritime Transport 2017", http://unctad.org/en/PublicationsLibrary/rmt2017_en.pdf

US Department of Defence, "Summary of the 2018 Department of Defence Artificial Intelligence Strategy: Harnessing AI to Advance Our Security and Prosperity", https://media.defense.gov/2019/Feb/12/2002088963/-1/-1/1/SUMMARY-OF-DOD-AI-STRATEGY.PDF

US, "Report to Congress on Navy Large Unmanned Surface and Undersea Vehicles", https://news.usni.org/2019/06/11/report-to-congress-on-navy-large-unmanned-surface-and-undersea-vehicles?fbclid=IwAR2COlubN-Eb5HmEvu1vo1ORx-LpsChj9Z7TkfDrgBbhvrX958WdgOJ_0KA

Secondary Sources

Books and e-books

Boukis, Christos, Aristodemos Pnevmatikakis & Lazaros Polymenakos, (eds) *Artificial Intelligence and Innovations 2007: From Theory to Applications* (New York: Springer, 2007).

Brümmerstedt, Katrin, Fraunhofer-Gesellschaft, Ralf Fiedler, Verena Flitsch, Hendrik Roreger, Benjamin Sarpong, Benjamin Scharfenberg & Fraunhofer

Verlag, *Digitalization of Seaports - Visions of the Future* (Fraunhofer Verlag, 2017).

Geerlings, Harry; Bart Kuipers & Rob Zuidwijk (eds) 'Ports and Networks: Strategies, Operations and Perspectives', https://books.google.co.in/books?id=pI84DwAAQBAJ&printsec=frontcover&dq=smart+ports&hl=en&sa=X&ved=2ahUKEwjX44T_loPrAhUZXisKHb_mC8UQ6AEwCHoECAYQAg#v=onepage&q=smart%20ports&f=false

Girasa, Rosario, *Artificial Intelligence as a Disruptive Technology: Economic Transformation* (New York: Springer, 2020).

Jackson, John E., *One Nation, Under Drones: Legality, Morality, and Utility of Unmanned Combat Systems* (USA: Naval Institute Press, 2018).

Jensen, Lars, 'Liner Shipping 2025: How to Survive and Thrive' (CreateSpace Independent Publishing Platform, 2017).

Kujala, Pentti & Liangliang Lu Marine (eds), Design XIII: Proceedings of the 13th International Marine Design https://books.google.co.in/books?id=b2C1 DwAAQBAJ &pg=PA 897&dq=big+data+shipping&hl=en&sa=X&ved=2ahUKEwiv1M abpIPrAhUEfSsKHR14CecQ6AEwAXoECAMQAg#v=onepage&q=big%20data%20shipping&f=false

Levit, Alexandra, *Humanity Works: Merging Technologies and People for the Workforce of the Future* (London: Kogan Page, 2019).

National Research Council, Division of Engineering and Physical Sciences, Naval Studies Board, Committee on Autonomous Vehicles in Support of Naval Operations, *Autonomous Vehicles in Support of Naval Operations,*

https://books.google.co.in/books?id=kcebAgAAQBAJ&pg=PA15&dq=drones+naval+operations&hl=en&sa=X&ved=2ahUKEwjYo53hp4PrAhUal EsFHQJOCREQ6 AEwAHoECAI QAg#v=onepage&q=drones%20naval%20operations&f=false

Pathak, Ashok, *India's Strategies for Information War & Cyber Deterrence* (New Delhi: Vitasta Publishing Private Limited, 2019).

Pauli, Gunter, *Blue Economy: 10 Years, 100 Innovations, 100 Million Jobs* (New Mexico: Paradigm Publications, 2010).

Sakhuja, Vijay, *Asian Maritime Power in the 21st Century: Strategic Transactions: China, India and Southeast Asia* (Singapore: ISEAS–Yusof Ishak Institute, 2011).

Shen, Xuemin and Tingting Yang, Mission-Critical Application Driven Intelligent Maritime Networks https://books.google.co.in/books?id=38Dc

DwAAQ BAJ&pg=PA2&dq=5G+maritime&hl=en&sa=X&ved=2ahUKEwiQofDFpYPrAhXUZC sKHeneCggQ6AEwAHoECAMQAg#v=onepage&q=5G%20maritime&f=false

Schwab, Klaus, *The Fourth Industrial Revolution* (UK: Portfolio Penguin, 2017).

Steven, Keslowitz, *The Digital Dystopias of Black Mirror and Electric Dreams* (North Carolina: MacFarland & Co, 2020).

Soares , Carlos, & Guedes, T.A. Santos (eds), *Progress in Maritime Technology and Engineering* (London: Taylor and Francis, 2018).

Soyer, Barýþ &Andrew Tettenborn, (eds), *New Technologies, Artificial Intelligence and Shipping Law in the 21st Century* (New York: Rutledge, 2020).

Soyer, Baris & Andrew Tettenborn, *Artificial Intelligence and Autonomous Shipping: Developing the International Legal Framework* (Bloomsbury Academic, 2021).

Talley, Wayne K., 'Port Economics', https://books.google.co.in/books?id=jJxADwAAQ BAJ&pg=PT281&dq=smart+ports&hl=en&sa=X&ved=2ahUKEwjX44T_loPrAhUZXisKHb_mC8UQ6AEwA3oECAcQAg#v=onepage &q=smart%20ports&f=false

Wilmsmeier, Gordon & Jason Monios, 'Geographies of Maritime Transport' https://books.google.co.in/books?id=a6_ZDwAAQBAJ&printsec=frontcover &dq=smart+ports&hl=en&sa=X&ved=2ahUKEwjC4M77l4PrAhUEbisKHV8vBBo4ChDoATAIegQIBhAC#v=onepage&q&f=false

Wang, Xiwen, *When 5G Meets Industry 4.0*, https://books.google.co.in/books?id=DErzDwAAQBAJ&pg=PA5&dq=5G+Industry+4.0&hl=en&sa=X&ved=2ahUKEwjdprzopIPrAhWWeisKHb3XBflQ6AEwAHoECAIQAg #v=onepage&q=5G%20Industry%204.0&f=false

Tao, Fei, Meng Zhang, & A.Y.C. Nee, *Digital Twin Driven Smart Manufacturing*, https://books.google.co.in/books?id=PvKGDwAAQBAJ &printsec=front cover &dq=AR/VR++Maritime&hl=en&sa=X&ved=2ahUKEwi3sajWpoPrAhWFcn0KHXsCCf0Q6AEwBXoECAYQAg#v=onepage&q&f=false

Raytheon, *Artificial Intelligence: The Frontline of a New Age in Defence*, https://cdn2.hubspot.net/hubfs/2097098/MCM120_BreakingDefense_AI_ebookR1%20(1).pdf

Articles in Journals and E-journals

Allen, Gregory C., 'Understanding China's AI Strategy', *CNAS*, February 6, 2019, https://www.cnas.org/publications/reports/understanding-chinas-ai-strategy

Daga, Radhika, "Technology 2019: Another Year of Breakthroughs", https://www.vifindia.org/article/2020/january/17/technology-2019-another-year-of-breakthroughs

Heller, Christian H. (2019), "The Future Navy—Near-Term Applications of Artificial Intelligence," *Naval War College Review*: Vol. 72, No. 4, Article 7, https://digital-commons.usnwc.edu/nwc-review/vol72/iss4/7

Kulbiej, E. & P. Wo³ejsza, "Naval Artificial Intelligence", https://www.researchgate.net/publication/318655874_Naval_Artificial_Intelligence

J. Fras, Y. Noh, M. Macias, H. Wurdemann & K. Althoefer, "Bio-Inspired Octopus Robot Based on Novel Soft Fluidic Actuator", *2018 IEEE International Conference on Robotics and Automation (ICRA)*, Brisbane, QLD, 2018.

Yadav, Rameshwar, "5G Technology: Transformational Synthesis for Armed Forces", https://www.vifindia.org/article/2019/june/24/5g-technology-transformational-synthesis-for-armed-forces%20%20%20%20%20

Reports

"Make In India: Through Indigenous Research and Development by DRDO/Industry-Part I, VIF Task Force Report, https://www.vifindia.org/paper/2019/february/27/vif-task-force-report-make-in-india

"Achieving Self Reliance through Indigenous R&D by DRDO /Industry-Part II", https://www.vifindia.org/taskforcereport/2020/may/20/Achieving-Self-Reliance-through-Indigenous-RandD-by-DRDO-Industry-part-II

INDEX